PERENNIALS

THRIVING FLOWER GARDENS
IN EVERY TYPE OF LIGHT

NEDRA SECRIST
Author of *Powerful Perennials*

Hobble Creek Press | An Imprint of Cedar Fort, Inc. | Springville, Utah

Front cover photo courtesy of Miranda Dejarnett. Back
cover photos (hens and chicks, aconitum, and peonies)
courtesy of Walters Gardens. United States Frost Areas map
reprinted with permission from *Compton's by Britannica*,
©2011 by Encyclopaedia Britannica, Inc.

ISBN 13: 978-1-4621-2136-6

Published by Hobble Creek Press,
an imprint of Cedar Fort, Inc.
2373 W. 700 S., Springville, UT, 84663
Distributed by Cedar Fort, Inc.,
www.cedarfort.com

LIBRARY OF CONGRESS CATALOGING-IN-
PUBLICATION DATA

Names: Secrist, Nedra, 1936- author.

Title: Perennials : thriving flower gardens in every type
of light / NedraSecrist.

Description: Springville, UT : Hobble Creek Press,
an imprint of Cedar Fort,Inc., [2017] | Includes
bibliographical references and index.

Identifiers: LCCN 2017046255 (print) | LCCN
2017053251 (ebook) | ISBN 9781462128587 (epub,
pdf, mobi) | ISBN 9781462121366 (layflat binding :
alk. paper)

Subjects: LCSH: Perennials.

Classification: LCC SB434 (ebook) | LCC SB434
.S437 2017 (print) | DDC 635.9/32--dc23

LC record available at https://lccn.loc.gov/2017046255

Cover and page design by M. Shaun McMurdie
Cover design © 2018 by Cedar Fort, Inc.
Edited by Allie Bowen and Kaitlin Barwick

Printed in Korea

10   9   8   7   6   5   4   3   2   1

Printed on acid-free paper.

DEDICATION

Dedicated to all of those independent,
free-spirited, Western do-it-your-selfers who
create their own, very personal spots to call home.

Cookie-cutter landscapes are not for them,
only their individual vision created by love, sweat,
labor, time, and desire for something special.

CONTENTS

INTRODUCTION: LIVING OUTSIDE THE BOX

What's new today will soon be old.
Only Earth's gifts really hold.

LIVING OUTSIDE THE BOX of our homes and tech devices is what outdoor living is all about. Available property sometimes referred to as "they just aren't making any more dirt" is a valuable commodity that is becoming more and more difficult to own. Homeowners with cramped elbows feeling the need to push for more room can lessen their confinement and desire for more space by simply moving outside the box of their homes and using their yards as outdoor space. The words "The Great Outdoors" are not a description of living inside an electronic box or house.

Western Rocky Mountain homeowners are urban, suburban, or rural dwellers. The U.S. census rates of urban residents versus rural residents in each state raises yearly. Rounded off numbers indicate that people living in city areas have raised as high as 90 percent in Utah, 86 percent in Colorado, 70 percent in Idaho, and 56 percent in Wyoming, and Montana residents who still crave their wide-open blue skies have only moved 56 percent away from their rural roots. It takes land—lots of land—to support the lifestyle of a rancher or farmer. Urban and suburbanites live in small communities or large cosmopolitan cities, but the outdoor requirements of both inhabitants boil down to the same desire: a place where one can withdraw from stress, feel safe, and call home.

URBAN OUTDOOR LIVING

Many communities are enlisting gardeners to teach and sponsor vacant lots as community growing centers. Much of the produce grown there is given to charities or food banks and some is donated to hard times residents, but there is always enough to take to the farmers markets to sell. A new healthy industry in the cities is being formed through the abundance of Mother Nature.

Urban gardens are the trend for the future. Many are growing their own vegetables or herbs on their terraces in planters or containers. People want to know where and how their food was grown, and it's amazing how many tomatoes can be harvested from one flower pot. Greenery adds creative privacy that helps restore our much-needed energy that we find is so depleted at the end of the day. Not only plants grow in gardens but people do too! (Photo courtesy of Karen Matthews.)

Housing suburbs are often limited in gardening space depending on the size of their property. By combining a variety of trees, shrubs, and perennials with a splattering of annuals, they are able to create a rich tapestry of color and still leave room for other needs. A homeowner may demand off-street parking, or storage space for garden equipment, firewood, outdoor furniture, and, of course, "Big Boys Toys," which are a must-have in the west. By listing outdoor desires and making a plan, a homeowner can fit, even on a small property, an important preference like a golf putting green right in their own backyard.

A miniature putting green tucked into a corner of a backyard gives hours of fun competition for this family. The golf green has an easy upkeep with man-made turf that can be used most any time of year.

A pergola tucked alongside a massive apartment complex offers a garden full of perennials for the enjoyment of residents. Many apartment complexes are also offering rooftop perennial gardens. The residents can gaze down and watch the energy of the sprawling city below. (Photo courtesy of Marsha Fryer.)

A partially covered patio off the back door of this home contains an outdoor kitchen/bar for grilling, a hot tub for funning, lounges for sunning, and a table and chairs for dining. Planning on this standard-sized suburban lot has given this small space a year-long season use of delightful outdoor living for a family.

Water! Water in rural areas must first find a source and purchase a use permit. A commercial hook-up would be the easiest but often water has to be pumped from a river, lake or through drilling a well. Individual well water used for human consumption must be tested, sanitized and monitored by state regulations.

This lovely home looks like a dream farmhouse, but is really a working farm. Painted in color-coded grey and white with a touch of pink, the landscaping is kept simple with heritage types of perennials, bleeding hearts, Turkish iris, poppies, peonies, and a few shrubs. Rural homeowners have more room for outdoor living but must also utilize space for making a living. A plan organizing space to include animal corrals, barns and feed, crops or fields, and farm equipment storage are necessities—plus infrastructures like roads, fences, gates, power lines, and water are the farmer's responsibility.

A gate that encloses a rural property is a legal responsibility for ranchers. Farm animals must be either fenced in or fenced out depending on the state laws. The original western spirit of pine tree inserts in the gate shows how original homeowners are when it comes to designing their own areas.

RURAL OUTDOOR LIVING

Persons living in the Western Rocky Mountains with its crazy topographical elevations are pretty much forced to take a more creative way to landscape. Many of these rural dwellers are choosing to live in mountain cabins. Westerners are flocking to the peaceful life style of high-altitude mountain living. Alpine homes may start out as vacation cabins, but many homeowners find the lifestyle so comfortable that a commute to work is well worth being able to live in the spirit-lifting health of the mountains. High-altitude gardens are totally natural with meandering paths through huge stands of pine trees lined with native wildflower perennial gardens. Vegetable gardens furnish superb food when a gardener plants to harmonize with the short growing season. Turnips, peas, beets, cabbage, carrots, and other frost-resistant edibles grow well. Potatoes thrive in this environment but are not frost resistant so must be protected with mulch and frost cloth in case of an unexpected freeze.

Alpine homeowners must take a more creative look at their outdoor space for there is still a need for water, septic

Mail delivery along with property exits and entrances are the rural homeowner's responsibilities. The above well-groomed gravel drive provides the driveways, and gated and fenced restrictions—plus, it adds a very attractive mail box.

The steep, rocky, mountain cliff side made it possible for the homeowner to landscape their mountain retreat with boulders—even adding a huge potato pit for storing winter vegetables behind one of their walls.

The A-shaped roofline of this mountain cabin gives it a stabilizing fit with the same peaked pitch as the surrounding mountains. The roof line also makes snow removal easy.

the record of having more sunny days than any other city in the United States. Phoenix, Arizona, is the second sunniest city. Homeowners in these states garden well by utilizing drought-tolerant perennials, trees, and shrubs. Russian sages, nepeta, and grasses add easy care to landscapes. With this much sunshine, all that is needed to grow most anything is water, and sadly that is what is lacking.

All of us need a place to regroup in the calming beauty of nature. Relaxing on the lawn or patio under the shade of trees to catch a breath of an evening breeze is the ultimate gift of outdoor living.

Plan a simple garden design so you can depend on your own resources of time, energy, and cost to maintain your vision. Decrease the many man-hours needed for yard

systems, electrical power, driveways, parking, and security. However, these same highs and lows in elevations can provide very unique landscaping if they are designed to contour to the site. Landscaping with the native flora and fauna plant material like alpines and sages makes upkeep and watering almost nonexistent. Using rock boulders found on the mountain home sites for retaining walls gives cost effective landscaping and flat spaces of property to increase spaces for fulfilling a mountain gardener's vision of home.

Sunshine is a major player when living in the desert climates of the west because of the low humidity and many days of sunshine. The real estate communities of St. George, Utah, and Denver, Colorado, brag about their three hundred days of sunshine a year. Las Vegas, Nevada, holds

Drought tolerant gardening is crucial in the western states but that does not mean it isn't attractive. The personal attitude regarding the geographic home is one that leans toward simplicity. Home owners dodge the bullet of palaces or manors that require services or hired yard care. Curtailing the amount of grass or lawn saves both time, money and most important, water!

A front yard planted with drought-tolerant, long-blooming perennials like the golden *coreopsis* and orange groundcover *zauschneria* stays attractive even through the hottest days of summertime. Hardscaping areas of properties by adding walkways, paths, hillsides, and courtyards cuts back on the amount of time consumed with the expensive care of turf.

upkeep by using the countless new mowers, trimmers, and and other technology available to gardeners. The installation of a sprinkling system in the sun-soaked, desertlike conditions of the west is a must to save both time and money.

Simplify your plan and eliminate unnecessary frou-frou from outdoor living—especially in the form of masses of annuals that require yearly planting, regular deadheading, and fertilizing that is detrimental to soil and water over the long run! Annuals are like frosting on cake to wildlife in the mountains, so they don't last long. Plant trees first,

Not a great deal of space or water is needed for a child's play yard other than a protective protection barrier of colorful perennials and a few rocks for playing tic-tac-toe.

fully realizing what their mature size will be and placing them away from the house for fire protection. Trees are free air conditioners, so they are valuable when blocking the prevailing wind, southern and western sun, or providing shade for a deck or patio.

Limit excessive planting of shrubs in rural areas. Wildlife enjoys munching on the woody stems of shrubs. Deciduous shrub-sized perennials are a great alternative and go underground in winter, not requiring constant pruning. Plant alpine perennials that grow well in the dry, rocky, alkaline soils of the mountains and add the variety of native perennials to your gardens for natives are conditioned to live in western environment. The end result will be a haven of repose in the "Great Outdoors," and you'll know you did this by yourself!

Peaceful space! What more could any homeowner wish for?

Start your outdoor living adventure now by enjoying *Perennials: Thriving Flower Gardens in Every Type of Light.* Our western winter walls have become more transparent with solar windows and power. Outdoor living is enhanced when living in the midst of our protective mountains for their magnificent vistas surround communities. Western homeowners are gifted with tall snow-blanketed peaks in winter and horizontal drifts of mountain colors in other seasons. The best part: it's all free, right there to be enjoyed by simply climbing out of the box and getting outdoors. Many simple techniques for enjoyment of outdoor living—such as adding decks, terraces, and patios that flow pleasingly from inside to outside the home to gain both visual and actual living space—will be explored here. Ways to climb out of a box and live life fully in your own space is now presented for your enjoyment!

Gardeners plant hats
on their heads
Instead of plants
in flower beds.

FULL-SUN PERENNIALS

GARDENING IN FULL SUN

A GARDENER needing a perfect employee to help generate a more stunning yard started a "Help Wanted" ad campaign. When potential employees showed up for an interview, the gardener had a check list of questions to ask.

1. Can you always be depended on to get here on time, even when we start earlier during summer months?

2. Will you work through seasonal changes like wind, rain, hail, or snow?

3. Is it okay if we work shorter hours in the winter?

4. Is there a possibility of you working overtime during the summer months, on weekends, and on holidays?

5. Will you work without complaints of needing time off and asking constantly for a raise in wages?

Not many of the jobseekers who answered the ad stuck around long. They had no intentions of saying yes to the gardener's outrageous demands.

With a sudden clarity, the gardener realized that she has a garden helper who already performs the entire checklist of services. Tilting her head upward, she gazed up at the precious sunshine and said, "Thank you! Thank you, Sun! You're the reason for my stunning garden. Thank you for doing your job even when I'm not around to supervise and for showing up every single day of the year—including holidays! And especially thank you for having such a dependable work ethic. Without you, there would be no gardens!"

The sun is a perfect employee, and his gift warms the soil, soul, and the back of the neck and is the reason we have gardens. Sometimes the sunshine varies in its intensity and may be extremely hot for at least six hours a day. This sunshine is called "full sun" and is where most perennials grow and bloom best.

There are other considerations for evaluating full sun as well:

1. LOCATION

The high sun of summer in the higher-elevation gardens of the west is more intense because the sun has fewer atmospheres (and less pollution) to pass through. This is why most perennials in our gardens perform better with some partial shade during high noon. Northern gardens' sunlight radiation may be more intense, but it is cooler than gardens further south. Full sun in Montana is cooler than full sun in Southern Utah. In gardens surrounded by cement hardscapes, sidewalks, or rock mulch, the sun radiates more heat. This explains why drought-tolerant perennials are planted in parking-lot gardens. In opposition to these extremely hot spots are full sun areas surrounded by lawns or located on the perimeter of a shaded area. These spots are still considered full sun but are cooler.

2. SEASON

Seasonal factors like the lower slanting of the sun's rays in spring and fall mean that the sun's heat will be different in June than it will be in October. The sun requirement for a full-sun perennial varies due to the strength of the sun. For example, the winter sun on dormant perennials can start a thawing cycle that will give the plant wet feet, causing rotting. Many seeds will not germinate and many perennials like tulips and columbine will not bloom without a winter's cooling dormancy.

3. TIME OF DAY

The time of day changes the sun's heat. The sun, as it moves from the eastern sunrise to the western sunset, is hotter at noon than in the early morning and evening. To calculate the

When you are choosing perennials, a label attached to the plant may show a full circular golden sun that means the plant you're looking at requires at least six hours of full sun to perform well in your garden.

Hot colors, hot flowers and hot sun are the elements that make up full-sun garden.

number of sun hours a day, a gardener needs to subtract hours before 10:00 a.m. and after 6:00 p.m.

4. WATERING AND SOIL

Another factor is the amount of water the plants receive and how well they are mulched (for mulch cools a plant in hot sun and provides help with respiration). Drought perennials find pumping water to resist the heat easier than other plants but still may show wilting at high noon. Shade perennials without the drought resistance and respiration pumping ability of full sun plants will turn crispy in high heat.

So what happens if a full-sun perennial is planted in partial shade? The plant may live, but the size and health of the perennial and its flowers depends on light levels. The shape of the plant will look lanky as they try to reach for the sun. Perennials planted in too much sun will have a yellow tinge to the foliage and will appear to be wilting or huddling, trying to protect itself from the sun.

For a clearer picture of the sun exposure in your garden, spend time in your yard. The best time of year to check the sunlight hours is around the time of the summer solstice, June 21, when the sun is at its highest point. Check the yard in the morning, at noon, and again around 4:00, observing the arch the sun's light makes. From this information a conclusion of six hours of full sun can be made. Gardens change over time and what was once a shady garden retreat will change if a tree is added or removed or another structure built so the hours of full sun will vary over the years.

For gardeners not satisfied with the results of standing in their yard and making a judgment call, a graph-paper drawing gives an easy visual of your yard. Start by sketching in permanent structures like the house, garage, and driveways. Draw in large trees, noting the size of the leaf. Large tree foliage gives denser shade than smaller-leaved trees. Trees grow, so this mapping will only be accurate for a while. Using colored pencils, color in the sunlight at different times of day in gardens. Or, if all else fails, a simple little tool called a light meter can be purchased. Most meters will record an all-day reading, so place the meter in the garden in the morning and pick it up at sundown. The meter will tell the hours of sun, partial sun or shade. Full sun is not a hard and fast rule in the garden valleys of the Rocky Mountains. Every experienced gardener knows that a full-sun perennial grown with a little partial shade is healthier and more beautiful. The hard and fast lines for planting perennials are blurred, but full-sun gardening is probably the most rewarding; flowers are bigger, colors are brighter, foliage is lusher.

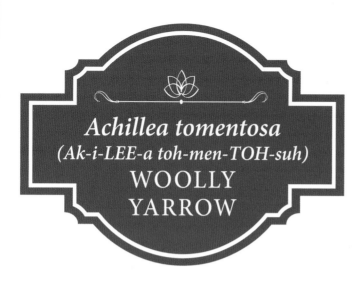

Achillea tomentosa
(Ak-i-LEE-a toh-men-TOH-suh)
WOOLLY YARROW

SHAPE	Horizontal mat with flat-topped clusters of flowers
HEIGHT	Six to eight inches
WIDTH	Spreads to fifteen inches
BLOOM TIME	Late spring through summer
COLORS	Yellow
SITE	Well-drained alkaline soils
LIGHT	Full sun
HARDINESS	Zone 2
COMMENTS	An alpine, rock garden perennial

Alpine perennials have evolved genetically from their original tropical regions where they once grew. Now they are the toughest of all the other perennials, for they have moved from the tropics to the high elevation mountains and conditioned themselves to thrive in cold climates, drought situations, and especially to team up with rocks.

Achillea's bright, cheerful, long-blooming center buttons are charming even after the flowers' golden ray t have dropped. The buttons persist on the horizontally growing foliage for several months giving this yarrow the reputation of being long blooming and the nickname of button flower.

The soft, velvety leaves of *Achillea* are one of these perennials' finest features. The leaves have a tendency to stay evergreen through the winter seasons, and its neutral silver-gray color tones down the many other greens in the garden.

Achillea tomentosa can be a robust spreader unless planted inside a rock barrier. *Tomentosa* has survived in this same spot in my garden for over thirty years.

GARDNERS MAY HAVE met us hanging over rock walls and along hot, sunny walkways or difficult curbside plantings, but we were probably not really noticed for we are such a low-key type of perennial that our name doesn't register. Hopefully after getting better acquainted, we will be recognized and our name remembered on our next encounter. It's not until our flat-topped golden flowers open in June when the gardener will smile and remember: Oh, there is that incredible little *Achillea tomentosa* that has been growing here forever! It is such a tenacious little thing with that delightful, feathery foliage!

We are a dwarf species of the well-known, indestructible *Achillea* that grows to three feet in height and was named after the physician, Achillea, who during the legendry Greek Wars treated the wounds of the Trojan soldiers with our leaves. We are still considered a folk remedy for our ability to staunch bleeding. Simply place a leaf over a cut, like a shaving nick, and the bleeding will stop.

Achillea tomentosa has a natural affinity for growing well in the alkaline-rich soil provided from the lime in the cement of a driveway or sidewalk. Curb-side plantings of wooly yarrow must tolerate the lime as well as the salt spray applied to snow-packed winter roads.

This is interesting information, but we are much more than an interesting ancient folk remedy. We belong to the toughest, most resilient group of plants on earth called Alpines. Alpines thrive where other plants dare not grow. We are right at home in the rocky troughs and hot, dry deserts of high mountain gardens and are famous for thriving in this challenging climate.

We are also attractive. The perky energy of our lemony-yellow flat-topped clusters with their tubular disk buttons and surrounding golden rays stands out in the masses of the garden greens like a bright beacon. We bloom in abundance on stems, about eight inches above attractive mat foliage, and we flower through June and July. The outside rays may drop from my center button but I'm just as attractive without the rays, and the center buttons will persist through late summer and often stay looking as fresh as the flowers did. Even our soft, silvery, fernlike foliage stays fresh-looking as it nestles naturally at the base of rocks.

We develop from a mat of fuzzy foliage, which is considered by many as our best quality. Each silvery-green leaf is divided, toothed, and hairy on both sides, giving us highly sought-after Xeriscaping abilities. When our foliage and flowers team up, we create a self-sufficient, very dependable, uniform perennial for rock gardens or other tough growing areas such as driveways and curbsides.

Our aromatic spicy scent and bitter taste is a deterrent to deer, rabbits, and other wildlife, but even if we were browsed, our tight root structure would prevent damage. We are popular with pollinators—bees, birds, and butterflies eagerly visit our blooms.

With the strong, tenacious root systems we grow, a sharp shovel will be necessary to dig divisions. Early spring, just as new growth starts, is the best time for dividing any perennial growing in the high mountain valleys. Dig up our roots, pull the root ball apart, and shake loose the *Achillea's* root sections. Plant these starts back in the garden making sure each root has a green nubbin showing. Water well. Woody centers will not propagate, so throw these in the compost heap.

We enjoy the alkaline, sandy, rocky, or clay soils of mountain gardens. We also like good drainage, so growing us in easily draining rock gardens or along cement walkways are where we thrive. Too much water will rot our roots. Low fertility and salty soils like in deserts and seacoasts are okay with us. We are more attractive when grown in lean soil, so no fertilizing is required.

About the only care we may need—and this really isn't as important for us as for other perennials—is a freshening-up trim after we bloom. We don't easily reseed because we may be naturally sterile, so we spread by our roots. The seasons are often too short for another bloom, so deadheading is only for tidying up my already neat foliage.

I have few problems except that I'm not readily available in many nurseries. A local nursery might have several *Achillea*, but they are rarely carry *tomentosa*. Most nurseries will custom grow perennials if a gardener makes a request but would not have me available until the next spring season. Box stores stock the big sellers and are distributers not growers. A gardener may find that I have to be ordered

Blue companion plants like wild geraniums are very showy when teamed with the gold of *Achillea tomentosa*.

online or through a catalog. Mail order companies, as growers will probably have hundreds available. Their plants may be priced slightly cheaper but remember that shipping costs need to be added. Usually, we are a smaller perennial when ordered directly from a grower, so a gardener may need to order a few more plants. Many nurseries time the arrival of a plant shipment by using local zip-code numbers and match it with the hardiness zone so the plants will arrive at the proper planting time. Mail-order shipments are packed securely so the perennial is protected from cold, heat, and lack of water. The reputation of the nursery and its guarantees need to be checked before ordering.

Another problem we may have is we are very robust growers if given plenty of room to spread. Planting us in a rock wall will curb this tendency, because when we reach the rock edge, we stay put. When planted in a flat garden such as along a driveway, a plastic barrier can be placed around our group. Rarely will we jump a barrier.

We look lovely as long-lasting cut flowers, and if picked just as our buds start to open and hung to dry in an airy, dark area, we dry easily for everlasting flower arrangements. The small size of our tidy, fuzzy foliage fits nicely into a container planting of perennials with the added bonus of a long season of our lemon flat-top flower centers.

Companion plants that we accent are unlimited for our neutral silver foliage provides a neat under planting for taller perennials and we blend nicely with other Alpines. Be sure to team other drought tolerant plants with us, so we will both enjoy the same environment. I bloom in June, the same season as scarlet oriental poppies and blue salvias. Together our primary colors are show-stoppers.

Several new wooly yarrows are now available. 'King Edward' grows in a small clump with primrose-yellow blooms. 'Goldie' and 'Aurea' are both smaller and more compact and while 'Golden Fleece' and 'Maynard's Gold' are new names, but the perennials resemble me.

Now we are acquainted, I'm sure you will find a ton of places to use *Achillea tomentosa* in your Alpine gardens!

ALPINES

ALPINES ARE VALUABLE plantings for sun-stressed areas of yards, driveways, curbs, and walkways. Their small size and tough hardiness give them status in the rocky high mountain gardens of the west. Cement is often an eyesore, especially if it is a carbon-copy just like the neighbor's cement. Creating a curved, colorful border of alpine perennials that grow naturally short to keep a driveway, curb, or walkway visually safe is the solution.

Alpine perennials are the small, tough plants that thrive in the harsh environments of their Rocky Mountain home. They perform in the lean, alkaline clay soils, the high desert aridness, the bitter winters, and hungry wildlife of western gardens. They grow naturally short with deep roots to preserve their energy even through a drought situation. They are so sustainable, requiring little care, plus they provide a tightly knit weed barrier in a garden.

There is a satisfying correctness when Alpines are planted in rock gardens because they are soul mates. The plants stay small to show off the rock, and the massive strength of the rock acts like a protector of the flowers.

Landscaping a problem sloping hill or bench where water drains off is doable when using the slope for a rock garden. Planting Alpine perennials in that rock garden simulates a natural mountainous site, so they both look amazing! Fortunately, rocks are readily available in the Rocky Mountains. Collect rocks appealing to you, but choosing rocks compatible to where you live are easier on the back and will look more natural.

Larger rocks placed at the bottom of a slope will help hold the structure. Plant the medium rocks upward to the mid-section, and use smaller rocks on top to give the garden a naturally evolving look. Bury at least one third of the rock underground to anchor it firmly while keeping the grain or strata of rock running in the same direction.

Adding your Alpines is the finishing touch.

An important design element for rock gardens is to use a variety of shapes and textures and all seasons of color in the rock garden. Choose plants that fit the size of the rocks—too large, and they may hide the rocks and change the rock garden into a bed or border; too small, and the flowers may disappear. The main point of a rock garden is for the rocks to give it character.

The following album of Alpines shows perennials that are sun loving for growing either in a rock garden or along a sun-stressed cement area of a yard.

Photo courtesy The Betty Ford Alpine gardens in Colorado.

ALBUM OF SPREADING ALPINES

THERE ARE HUNDREDS of Alpine spreaders that both mound and spread. The rock cresses and *Aurinia*, or basket-of-gold, are spring favorites. Basket-of-gold's brilliant yellow color contrasts with the dramatic dark-purple beauty of *Aubrieta* and its look-a-like,

pink and white *Arabis*. The three together bring a lively sense of spring and are eye-catching in both a rock garden or along a sidewalk or driveway. Spreading alpines similar to the rock cresses can be found for every season and in every color, so there is no limit to perennials for rock gardens.

Aubrieta, or purple rockcress, is a fine rock-garden perennial with masses of deep-purple flowers that carpet the ground in spring.

Bright lemony-yellow *Oenothera missouriensis*, or evening primrose, colors the garden from early summer to fall with pale-yellow, luscious-looking blooms.

Artemisia, 'Silver Brocade,' with its intense silver ground-hugging color easily forms a frame around the red geraniums, and this is only one of its many talents.

Sedum, 'Sunset Cloud,' with its rich-red foliage is just one sample of the huge variety of colorful *sedums* that grow well as alpines.

MAT OR FLAT-GROWING ALPINES:

Mat or flat-growing alpine perennials are the perennials that carpet or creep to cover the ground. These are the best weed barriers available for gardens. All of the creepers are invaluable due to a long blooming season, winter evergreen tendencies, and excellent foliage. Alpine perennials that hold their foliage through winter slow down melting snow problems so the soil won't wash out. The flat alpines are carefree and look attractive without any TLC the full season.

The short *Veronicas*, like 'Crater Lake Blue,' are just one of many spreaders that start their color parade right after the rock cresses fade.

Cerastium, or snow-in-summer, forms mats of silver-gray carpet with white snowflake-shaped blooms in early summer.

Veronica liwanensis, or Turkish speedwell, is stunning with its true cobalt-blue miniature flowers that cover a mat of fine, waxy-leafed foliage that blooms mid-spring.

Yellow Delosperma, or ice plant, is the hardiest of these succulent spreaders. Its flat carpet of evergreen foliage turns red through winter.

Thymus, or thyme, forms a low, sweetly scented carpet of fine foliage that will cover a dry location, stay evergreen, and can be walked on.

ALPINES WITH STEMS OR TUFTS

Alpines with stems and tuft shapes add a different accent and texture to the garden. The stems of spring-blooming bulbs like daffodils and tulips are well-recognized examples of the foliage variety these alpines add to the rock garden.

Potentilla, or five fingers, forms a fine, tight, lacy mat that covers itself with delicate yellow flowers in summer.

Armeria, or thrift, form grassy, twelve-inch spikes topped with intricate rosy-, lavender-, or white-colored balls. With deadheading, thrift will bloom off and on all summer right up to frost.

Early blooming, short-crested *Iris* with their intricately colored blooms add a spiky foliage effect to an alpine garden all season.

'Stella de Oro' is a dwarf, ever-blooming daylily with spiky, grassy foliage. New colors of 'Stella' like 'Purple de Oro' and 'Red de Oro' are also being offered to use as alpines.

MOUNDING ALPINES:

Alpines that form a mound are the most prevalent shapes and give gardeners a huge choice of perennials. Mounding plants give gardens a natural-looking appearance.

Alpine poppies add a spiky texture and bright-colored flowers and bloom in the coolness of spring and fall. Poppies reseed readily so their bright colors will dot themselves all over the rock garden from year to year.

Artisimia or 'Silver Mound' adds an all-season, soft-feathery silver shape to a sunny rock garden or walkway.

Any short grasses like the blue *Festuca* add a short evergreen spike that are so drought tolerant they belong in a sun-stressed area.

Asters x dumosus 'Woods' series are dwarf, late-blooming perennials that furnish fall color with bright-colored mounds of purple, violet, and pink.

Euphorbia polychrome, or spurge, forms a brilliant yellow mound in springtime, turning to rich bronze foliage the later part of the season.

Leucanthemum, or shasta daisy, in dwarf sizes like 'Snow Lady' or 'Silver Princess' are favorites because they add a pop of white, which accents the rest of the garden.

Dianthus, or pinks, bloom in June in every shade of pink, red, and white, plus bi-colors of mounding alpines. *Dianthus* enjoys the alkaline that washes from the cement edge of the driveway.

An excellent new hybrid *Sedum* is 'Zenox,' which grows and stays in a tight, ball-shaped mound.

ALPINES WITH LEAF ARRANGEMENTS CALLED ROSETTES

Rosettes are handy in a rock garden because they can be tucked into small rock crevices. A simple example of a rosette is the foliage of the ubiquitous dandelion weed that we wish we were not so familiar with. The dandelion grows in a rosette with a hard-to-pull taproot. Alpine perennials have these same spoon-shaped leaves the same tenacity. Here are a few examples of alpine rosettes.

Gaillardia 'Arizona' series forms a brilliant hot-colored mound that blooms summer through fall.

Coreopsis, or tickseed's rosette, stems are late to emerge in spring, but by June, this gorgeous perennial has developed into a one-foot mound of needle-like foliage that covers itself with small yellow daisies from June through frost and gives constant summer color in the garden.

Sempervivums, called hens-and-chicks, grow with very intricate rosette-shaped petals. Each little chick can be removed by tugging the root from its mother to be planted between rocks or as a driveway edger.

Geum grows from a circular rosette and blooms in hot pinks and whites. Without snow cover protection, *Geum* is prone to winter kill.

Silene, or campion, starts out as a rosette then blooms in August as a tidy-shaped mound covered with fuchsia-pink flowers.

SUB-SHRUBS

Sub-shrubs are small woody shrubs that are really perennials. These sub-shrubs are so short and drought tolerant that they are excellent alpines.

Any gardener who lives in the high mountain valleys of the Rockies will find a need for growing Alpines. They are carefree and handsome with a lot of versatility as to shape, size, and bloom-time—plus hardiness is simply assumed. A gardener may find alpines to be their favorite perennial.

Linium, or flax, is a North American native that grows from a central rosette. Flax blooms in one of the truest blues available.

Iberis, or candytuft, is a small, tough evergreen shrub that adds a white lacy flower to a spring garden.

Dictamnus, or gas plant, is definitely a sub-shrub, but it does go underground in winter and is slow to break dormancy.

Lavender has long been considered a shrub due to its woody stock. Lavender blooms in shades of blue and purple during mid-summer and is fragrant. It is touchy about cold temperatures and stays stronger when planted with the heat sink of rocks.

Potentilla's woody stems are so tough and roots are so strong that this long-blooming small shrub can be planted in high-mountain rock gardens and to soften the hardscape of cement drives. Maturity may increase the size of *Potentilla* from a sub-shrub to a regular-sized shrub.

Helianthemum is a dwarf shrubby evergreen for alpine rock gardens and along cement edges.

Aster
(AS-TUR)

SHAPE	Mound or bush with daisy-shaped flowers
HEIGHT	Depends on the variety
WIDTH	Equal to height
BLOOM TIME	Late summer to fall
COLORS	Every shade of blues, purples, pinks, fuchsias, reds, and white
SITE	Average well-drained soil of western mountains
LIGHT	Full sun
HARDINESS	Thrives in high elevation, cooler temperatures, and cold winters
COMMENTS	Valuable for the fall gardens

Aster novae-angliac, or New England Aster, 'Alma Potschke,' is spectacular with its dense mass of glowing rose-pink flowers. Alma reaches three feet in height and width, bringing an impressive spot of color to the fall garden. Alma is an early bloomingaster, often coloring in September. Taller asters like 'Alma' are more attractive at the back of the border where their height fills in a back fence line.

REMEMBER THAT OLD saying? "Last the best of all the game?" Well, I may be the last in line to bloom but the dramatic drama that my royal colors bestow on the fall garden brings a rousing "Grand Finale" to the end of summer. My intense shades of purple, blue, pinks, fuchsias, reds and white mounds of dense daisy-shaped flowers act as a farewell celebration not only to gardeners but to the pollinators stoking up on food for winter.

I'm named *aster* because the father of plant names, botanist Carl Linnaecus, named our family the Greek word for "star," *Astron*. Our family of star-shaped bloomers is enormous—we are the largest family in the plant world. Our flower centers are composed of tightly packed individual florets that appear as a single center. Rays or petals that often vary in length surround our centers and can be singles or doubles. Many of our relatives are revered for their beauty like dahlias, coneflowers, daisies, and zinnias, so it is obvious we genetically have the same gorgeous beauty traits. Our specialness is rewarded by us being chosen as the birthday plant for September.

Asters are original North American natives that displayed a very wild relaxed floppy growth habit at the time of discovery. Their huge underground rhizomes would spread into a broad mass that would smother any other plant in their vicinity. Tall gawky stems would flop open and reveal a dried, dead-looking base with desiccated petals that was an eye sore. Fortunately, we are more disciplined now, especially my shorter hybrid varieties that are more attractive and carefree. Here are a few of these very special stars in our family.

ASTER, 'PURPLE DOME'

Aster, 'Purple Dome,' is an exceptional New England aster with its compact mounded shape. The following views of 'Purple Dome' will show how well we fit into the garden throughout the summer until our fall show starts to color the flowerbeds.

View 1 is Midsummer: 'Purple Dome' is the nice mounded, all-green, shrub-looking bush on the bottom right, front edge of the picture. We break dormancy late spring, so we are just forming our attractive mound of tight, dark green foliage. Behind me is the golden helianthus, 'Summer Sun' that adds eye-catching golden color from June until I start to bloom.

View 1

View 2

View 2, Late Summer: In view 2, the 'Summer Sun' have been cut back to the ground so the berm should look blah, but it doesn't. The 'Purple Dome' asters are now forming buds and starting to color. The raspberry-colored aster, 'Winston Churchill,' is starting to bloom behind me. Companion plants for asters are any perennial that blooms early and needs cutting back for I'll camouflage a bare spot.

View 3, Fall: A close up of the eye-catching contrast between iris, *Pallida* and 'Purple Dome' aster.

View 3: Another companion planting technique for asters is using perennials with exceptional all-season foliage like the striped iris, *Pallida*. The striped iris accents 'Purple Dome' attractiveness and eliminates any downtime before it blooms.

One warning about this favorite perennial: Sometimes hybrids will revert back to the species we were originally bred from. This probably happens due to age, for asters remain more vital if divided at least every four years. Most of the reverted perennials are seedlings, but often this compact hybrid perennial will get tall and lanky again. It would be wise to only purchase vegetative starts or divided roots and cuttings of 'Purple Dome' to make sure your aster will be as exceptional as it should be. The vegetative starts are a clone of the aster so will stay compact. If you choose to keep the unruly reverted plant, cut six inches off the top growth early in the season for the removal of the height will strengthen and thicken our stems. It will probably never have the neat tidiness of the true hybrid but will still provide fall color. Like most fall-blooming perennials, asters are slow to break dormancy in spring, so give us time to gain some height before cutting back.

The tall, lanky aster on the right side of aster, 'Purple Dome,' in the above picture has reverted. By the end of fall, the stems will lay tumbled, revealing browned and brittle mildewed leaves. These reverted asters are not well-behaved and very unsightly, so I remove them. Mildew is weather- and climate-dependent, meaning the asters have been watered too much or too little or have been overcrowded.

ASTER, 'RED ALERT'

Picking a favorite aster is foolhardy, but the New York aster, 'Alert,' is one of my top ten outstanding perennials for many reasons. First: 'Alert' has never reverted and always comes back healthy from even the coldest of winters. Second: 'Alert's' brilliant fuschia-red-colored rays that surround a golden center have never lost their richness, and red shades are hard to come by in a fall garden. Often, aster colors will fade in western alkaline soils, but not 'Alert'. Third: it has a sturdy, fifteen-by-fifteen-inch size that when planted along a front garden border furnishes neat compact color masses. Fourth: 'Alert' has been in my garden for years and never been divided. Perhaps the hybridizing on 'Alert' is more permanent for it grows a little larger but has stayed in its neat tidy size and shape.

Our New York asters, or *novi-belgii*, are outstanding members in the family of asters. The family traits are so similar to the New England types that it's almost impossible to tell us apart. Our flowers look the same, but we grow shorter, two to four feet tall. New Yorkers have thinner stems and smooth light-green leaves that are more prone to wind damage. 'Winston Churchill', one of the New York asters, has double, inch-and-a-half blooms of a brilliant raspberry color. Winston grows to about fifteen inches in height and width, but should he revert back to his species, he often reaches five feet in height and will flop.

NEW YORK ASTER, 'WOODS' X DUMOSUS SERIES

Asters, 'Woods Series,' in rose and pink grow about twelve inches in height, giving them priority as container plants. 'Woods' asters are so dependable that they will overwinter easily in pots as long as the soil is kept moist and drains well.

A readily available favorite of New York asters is the hybrid dwarf, 'Woods' *x dumosus* series. They bloom in 'Woods' blue, purple, rose, pink, and white, and are so close to the ground that they make a colorful edging along the front of the border. Rust and mildew disease problems are nonexistent with the 'Woods' series. 'Woods' aster, white is also partial shade tolerant, which is nice, for most of the larger asters will mildew if planted in shade.

The 'woods' asters are indestructible due to their compactness. This is another reason to choose the shorter asters—not only are they superior but they do not suffer from the disfiguring mildew or rust diseases that have always plagued taller asters. Tall asters appear healthier when planted at the back of the border with other perennials such as the contrasting yellows of *Solidago* or Golden Rod or the solid shapes of sedums positioned in front to hide any desiccation of our bottom leaves. Asters need plenty of room; crowding is a factor that can cause mildew, as is too little or too much water. Overhead sprinkling is also hard on asters. If you are already stuck with sprinklers, water just after sunrise so the plants will have plenty of time to dry before temperatures cool off. Rust in humid areas can show up under the leaves and on stems as orangey pustules, but this rarely happens in the arid climate of western summers.

Dividing asters every three to four years is the easiest way to maintain vigor and prevent mildew and rust. The only problem is that by spring gardeners forget where we are planted and in turn forget to divide us. A marker like a wooden paint-stirring stick with a name and reminder to divide placed in the ground during the previous fall clean-up will tell the gardener of our location. Asters do not break spring dormancy until nighttime temperatures become a consistent 65 to 70 degrees, for we are late breaking perennials. Divide us as soon as any growth appears, for once we break dormancy, our exurbant growth pushes our height so fast that waiting will make it too late. Save only young starts and compost the woody center section when dividing, and deadhead our fall blooms as soon as they freeze so we won't self-seed.

Our family loves the cooler growing temperatures of western mountains. We fit well here because we have deer resistance due to the turpentine smell of our crushed leaves, but I've known cattle and rabbits to occasionally browse a bite. I really prefer a lean soil like that of the high valley gardens, but I will bloom nicer with a layer of compost added in spring. All in all, I'm an easy-to-grow, long-lived perennial and will always return even after the most difficult of winters. But most important, I make fall the best time of year in the garden, and don't forget I'm known as a symbol of love.

Typical of the short asters is 'Snowball' which grows so close to the ground that it never ends up with bare knees. Dwarf asters are more versatile, and 'Snowball' grows in the heat of the rock garden but performs well in a shady area or even under a pine tree where it has spread as a ground cover.

Bees and other pollinators swarm the late-blooming aster nectar because we are their last opportunity of feeding to help maintain the hive through winter.

FALL'S FOLKLORE WEATHER PREDICTIONS

SUNFLOWERS ARE FOOD for the winter birds, so when an excessive multitude of these golden blooms fill areas, nature is trying to provide a feast for the birds. Sunflowers' tall height on strong stems will stand above the snow so birds can find their seeds easily.

Asters are almost the last flowers of summer, and their blooms tell a gardener that it is time to start preparing for winter. Asters also give hints as to the type of winter to expect. The later in the season that Asters bloom the more severe the winter will be. Folklore weather prophecies also say that a warm November is a signal of a bad winter.

A mass of wild sunflowers filling road mediums, ditch banks or fence lines is an old folklore indicator warning that a gardener needs to prepare with a strong winter defense because the winter is apt to be cold and wet.

Bees flock to the aster blooms to stock up on nectar for the winter months. A gardener can often judge how difficult the winter will be just by observing the activity of the bees on asters. The more frenzy displayed by the bees, the earlier and probably the colder the winter. Folklore advocates say that "bees will not swarm before a storm" and bee activity slows almost to a standstill before the first snowstorm. They are probably getting their queen situated for winter.

Asters and bees are not the only forecasters of what to expect from the winter months.

The timing of the tree leaves turning color and falling can also indicate the weather.

If the leaves fall early, the fall and winter months are usually mild. When the leaves hang on and drop later the winter is usually severe. It said that the brightness of the fall foliage also indicates cooler weather.

Another sign of a mild winter is when snow falls before the ground is frozen. Snow is often referred to as a poor man's fertilizer because snow covering serves as an insulating, high-nutrient mulch on gardens. Snow protects plants, while frost is called a plough because of its ability to soften and break the ground. Folklore says a deep snow winter always forecasts the next season's year of plenty.

Besides how fall's asters bloom are many animal indicators foretelling what the winter season will bring. The most famous animal weather predictor is of course the ground hog who if it sees its shadow on February 2nd signals six more weeks of winter.

Deer will disappear with an approaching storm and hunker under the cover of mountain pine trees, shrubbery, or sage brush. This seems to be an accurate marker of when hunting season begins because the first snow fall seems to always arrive during the first day of deer hunting and hunters struggle filling their tags.

Domestic cattle and sheep will grow fatter with a heavier layer of fur when the winter is going to be harsher. An observer will notice the fur of these animals will look rough and be much thicker, especially on the nape of the animal's

Birds that do not migrate south will find a protective winter home in pine trees so a thicker than usual crop of pine cones is a gauge for how cold and long the winter might be.

necks. Check out your animals or pets for an excellent weather lore gauge that the upcoming winter will be severe.

When raccoons have thicker tails with bright bands or when a muskrat builds its nest far from shore, a gardener is being told that a frigid winter is coming. A muskrat nest close to water's edge is a sign of a mild winter. The old saying "The fatter the rabbits in September and November, the colder will be the month of December" holds true with folklore forecasters.

Insect behavior is often claimed to benchmark a harsher than usual winter. Anthills built higher than usual while spiders spinning larger more intricate webs are a few of these.

The location of a wasp's or hornet's nest is an indicator of the type of winter a gardener can expect. If the nest is high off the ground in the tops of trees, the winter will probably be mild. When the nest is located lower to the ground, expect a frigid winter season.

One of the most popular forecasters of a colder than usual winter is the color and stripes on a wooly caterpillar's coat. It is said that the darker the color of its coat, the colder the winter. An orange-colored band in the middle of the coat warns of heavy snow in mid-winter while a dark stripe at its head indicates a colder start to winter. A darker stripe at the caterpillar's tail indicates severe weather in spring.

If the apples show tough skins at harvest, a gardener can prepare for a rough winter by a complete and through soaking of the flowerbeds in fall. This is a wise time to stock up on gardening books to read so you are ready to hibernate along with everything else.

Birds even display folklore forecasting with their behavior. The migratory flights of monarch butterflies and birds can be observed as a winter weather indicator. The earlier the flight, the earlier winter arrives. If the migraters hang around, the winter will be mild. The higher the birds fly, the fairer the weather. The height that birds fly due to weather conditions is probably caused by the dropping of the barometric air pressure, which affects many birds' hearing, so this old saying has a scientific basis backing it as truth. Barometric pressure can also affect children and adults, making them more impulsive. The group honking conversation of geese as they form their V-winged formations to fly to a warmer area has always been one of the indicators of an approaching winter.

Birds will frantically search for food a day before a snow storm and often will display abnormal behavior.

Vegetables and fruits also act like the national weather forecasters by predicting a cold winter by the thickness of their skins. Folklore says that onions', apples', and corn husks' outer layers will be thicker than usual.

Thunder in winter is unusual and caused by a drop in the jet stream that replaces warm air with cold. An old folklore saying that seven days after a thunder storm, temperatures will still be low enough for moisture to fall as snow has been around for a long time. Added to this is the saying that if it thunders in February, it will frost in May, so weather signs occur all year.

Weather forecasts provided by nature are not only entertaining but are often right on the mark. A more accurate way to know exactly what the weather is doing is to be your own anchor/weather reporter by having your own rock weather station. Go outside and look at your rock. If the weather station is feeling cool and damp, the forecast is spring. If the weather station is hot to the touch, it's telling you its summer. A wet weather station tells you that it is raining. If the weather station is surrounded by falling leaves, it's fall. If it is covered with snow, you know it's winter. This method is always correct. Now any gardener can be their own forecaster!

TIPS FOR PREPARING THE GARDEN FOR WINTER

1. Leave tall asters standing in the garden over winter. Their strong stems hold their form nicely and protect the plant. This also simplifies finding the plant in the spring should it need dividing, as most asters do. Tall, strong-stemmed perennials offer a feeding perch for winter birds. They also trap beneficial blowing snow around their stems.

2. Mulch, mulch, mulch: Mowed leaves picked up by your lawnmower make excellent mulch for flower beds. The ground may be frozen, but the underground activity of plant's roots, earthworms and microbes increases, and your leaf mulch will all but disappear over winter. Wait until after the ground freezes before applying the layer of mulch. Rodents looking for an easy winter home will tunnel under soft mulch, but by waiting to apply the mulch until after a deep frost, the rodents will have already found a home. Mulch also helps the ground stay frozen, so it curbs the freeze-thaw cycle that damages so many perennials.

3. Cut down and remove other dead plant material to tidy the garden and place them in a compost bin or pile. Composting will destroy any seeds or diseases, and there will be fluffy compost ready for next spring's planting.

4. Get yourself a good gardening book to help you dream and ease yourself through those long, dark, winter days. Above all, use winter as a time to rest like the plants do.

Aurinia
(ow-RIN-ee-uh)
BASKET-OF-GOLD

SHAPE	Mounding mat with clustered flowers
HEIGHT	Short groundcover
WIDTH	Fifteen to twenty inches
BLOOM TIME	Mid to late spring
COLORS	Vibrant, intense yellow
SITE	Drought tolerant
LIGHT	Full sun
HARDINESS	Zone 3
COMMENTS	Deer resistant

No spring would be as bright without *Aurinia*, or Basket-of-Gold: AKA; Alyssum Golden Tuft, Dwarf Golden Tuft, Golden Alyssum, Gold Dust, Yellow Alyssum, Dwarf Golden Tuft, and Montanum Mountain Gold, which is the hardiest of all of the *Aurinias*.

Aurinia, 'Summit,' is stunning and grows a little taller in a more uniform, compact clump rather than as a spreader. The foliage and flowers grow thick and dense forming a perfect compact mound.

Aurinia's natural element is growing in a rock wall. The rock helps provide the good drainage that *aurinia* demands and the alkaline (meaning mineral, for minerals are what rocks are made of) type of soil that *aurinia* thrives in.

The vibrant, golden spring color of *aurinia*, 'Compacta,' or basket-of-gold, gives this perennial its popularity. The cement in the sidewalk adds alkaline elements to aid *aurinia* to grow and bloom in all its loveliness.

I REALLY WONDER HOW any gardener could find a small, unassuming perennial like me in a nursery by simply asking for me by my name, *Aurinia*? With such a long list of other names it would be impossible. The worst of my common names is madwort. I earned this name from being a famous folk remedy. The word *wort* always means plant and mad came about for it is said I was used to cure dog bites or rabies. I'm even harder to find now that my new family classification is part of the mustard weed family. Our flowers are definitely the same bright colors but I'm a traditional low growing Alpine perennial that turns on spectacular lights in spring garden displays and Mustard weed is a tall gangly seed spreading machine. Scout troops and horticulturists in the western mountains volunteer long hours trying to irradiate this nuisance. I really don't want to be related to mustard weed. One certainty about my name is the genus of *aurinia* for it means golden but the adjective *saxatatilis* behind my name is a dead giveaway for *saxatatilis* in Botanical Latin means "of the rocks," and this explains who I really am. I'm a gorgeous golden perennial that grows in rocks, especially when I'm allowed to drape over a rock wall. After all of this name confusion, I hope a gardener will understand the importance of a perennial's Latin name and the adjective that follows behind.

For a little more confusion, here are a few other names we've been called by hybridizers. We prefer to germinate ourselves so our resemblances are similar for we are all gold and look and grow the same. 'Citrina's' tiny clusters of golden flowers are more delicate in appearance and coloring. 'Compacta' only grows eight inches tall but will form a large fifteen-inch prostrate mound. 'Gold Ball' and 'Gold Dust' are so similar with the exception of 'Gold Dust's' more buff yellow blooms that they could be the same plant. And then there is the *aurinia* named with the name of Idaho as its adjective, *aurinia idaeum*, which shows how rooted I am to living in the west. I suppose you could say that "*aurinia* by any other name is still *aurinia*."

A rock wall allows the good drainage I need, because I will rot with wet feet. Even gravel soil mulch is to my liking. Small hairy leaves cover my smooth, spoon-shaped leaves turning them silvery, a signal that I'm indeed a drought-tolerant perennial. I'm often listed as a water-wise or xeriscaping perennial in flower manuals because I survive even the hottest of summers. Excess water or fertilizer encourages an untidy soft growth and reduces my flowering and winter hardiness, so plant me in dryer alkaline rocky soils with poor soil or low fertilizations levels. In other words, plant me in the hot, dry, lean, arid soils of the high Rocky Mountain gardens where I'll thrive. My best time for fertilizer is right after an early spring snowstorm. Sprinkle the fertilizer on top of the snow and as the snow melts in the warmth of spring sunshine the fertilizer gradually soaks into the ground along with the melting snow.

Another preference I have is growing in a cool climate so plant me in the upper elevations of the mountains with their cool summer nights and the bright light of their unpolluted sunshine where I'll find my comfort zone. Basket-of-gold, or *aurinia*, is pest free and wildlife resistant and has no disease problems. I was actually discovered in Central Europe and Turkey, places with similar environmental conditions, but my new home is growing in the cooler zone-three climate of the west.

Spring blooming is a must for me because I have the very important job of providing early food for beneficial insects. I win the award for being the most-visited spring perennial by pollinators because I provide early food for the beneficial insects like lacewings, flower flies, and parasitic wasps. These are the insects that take out fruit flies, aphids, spider mites, and white flies. The beneficial insects, or the ones we want around, feed on the early nectar or pollen food sources found in the profusion of my blooms. This food helps sustain them and allows them longer survival and more prodigy. I'll explain how I work to provide beneficial insects by using the parasitic wasp as an example: The wasp will lay their eggs over the preying non-beneficial insects like aphids or insect's larva. When the wasp's eggs hatch inside that larva, the wasps devour the aphid larva. It's a very positive feeling when planting an exceptionally beautiful perennial like *aurinia* to welcome in spring, but even more rewarding when a gardener knows they are really providing food for the pollinators that in turn are natural insect controls.

Aurinia, or basket-of-gold is a fine edging plant for along a path, rock gardens, sidewalks, or driveways. All are perfect spots to grow basket-of-gold.

This unusable area of the yard was located between the higher level of a highway and the homeowner's lawn. The grade was steep, but with the rocked retaining wall, the hill is now usable.

Other alpines, like the creeping *phlox*, 'Emerald Blue,' prefer growing in the same conditions of well-drained rock gardens or along an edging of cement, so they are great companion plants for *aurinia*.

The rocked wall of this unusable property is now a place to show off the gardener's favorite flowers. Mixing grass clippings and manure along with the original clay, as the wall was filled, gave the perennials what they needed; well-drained, compost-rich, amended soil.

Propagating me is easy. A gardener never needs to bother with divisions for they are not successful nor are cuttings. The best way to start *aurinia* is to allow me to do my own seeding. As soon as my flowers begin to fade my stems can be snipped off. I look nicer if my stems are cut back to about one-third of my regular size then I'll stay nicely compact. Shake out the cut stems or rub the seed heads between your hands to help them scatter where you want them. The wind will pick up pollen from one plant and send it to another for fertilization. When planted on a slope or rock garden I naturalize easily and if the wind blows my seeds into cracks in sidewalks or rock walls I'll happily germinate there. I'm not the only Alpine perennial that finds pleasure when growing in a rock wall the others do also, so build a rock wall where these delightful plants can grow.

BUILDING A ROCK WALL

Rock walls are used primarily as a soil barrier or retaining wall when a change of elevation is required. The rocks are set into a trench and then backfilled so no mortar is needed. Collect the rocks first. The heavier and flatter the rocks are, the stronger the wall will be so use the largest rocks available. Don't worry about trying to fit the rocks perfectly in the wall for cracks left between the stones, supplies drainage or a place for the self-seeding of Alpines like *aurinia*. Dig the wall trench deep enough to bury at least one-third of the rock. Angle the stones at a slight incline for greater stability. Use a hammer or a chisel to break off any weird tips or edges for a smoother, tighter fit. Back fill and tamp the dirt down as each rock is set so the rocks won't shift.

Use broken or small pieces of rock to help with the backfill. A raised flower bed like this can be filled with grass clippings, manure or other organic materials mixed in with the original soil. Amending soil with these materials will prove miraculous for growing outstanding perennials.

Rock walls raise flowerbeds up so the plants can be easily viewed and admired. Imagine this garden without the rock wall. The garden would be a bust! Rock walls are a valuable design element.

The rock wall was so successful that the gardener decided to raise the side beds by rocking another fifty-foot retaining wall. When building a long wall, curve the wall for strength but don't try to make the curves too fancy. To simplify a wall, use a hose for the pattern and then check the line by running a lawn mower over it to see if the curves are shallow enough for mowing.

Perennials like *aurinia*, rock cresses, and other alpines are naturally suited to thrive in the high mountain valleys of the west because they are suited to growing anyplace there are rocks.

ROCK WALLS & CASCADING PERENNIALS

PERENNIALS THAT SPILL over rocks or the edges of planters and containers, such as basket-of-gold, are valuable assets to any garden. These perennials are the tough, small rock garden or alpine plants that are cold hardy, low maintenance and often evergreen that characterize alpine perennials. The following group of perennials could be called cascading or spiller perennials for they tumble over rock walls with a natural grace and beauty. Their foliage is also unique; some are silver or burgundy colored, others have masses of tiny leaves with evergreen foliage, but all add a simple abundance to the rocked edges of flower gardens. Starting with spring-blooming perennials and working through the seasons, here are a few samples of hardy perennials that spill in the same tradition as *aurinia* or basket-of-gold.

Creeping *phlox* with its many colors of pinks, blues, purples, rosy reds, and white, blooms in spring and contrasts nicely with *aurinia's* golden blooms. Trim creeping *phlox* back to a tuft after it completes its blooming to keep the foliage always looking healthy.

All rock cresses like *aubrieta* and *arabis* cascade along with their best bud, *aurinia*, for their bright-purple blooms contrast with *aurinia's* golden-yellow, causing an element of excitement and energy between the two spring-blooming plants.

Veronica austriaca, 'Crater Lake Blue,' is a cold hardy, early blooming, long-lived perennial that spills nicely. It's difficult to find a true blue color in the plant world, for most of them have lavender tones, but this *Veronica* is true blue. Photos of blue flowers rarely photograph the true colors of a blue blossom.

Rock retaining walls are a natural part of high mountain gardens in the west for there are plenty of rocks available. They make long-lasting garden structures that an ambitious gardener can build themselves. Locally quarried rock is less expensive and more available. Rock walls act as garden bones, but it is the addition of the lovely look of cascading perennials that softens the hard edges of the walls when they really reach their potential. Cascading perennials are the "rockstars" of western gardens and will add a colorful palette throughout a full gardening season with their variety of different flowers, colors, and foliage. Once the perennials are established, a rock wall will be maintenance-free other than a little trimming. How lovely to be able to create such a delight in the garden by using these wonderful perennials and a rocked wall!

Cerastium grows so easily that it can even cover this enormous wall of boulders. The white snowflake-looking blooms on silver foliage are superb in any garden.

Soapwort is a very popular perennial for western rock gardens for it spills over edgings and rock walls in late spring and early summer, a gardener's favorite outdoor time. Soapwort seeds easily by trimming seed stems from the plant and tossing them back in the garden. The greenery on soapwort stays nice all season even under a covering of snow.

Dianthus deltoids are the cascading form of *dianthus*. *Deltoids* are drought tolerant due to their tiny waxy, dark-green foliage that drapes beautifully over walls or containers, frequently staying evergreen throughout winter. In June, *dianthus*'s trailing stems will be covered densely with small, brilliantly colored flowers.

'Druett's Variegated,' with its tiny balloon shaped buds that open white over a creamy-edged rosette from May to September, is an outstanding perennial. 'Druett's' long bloom time in partial sun is valuable because of its pretty form and hardiness. It's strange, but this fine hardy perennial is not readily available in the market.

Winecups begin their never-ending blooming in mid-June and keep blooming and spreading to a full four feet by the end of the season. The wine flowers with small white centers and the green lacy foliage are lovely when decorating a rock wall.

Cranesbills are care-free and will spill beautifully over an east- or north-facing rock wall. The cranesbills are long lived, long blooming, and dependable; once a cranesbill is growing in a garden it stays. They grow well in partial shade but will do sun in cooler high mountain valleys with adequate water.

In full hot sun, evening primrose will flower summer to fall. Deadheading the interesting pepper-shaped seedpods helps prolong the blooming, and by tossing the weird pods into the garden, they may reseed and keep this delightful perennial in the garden, for evening primroses are not famous for living a long life.

Cerastium tomentosum
(sir-AS-tee-um)
SNOW-IN-SUMMER, 'SILVER CARPET,' 'YO-YO'

SHAPE	Groundcover with clusters of flowers
HEIGHT	Four to eight inches
WIDTH	Twelve to twenty-four inches
BLOOM TIME	Late spring to early summer
COLORS	Silver foliage, white flowers
SITE	Dry, sandy, well-drained soil
LIGHT	Full or part sun
HARDINESS	Zones two and three
COMMENTS	Extremely hardy silver groundcover

The silvery foliaged, white flowering groundcover, *Cerastium*, Snow-in-Summer, is the first plant to draw a viewer's eye to this garden. It appears so brightly luminescent that it can't be ignored.

s attractive garden would never be as appealing
 hout *cerastium*'s gorgeous flowers and foliage
 gging to encase the immense boulders. Far more
 n just being appealing, *cerastium* stops erosion by
 ping the rock and soil right where they belong.

Lamb's ear is another silver-colored felt-feeling groundcover with many similar traits as *cerastium*. The leaves are much larger and softer, shaped like a lamb's ear, making it delightful for children to touchc but Lamb's ear will also rot if not planted in a drought area.

Snow-in-summer nestled at the feet of the hot-colored *Gaillardia* anchors the perennial to the ground and hides its knobby knees.

MY REAL NAME was coined from the Greek word *keras* meaning "horn," probably because my starlike white flowers lift up and bend slightly about eight inches above my foliage. *Cerastium* is my proper name, and I like it much better than when I'm tagged with Mouse-ear Chickweed that makes me sound like a weed. Often, my name is listed in catalogs as *Cerastium tomentosa,* for *tomentosa* means felt-feeling foliage, and my foliage is covered with tiny hairs that make it feel like felt. These hairs give foliage drought tolerance and a silvery coloring so all plants with this type of foliage are drought plants. When all is said and done my name sort of suits me but I'm really pleased when I'm called by my common names: Snow-in-Summer, or hybrid names 'Silver Carpet' and 'Yo Yo' for they are delightful names. Now you know who I am, let's get better acquainted about what I do.

I'm a small ground-hugging perennial that adds a unique quality in the garden. Silver-foliaged groundcovers are rare, especially when they mass themselves with small white snowflake flowers. I furnish a clean, refreshing look anywhere I'm planted. As a groundcover, I can carpet a large area, spreading slowly and vigorously, but never invasive. I'm efficient at curbing erosion on steep banks that are difficult to water. My small, hairy, mouse-ear leaves give me the characteristics of drought-type perennials, so this makes me an excellent substitute for thirsty lawns. Too much water, or even a soggy wet winter, will rot my foliage.

After I finish blooming and need to be trimmed, I'm mower- and weedeater-friendly so maintenance is almost nonexistent. A high setting on the mowers that only snips the blooms will leave my foliage looking nice for the rest of the season, but don't trim me too short. As I age and my stems get long and lanky, it's tempting when hand trimming to pull out too much foliage, leaving me looking ratty with dead patches. Cutting me back by shortening my stems will tighten my foliage for a more uniform look. My foliage stays evergreen, providing attractive winter groundcover in the landscape. A spring tidying with a wispy rake or broom to remove any dead tree leaves or debris that has blown in over winter is all I'll need to look great for the new season. My colors not only lighten a pathway, but I can be walked on and mowed, making me a good groundcover between stepping stones. The denseness of my foliage also creates a solid weed barrier for wherever I'm planted.

Planted in a rock garden, silver brightens every other color simply by the contrast of my foliage mixed against a sea of other greenery. Grey or silver are neutral shades that when planted between drifts of other perennial eases colors transitions that just may clash. A break of silver colors between plantings gives extra drama to the other perennials.

In spring, I'm especially attractive contrasted with early blooming groundcovers like purple *Aubretia* and creeping *Phlox*. As an under-planting for spring bulbs, I'll look spectacular in the garden, and I'll hide the bulb foliage when it dies back after blooming. As a fine border edger, I'm highly valued as a drift between other edging perennials like blue wild geraniums and rosy-pink thrift. Any contrasting foliage of bronze or red like that of sedums is striking against my silvery leaves.

Along a rocky ledge where water tends to drain downhill, I'll form a tight carpet that will hold the water and stabilize the soil. I can also be moved into bare spots because my roots are easy to propagate. A small piece dug from around a mother plant can be pushed into small cracks in a rock wall, and in no time, I will be cascading over and down the rocks. I also spread from seed, so plan on me releasing seeds to fill in other bare rockery spots.

As if this wasn't enough talent, I add to container planters by spilling nicely over the edges. 'Yo-Yo' is a smaller, tighter

Using a trowel, remove a plug of *cerastium* from a thick part of its clump and replant it immediately. This easy-to-grow perennial will never miss a heartbeat and will start to perform on planting.

cerastium and is the best for pots or planters. My hardiness is legendary, and many growers consider me a lower zone than the zone three listed, so I winter well in pots in cold western climates as long as the pot gets laid on its side so I don't get too much water through snow fall and rot.

Any problem garden spot like a sun-stressed border along a driveway, curb, or sidewalk is a priority spot to plant me because I'll keep the edges looking fresh and weed free. In fact any difficult spot in the garden can become more beautiful and carefree by using my flowers.

Speaking of flowers, I haven't told you yet how pretty I am. My sparkling-white one-inch flowers are petite five-petaled delights with bright golden eyes. My flowers stand above my foliage on two-inch, wiry stems that bloom so thick that I resemble star-shaped snowflakes, thus my common name, snow-in-summer. When I bloom in late spring and early summer, the combination of my flowers and silver leaves gives the garden spot where I'm planted a look of luminosity both during the day and nighttime. My coloring is a delicious highlight in a moon garden, and many gardeners who work during the day find that moonlight perennials are their favorite plants. My foliage is more silver when I'm planted in full sun rather than shade. I don't do well in shade because my blooms and foliage deteriorate. Eventually, I'll turn mushy and expire when planted in shade. Hot, humid climates and I do not get along either, so just let me thrive in the Rocky Mountains gardens where I belong!

I grow in three sizes. The largest, like a Papa Bear in the Goldilocks story, is the most common size and is named snow-in-summer. Broader leaves, more vigorous growth and an almost rampant disposition are traits of snow-in-summer. 'Silver Carpet' is like a Mama Bear, a smaller medium more restrained size of *cerastium*. 'Silver Carpet' flowers freer, has whiter leaves and is easier to trim. Baby Bear, called 'Yo-Yo,' is the smallest with four-inch-tall foliage that is more gray-green

These potted *cerastium* plants were started in early spring and are blooming in June. This is how easy *carastium* is to propagate.

in color with a tighter, more delicate texture. 'Yo-Yo' has no aggressive tendencies but will spread nicely and is the best *cerastium* for pots.

None of us are particular about soil type or pH factors. We are tolerant of urban pollution and will grow in inner-city environments, so I know I'll grow especially nice in my comfort zone of the mountains.

'Yo-Yo' is the smallest and tightest growing of the family of *cerastium* and is slower growing. 'Yo-Yo' produces tight, almost solid, gray carpets over rocks that prevent erosion.

WHITE, THE BRIGHTEST COLOR IN THE GARDEN

JUST LIKE *CERASTIUM* with its adorable white flowers, white brightens and makes any perennial garden pop! Personally, I can't resist white, and as a grower, I offer many of my favorite perennials in white colors. They never sell! Even the white annual snapdragons, 'White Rocket,' and the white Zinnas, 'Profusion', grown for Mother's Day gifts are always left over. Gardeners seem unaware of the power of white!

Perhaps gardeners feel that white is a non-color, but **White is Light!** Put together every color of the light spectrum and the result is a bright shining white light! Combine all the other flower colors into one and a muddy gray is the result. White contrasts or accents any other flower color. Darker colors often lose themselves into the sea of foliage, like dark-red roses that really don't show up unless mixed with light-colored or white roses. Only then do the darker-colored roses stand out.

The nine-to-five workforce often gets the most enjoyment from their gardens in the evenings or dusk. Summertime temperatures have the tendency to push gardeners out of the heat of gardens during daylight hours so this is a prime time for white flowers to bring maximum enjoyment. Not only do night-blooming perennials release their enhanced fragrances more at night but the white colors glow in diminishing light. Equate white flowers to flying in an airliner over the United States at night. No matter how high the plane is, lights on the ground can still be seen. The rest of the terrain appears dark and flat: trees, fields, gardens and parks no matter how colorful they are during the day now look like mud but the lights stand out! The explanation for this is that white is actually a mixture of all of the visible light wavelengths. This is probably the logic behind the fact that most shade-flowering perennials bloom with white flowers.

A plant with silver leaves like the *Cerastium* and members of the *Artemisia* family, create an evening as well as a daylight glow. The white variegation on the foliage of perennials like the *Lamiums* and *Hostas* add a bright eye-catching accent to the garden and always stand out day or night.

Too much white can change a garden from a vibrant, exciting haven to a feeling of sterile isolation. Overdoing white gives such a sense of order and efficiency that it can stifle a garden's spontaneity. Excessive white flowers give the same feeling as that of just entering a hospital surgical center. Use white sparingly. Small drifts of white perennials spotted here and there in the garden, season by season, do entirely the opposite of boring or sterile by adding excitement and will separate and brighten the other colors. The value of white can be shown by the following examples of gorgeous white flowers in every major group of classic popular perennials. Starting with the early spring-blooming perennials and moving through the rest of the seasons, there are many pristine examples of what can be used to make your garden more luminescent. Below are only a few white perennial examples offered in hopes of opening a gardener's mind to white's creative possibilities. White as a symbol of new beginnings or a blank canvas is the perfect color to start with in the early spring garden.

Every color seems to fill this flowerbed, but it's the simple, white shasta daisy, 'Snow Cap,' that jumps out, drawing the viewer's eye and grabbing all the attention! White is the brightest color in the garden.

EARLY SPRING WHITE PERENNIALS

Aquilegia, 'Dove,' is so pure of form that it brings peace, calm, and order to a garden. It also adds light to a partial shade spot with its large intricate flowers.

LATE SPRING WHITE PERENNIALS

Iberis sempervirens, or candytuft named 'Snowflake,' has white flowers as pure as its name. The clean, consistent, evergreen foliage of Candytuft forms large cushions of fine leaved circular whorls that will be smothered in reflective pristine white. Candytuft is a sub-shrub that stays evergreen through winter.

SUMMER WHITE PERENNIALS

Paeonia, 'Ducchess-de-Nemours' is a traditional flower in the traditional color of pure white. The prolific blooms of this classic garden perennial are fragrant and held aloft on strong stems that stay attractive all season.

MID-SUMMER WHITE FLOWERS

White Lilies have always symbolized purity, but 'Asiatic' *Lilium*, 'Casa Blanca,' does it better than any other. The flowers are hugely magnificent and fragrant with white, waxy, curved petals that are centered with curled burgundy stamens.

LATE SUMMER THROUGH FALL WHITE PERENNIALS

White *Asters*, both tall-uprights and short-mounds, help balance the overexuberance of colors in fall gardens. White *Asters* have small star-shaped daisy-like flowers with yellow button centers that lighten and brighten the other garden colors.

Bypassing touches of white in a garden as a non-color usually means that the power of white has not been recognized. Container plantings without white are not near as freshly enjoyable as those with a little white lacy spiller-type flower hanging over the edges. Shade garden perennials seem aware of the luminescent quality of white and most flower in white. Moonlight gardens are brought alive with the white of the flowers reflecting the moon. Every other garden becomes more alive with lightness and brightness with the addition of white.

Chrysanthemum
(kris-ANTH-e-mum)
'CLARA CURTIS' or MUM

SHAPE	Neat clump of daisy-shaped flowers
HEIGHT	Shorter, ten to twelve inches, second year grows taller
WIDTH	Will spread as a ground cover or can be kept divided for a mound
BLOOM TIME	August through October
COLORS	Large pinks petals surround a gold center
SITE	Neutral, alkaline: best Chrysanthemum for intermountain areas
LIGHT	Full sun to partial shade
HARDINESS	Zone four to eight
COMMENTS	Survives and thrives in my Idaho garden

The softness of both 'Clara Curtis's' color and the roundness of her flowers is so fresh and delightfully appealing to gardeners that she belongs in every garden.

The golden tightly packed center florets of 'Clara Curtis' contain both male and female seeds, but the outer rays have only a single production capacity.

Everything about 'Clara Curtis' *chrysanthemum* is warm and friendly. This beautiful perennial without any pinching, fertilizing, or fussing winds her way through a bed of other late blooming perennials making them more natural looking and lovelier just because she is there.

'Clara' is still brightening the garden along with the fall-blooming *Sedum* 'Purple Emperor.' The soft-pink shades of the *Chrysanthemum* contrast beautifully with the rich burgundy shades in the *sedum*.

PLEASE, JUST CALL me a Mum, short for chrysanthemum or 'Clara Curtis.' My chrysanthemum genetic parentage may leave a gardener confused. It's not that I have changed, for I'm still the tried and true, old-fashioned Mum that has never been patented or hybridized, but the name changes are due more to the botanists having a problem with changes in family names. To simplify, let's start over:

Hi, my name is AKA *Chrysanthemum X rubellum*, 'Clara Curtis.'

But AKA *Dendranthema zawadskii*. Clara Curtis has also been pinned on me and I'm also referred to as:

AKA *Korean Chrysanthemum*, zawadskii, 'Clara Curtis,' or for short called a Korean daisy.

Talk about confusing! I'm sure I feel more confused than you at my triple genetic AKA but the bottom line is breeders have been searching for a hardier *chrysanthemum* that doesn't end up in the compost heap at the end of the year. Gardeners assume that fall mums called Hardy Mums seen in garden centers are perennials. Not true with the exception of the *Korean* and *rubella* like me. Fortunately, my genetics come from old, old stalk that is hardier and is an answer to this quandary. Clara is nice and short, much easier to remember than Korean and Rubellum so use Clara for it suits my low-key life-style better.

Now I've explained, let's talk about my important qualities; I'm the hardiest, earliest, mid-summer, blooming mum available and grow well in northern climate environments. Some reports are saying I'm a zone three perennial but I feel more comfortable in a zone 4 climate. I also grow well in the well-drained alkaline soils in the west.

More and more of our family members are starting to appear on the market. Until I came along, Mums required the constant attention of pinching back numerous times a year, along with an intense regular fertilizing and watering schedule.

The other varieties that are typically offered are the commercially grown, cellophane-wrapped, potted *chrysanthemums* that are displayed as over-fertilized, full-blooming pots, at holidays like Mother's Day, Memorial Day, and a few for fall. These *chrysanthemums* are used for decorations and are very pretty with their full mounds of jeweled colored blooms but remember, they are grown as hot-house annuals.

In late fall when the asters have blackened with frost and the dahlias are turning to mush, commercial mums, which are November's flower of the month, become available again to brighten porches or planters. These symbols of fall's glory have been greenhouse grown as annuals also. Occasionally many obsessed gardeners will use their green thumbs to pot these inexpensive potted plants into their perennial flowerbeds and just may luck out if the soil is still warm. They may grow and they may return in spring and start to grow but they are susceptible to winter injury, will stay fragile and take dedication to grow. Many gardeners do not try to save regular varieties of mums and order new ones for spring. This helps curb pathogens that might have wintered over in the soil with these types of finicky *chrysanthums*.

The two main problems of trying to grow hybrid types of *chrysanthemums* is their need for constant pinching back so they will not end up a tall gangly flop and their puny non-winter hardiness.

A COMPARISON OF A 'CLARA CURTIS' CHRYSANTHEMUM AND THE OTHER CHRYSANTHEMUMS

- Growing other breeds of *chrysanthemums* has a set rule of requirements: Plant early before the last frost or plant the *Rubellas/Korean* anytime they are available. I'm not as easily found as the other Mums so grab me from the nursery shelves whenever you can find a 'Clara' for I plant well anytime. Avoid planting in sites with poor drainage. Mums do not tolerate wet, especially winter wet soils. Water Mums regularly.

- Pinch the other *chrysanthemums* at a nodule several times between late spring and early summer. Most of these cuttings are too immature for sticking as starts so they are wasted and the plants may still require staking to prevent them from flopping anyway. 'Clara Curtis' requires one cutback, four inches before the fourth of July and these cuttings can be stuck in nursery pots to root. Pot them up to winter in a cold-frame, then plant then in the garden come spring. If a relaxed cottage garden look is a gardener's desire then leave me alone without any pinching and I'll weave gracefully through the borders adding a pop of my fresh pink daisies poking their flowers up here and there among the late-summer flowers. With an early shearing, I make fine groundcovers that will spread attractively. Pinching always delays flowering by several weeks, but with my earlier bloom time, this doesn't really cause a problem. The sturdy stem of 'Clara Curtis' rarely needs staking, but if a rogue stem or two spirals upward, just snip it level to keep it looking tidy.

- A constant fertilizing regimen is required for hybrid *chrysanthemums*. They require a regular fertilizing program until they bloom. Then cut the stems, removing the first flowers trying to bloom. This removal of the first flower stems is to make way for new ones. This step is mandatory to create the solid domes of regular 'chrysanthemum' blooms seen at nurseries. I flower exuberantly without my stems getting cut. In summer, I'll burst tons of pink single-mop-heads that smothers the entire plant for over two months. These blooms are held aloft on light green stiff stems of intricate lobes of Mum type foliage. Deadheading me as my blooms fade, for a slight improvement in my appearance can be the gardener's choice and if the season holds, I may bloom again.

- The hybrid *chrysanthemums* require a regular dividing of the plant in the spring every two years. Remove the central dead material and throw it to the curb, for these hybrids are prone to disease. Replant the healthy starts, making sure each start has a thick crown, and let the watering, pinching, and fertilizing program begin. To propagate me is easy. In spring, babies form around my base and are easily pulled from the outside of my plant's crown for replanting. Only take the babies from around my edges for these are easy to replant, quick to take hold, and may bloom by fall. I only require division occasionally when my centers become woody. In northern gardens winter self-seed sowing is rare.

- After the hybrid *chrysanthemums* finish blooming they again demand cutting and mulching for they are not, even when listed as a zone 5, a hardy perennial. *Chrysanthemums* planted in the high Mountain valleys of the Rockies must be planted in some type of a protected micro climate in full sun to survive. My only winter survival skill is to not remove my stems during fall clean-up. These stems will trap blowing snow, wrapping like a blanket around me. This snow cover is all I require to sail through winter. Leaving stems to overwinter on many perennials gives the plants the extra winter protection they need in both a full sun and partial shade locations.

- The other hybrid *chrysanthemums*, called Exhibition Flowers, are bred to bloom with huge fanciful flower heads. Some are poofed and rounded or their rays may tip up like spoons. In Japan, these exhibition *Chrysanthemums* are a big deal. They even have a *Chrysanthemum* Festival of Happiness. These blooms are artistically tortured into forms like topiary or bonsais while I'm defined by my uncomplicated ability to produce an abundance of blooms without mechanical assistance and being capable of wintering in northern latitudes.

Clara shares the garden with all of the late-season blooming perennials like this spike *Veronica*. She is short enough to snuggle up under the feet of the other perennials.

I've hope I've explained our differences and it comes down to me being simple to grow and the hybrids are difficult and very high maintenance.

Another very hardy fine *Rubellum* or *Korean Chrysanthemum* sibling is 'Mary Stoker.' Mary's flowers are taller, up to fourteen inches, and bloom in a buff-straw color with some pink shading that almost looks apricot. These colors are very attractive as a color ploy to the masses of intense fall colors. Other varieties of hardy *Chrysanthemums* are being bred every day, so perhaps a wider choice of colors will soon become available. But for now, Clara Curtis's clean, fresh, pink, daisy-faced flowers that are attractive with every other perennial in the garden are perfection.

From a late summer blooming into fall's flower display is when 'Clara Curtis' with her freshness makes perennial gardens shine. There is not a perennial that blooms through this double long season that does not look better with 'Clara's pink daisies at their side.

She stands beautiful at the feet of *Veronica*, 'Sunny Border Blue' and *Helenium*, 'Red Jewel.' The white *Phlox* 'David' stands out in the garden and 'Clara' adds to its luminescence. Fall companion plants like Sedum 'Purple Emperor" and blue Monkshood, colorful *Asters* and Joe-Pye-Weed are complemented by my easy-going daisies.

DAISY-SHAPED FLOWERS

THE CHARM OF the smiling daisy-shaped flowers like 'Clara Curtis' is the joy they add to the eye and garden because of their easy, clean, daisy-shaped form. Everyone loves daisies for they are the first flower drawn by school children all over the world. The real meaning of the word *daisy* is "Day's Eye" because the petals open at sunrise and close at sunset with the flowers seeming to just be in the garden so they can bask in the glory of the sunshine. The typically flat, horizontal blooms of 'Clara Curtis' and all daisy-shaped flowers are pollinator platforms where insects and birds can land and feast from the packed pollen filled center disks that will eventually become thousands of seeds. Daisy-shaped flowers grow in all sizes: some are tall, others short, and even the tiny ones act more as a natural complement to the other perennials that stand around them. It is almost as if they play a light-hearted, back-up role to the spike, trumpet, and ball-shaped blooms in a garden. The round-faced openness of daisy-shaped flowers partners with everything that blooms in gardens because it is so uncomplicated. These flowers add a sense of running, laughing children in a garden by bringing that same energetic, joyful feeling wherever they grow. There are hundreds of perennials that bloom with rounded flowers but the samples below are totally at home in western gardens.

Asters are a typical daisy-shaped flower that brings masses of royal colors to fall gardens. The dense mounds of *Asters* bloom at just the right time to provide pollinators their last chance for food before winter. *Asters* grow in all sizes, are easy to grow, and they prefer sun, average water, and the cool nighttime temperatures of higher elevations.

Doronicum, or leopard's bane, is the first daisy to bloom in spring and often pops up with the tulips. Their rich-yellow blooms have a double set of daisy-like ray petals packed around a darker center disk. *Doronicum's* dark-green serrated leaves resemble holly leaves but are soft and pliable to the touch. Plant *doronicum* in partial shade, for the plant will go dormant in too much sun.

BOUQUET OF DAISY-SHAPED PERENNIALS

Coreopsis grandiflora brightens any garden with its sun-colored smiley faces. *Grandiflora's* twelve-inch clumps are long blooming and will naturally self-seed to spread their golden daisy smiles all over a sunny garden. *Verticiata* is a shorter, mounded *coreopsis* with ferny foliage and small yellow daisy-like blooms.

Gaillardia, 'Apricot, Arizona Sun,' furnishes the garden with bright apricot and golden, sunshine-looking disks. Other varieties of this drought-tolerant, sun-loving perennial, blooms in the hot-colors of orange, gold, mahogany and burgundy. Adding *gaillardia* to any garden is like adding daisy-shaped sunshine.

Echinacea, or coneflower's 'Alba,' is delightful, lovely, and dependable. The daisy-shaped flowers are even more interesting due to their unique spiky, lime-colored centers that are tightly packed with seeds. Coneflowers as native perennials bring all of those fine traits, like deer resistance, drought tolerance, hardiness, and food for pollinators to the garden.

The thirty-inch height of *Helenium* brings the brilliant fall colors of burnt red, yellows, rusts, oranges, and mahoganies to the late-summer garden. *Helenium* furnishes the back of the garden with daisy-like flowers on strong stems just as many flowers have finished blooming.

Erigeron, or Fleabane, is a native, sun-loving, self-seeding wildflower in the Rocky Mountains and blooms over a long season with lacy, feathery flowers in blues, purples, pinks, and white. Short fleabane forms tiny fairy-like clumps, while the taller varieties have a grassy quality of foliage.

Heliopsis, 'Summer Sun,' never stops bringing its golden smiles to summer gardens. 'Summer Sun' starts blooming in June and continues through Labor Day, one of the longest-blooming perennials. They form magnificent shrub-like clumps of strong-stemmed daisy-like blooms that through size and color brighten any garden.

Leucanthemum, or shasta daisy, with their large, showy, white rays surrounding a huge golden center disk are the classic daisy-shaped flowers. With their traditional fame of "He loves me, loves me not," they bring a sense of joyful frivolity to a garden.

Rudbeckia, or Black-eyed Susans, fill the late-summer, sunny garden with their striking, bright-colored, long-blooming daisies. Black-Eyed Susans are so popular and so easily recognized that they are a favorite in every garden.

Scabiosa, or pincushions flowers, bloom most of the summer in a profusion of lavender, blue, pink, or white daisy shapes. The intricate center disk is dotted with interesting stems, thus giving the perennial its name. Pincusion is long lasting in the garden as well as a cut flower in a vase.

Tanacetum, or painted daisies, are large, spring blooming daisies with huge golden circles. Painted daisy flowers also bloom in soft pinks through rosy reds and white. Painted daisies are strong-stemmed perennials with luscious rich-green ferny foliage that is an excellent cut flower.

All of the above flowers belong to the biological classification of *Asteraceae* and includes plants like asters and sunflowers because all *Asteraceaes* resemble daisies. Family members from this grouping make up nearly a tenth of the entire floral population of the world. They all appear as a single flower composed of petals called rays and centers called disc flowers. They are usually arranged in a symmetric with identical shaped petals in a circle around the center heads. The inflorescences, or disk heads, are composed of many tiny flowers called florets and can often contain over one thousand tiny individual florets.

The daisy shapes of the flowers are pollinator magnets because their open flower petals give a nice landing spot and easy access to insects. *Asteraceae* flowers have the tendency to open in the mornings, follow the sun through the day and close at night.

Asteraceae seed dispersal is done by a single tubular, ribbed seed called an achenes which is designed to prevent self-pollination and forms in the florets where both male and female reproduction team up. The ray petals have only single reproduction abilities.

Most are considered herbaceous perennials for they have stems and little or no woody tissue, but then nature still throws in a curveball for dandelions are also members of the enormous *Asteraceae* family.

Echinacea purpurea
(eck-i-NAY-see-uh
CONEFLOWER

SHAPE	Sturdy clump with flat, round, daisy-shaped flowers
HEIGHT	Twenty-four to thirty inches
WIDTH	Fifteen inches
BLOOM TIME	Midsummer
COLORS	Pinkish petals, darker cones
SITE	Well drained, variety of soils
LIGHT	Full sun
HARDINESS	Zones three to eight
COMMENTS	Northern America native perennial

Coneflower's unique "hedgehog" cones start the summer as a bright lime green, and as summer temperatures heat-up, so do the cones by changing to a swollen, coppery-colored, intricately packed cone-head of birdseeds.

Echinacea has seeded among a variety of other perennials. As Echinacea matures, the flat daisy-shaped petals lighten to pale pink, making them appear larger.

Echinacea shines from the summer garden with a pure energetic vitality that almost questions its long-lived bloom time and hands-off care. The background, companion perennials (blue Russian sage and 'Raspberry Wine', Monarda) also enjoy a full-sun garden spot.

Gardeners now have a choice of planting the tried-and-true classic pink coneflowers in their gardens or adding this new hybrid called 'Marmalade' to the landscape. Many of the new hybrids bloom in different colors like coral 'Solar Flare,' orange 'Sundown', and 'Sombrero' which offers both 'Lemon' or 'Salsa Red.' Winter survival of these new hybrids in my higher elevation gardens has been zero. It would be wise to check with other gardeners in your area before investing in a new hybrid one-season wonder.

"HO." THAT MEANS "hello" in my Native American Plains Indian tongue, for my origins are the plains or prairies of the USA. That means I'm a tough survivor, for life on the prairies cuts no corners for tender loving care. Originating on the plains gave me my deep-rooted staple traits, for I'm a drought-tolerant, long-blooming, low-maintenance, and dependable perennial. I can be counted on to add a rugged, striking beauty to the garden year after year. With luck, I'll spill a few of my seeds and they will germinate adding more plants year after year.

I'm a handsome symbol of summers all across America for my blooms are at their height in July and August. I'm so dependable that I instill in gardeners the feeling of nature's stability and that "all is right with the world." I was even awarded the Perennial Plant of the Year award in 1998 for my many values. In other words, I'm as close to what a Rocky Mountain gardener wants in their yard as a perennial can be.

My foliage forms a rich dark-green clump that is tall enough for growing in the back or mid-section of flower beds. Oblong, crinkly textured leaves grow opposite on strong stems that never require any staking. The uniqueness of my shuttlecock-shaped flowers with their reflexed or drooping petal rays surrounding a tight center cone is a quick giveaway that I'm a member of the *Asteraceae* family of flowers. I bloom and bloom, opening in mid-summer or July, and bloom through August into September and often I'm still flowering next to the fall asters.

Echinacea's sister plants are golden *rudbeckia* or Black-Eyed Susan and the white versions of coneflowers. The white blooms sparkle, adding an attractive contrast to the soft rosy colors of *echinacea purpurea* or purple coneflowers. As genetic companions, they grow well together for they are all drought-tolerant, extended bloomers, full sun, and deer-resistant perennials. Several of the white *echinacea* varieties are fragrant, giving them extra deer protection.

I never require a lot of fussing once my roots are established. My natural affinity is being left alone to just do my own thing and grow, for I'm lovelier when left to naturalize. I thrive in any type of soils be it lean, poor or rich. Slightly acidic soils like that of the prairie is my preference but I grow fine in western alkaline, so the type of soil isn't an issue. My survival skills have learned to make do with what is, but I admit there is one soil I really dislike! The soilless mix products that many growers use in their greenhouses or gardens are not for me! Most soilless products or "Designer Soils" as seen on TV are not dirt but made up of sterilized peat moss, vermiculite, and perlite. These pricy plastic bags of mix even sport designer names like Black Gold or Sunshine, and their sales are a tribute to how great the American marketing works.

Peat moss's main value is that it is a highly absorbent, water-holding product that prevents compaction. The biological process of mosses and other living material left to decompose to create peat moss takes thousands and thousands of years making it a nonrenewable product. Our local sphagnum peat fields in Downey, South East Idaho are a good example. This soil evolved from the flora and fauna dropped by the mad headlong rush of ancient Lake Bonneville when it flooded and created the Snake River Valleys.

Perlite is another local, Idaho product that is mined volcanic glass. The moisture left in the glass or silica explodes when heat is applied and this added to the soilless mix aids in drainage. Vermiculite is a lightweight, natural occurring mineral that expands when heated and holds moisture.

All of these products are natural, and when used in soilless mixes, peat and vermiculite hold water in opposition to perlite for good drainage. This is fine and good, but the next step is the hot sterilization process that kills the biologic make-up of good soil for good soil is rich in worms, seeds, spores, fungus and all kinds of pathogens. Plants need essential nutrients to grow and sterilized soil has no organic material and must be fertilized. If you find an *echinacea* in full bloom on the Garden Center's shelf it's certain that I have been greenhouse grown and fertilized with almost every watering. My flowers may look good on the nursery shelf but I guarantee my roots are nonexistent. Why would I bother to form roots when I can get fat and lazy on regular fertilizing without having to push so hard into the earth to grow? The main point is that I prefer natural soils and compost offers similar benefits as peatmoss and is a renewable resource.

I really detest being greenhouse grown. My leaves curl and my blooms will get too tall and floppy and lose their color. Aphids are known to attack me when I'm grown or wintered on the greenhouse shelf, but when I get planted outside in the earth where I belong, nothing seems to bother me. If I need to be wintered in a container pot rather than the ground, then place me in an unheated cold frame. This will give me a better comfort zone for a winter resting spot where I'll stay healthier. For goodness sakes, get me planted in the ground as soon as possible. I'm a perennial that thrives in a natural environment, and that is not a greenhouse.

I've been blessed with thick fleshy tap roots that are full of healing powers. My roots were the most widely used medicinal herb of the North American Plains Indians. I helped heal everything from toothaches, sore throats, rabies, blood poisoning and even snake bites. One old time story tells about an enterprising peddler who used Echinacea in his Snake Oil cure. He demonstrated the Snake oil's effectiveness by being bitten by rattlesnakes and cured himself with his own medicine. That story sounds a little overboard but if you ever find yourself in an emergency snake bite situation, mix some *Echinacea* powder with mud and a little water and plaster over the bite until you can get to an ER hospital. Echinacea can now be found on every natural remedy shelf in every store across the country and should also be found growing in every garden.

A closeup of an *Echinacea* bloom shows the thousands of seeds tucked in the center cone of its blooms.

All soil is not created equal Peat moss is a useful amendment but has an acidic ph level and is not beneficial to plants that prefer alkaline soils. Both clay soils and peat moss hold water, so this isn't good because almost all plants prefer well-drained soils. Peat is great in sand or rocky soils for its moisture retaining quality so the use of unrenewable peatmoss needs to be considered before investing. Remember, compost offers similar benefits.

My prime healing power works at stimulating the immune system and fighting off bacterial and viral infections. For example, when I'm used at the first signs of a cold, flu, or sore throat, natural *echinacea* will help lessen symptoms so they subside sooner. Studies have found that I enhance the movement of white blood cells to any area of infection. I zero in right to the problem so I can inhibit the bacterial growth such as staph infections. Topical *echinacea* applications do the same thing. The *echinacea* salves heal wounds and are effective on skin diseases including psoriasis. But too much of a good thing requires caution, so limit my use to less than a week and never over two weeks.

The best way to propagate me is seed. My long, fleshy taproots don't take kindly to division and never really bloom well afterward. My seed is formed in the hedgehog-like bristles of my cone. The name *echinacea* originated from the Greek word for "hedgehog," so it is an apt description of the spiky centers of my flowers. These distinctive cones stay solidly on their stems for birds to feast from in the winter landscape. Harvesting my cones to use as dried flowers adds a unique texture to flower arrangements or fall decorations. Enough seeds will escape my cones for me to seed nicely—not vigorously, but nicely here and there in your garden. It's interesting that these seedlings will be stronger and cold hardier than the parent plant. My seeds germinate better with a thin layer of soil over them, for light prohibits germination, so I'm not really a self-seeding perennial. Like most late-blooming flowers, I do not break spring dormancy until temperatures become comfortably stable, so seedlings will not show up until later in the season. Seeded *echinacea* starts are slow to get their roots under them and will probably need three years of development before blooming, but like most worthwhile things, we are worth the wait.

I'm in full open bloom during summer when gardens are at their peak. I don't play the show-stopping role in the garden like *Delphiniums* or *lilium*—I'm more the backup or orchestra music that accompanies the summer production. I'm happy being the way I am, so why change perfection?

Echinacea's appearance in the garden announces high summer is here.

KEEP THE SIZZLE IN SUMMER AND PERENNIALS OF THE SUMMER GARDEN

ECHINACEA IS A classic summertime garden flower. The splendor of the summer perennials is the gardener's reward for all the love, toil, and expense that brings a garden to this point in time. Summer comes later in the high valleys of the mountains and is usually the months of July and August. No more waiting for here are a few of summer's splendors.

A collection of some of high summer's sizzlers follows. The following are just a few of the back bones of the summer gardens and all are hardy in high-elevation gardens.

Delphiniums are the essence of western summer gardens because they prefer cool temperatures. Their tall, densely packed spikes of spectacular blooms become center stage no matter where they are located in the garden.

Achillea, 'Moonshine,' will bloom steady until mid-October, for it is a sterile, well-behaved hybrid that never sets seeds. This long-blooming, bright-yellow, perennial stands strong at around twenty inches and is the most popular of any *achillea*.

Hemerocallis, or daylilies, are considered mainstays of every summer garden. They are no-fail plants that live and bloom forever. Without these rulers of the summer garden with their glorious trumpets in rich vivid hot colors, there would be no summer garden.

Coreopsis 'Zagreb,' does not break dormancy until June, but by July, its golden flowers turn on like a lightbulb in the garden. 'Zagreb' is the hardiest of the small-mounding, ferny-leafed *coreopsis, verticillata*.

Heliopsis or Sunflower, 'Summer Sun', never stops blooming in high-elevation gardens. Their strong, sturdy clumps reach about thirty inches in both height and width. Their golden blooms, reminiscent of dahlias, are covered with flowers from early summer until mid-September.

Lilium is the elegant essence and fragrance of the summer garden with their tall, tropical looking foliage topped with trumpets in every color of flowers.

Oenothera, or evening primrose, with their large crêpe-paper-like flowers will bloom all summer through frost if their interesting bell-pepper-like seed pods are kept picked.

Monarda, or Bee Balm, have unruly, spiky blooms that are attention getting not only for their rowdy appearance but also for their array of hot colors and woodsy smelling foliage.

Phlox paniculata, or Tall Garden Phlox, brings huge rounded clusters of romantic colored, fragrant blooms to light up a summer garden. Phlox blooms right through into fall and grows in both tall and medium heights.

Summer perennial choices are generous with numerous favorites in every color, shape and size. Here are a few more flowers to light up the summer garden display.

ANTHEMIS OR GOLDEN MARGUERITES
Anthemis, or golden marguerites, bloom with small gold and yellow daisy shaped flowers on bushy lacy foliage.

ARUNCUS OR GOAT'S BEARD
Aruncus, or goat's beard, acts as specimen or hedge planting in the garden. The perennials have creamy white feathery flowers.

CAMPANULA OR BELL FLOWERS
Campanula, or bell flowers, grow both tall or short but all bloom in various shades of delightful blues.

ECHINOPS OR GLOBE THISTLE
Echinops, or globe thistle, flowers are spiky-looking globes of metallic blues on tall twenty-inch stems.

Nepeta, or catmint, in the summer border furnishes quiet shades of blues and lavenders. The soft coloring of *nepeta* fits well with all of the summer-blooming perennials. Cut *nepeta* back before it goes to seed and it will bloom again right up to snow.

FILIPENDULA or MEADOWSWEETS

Filipendula's, or Meadowsweets', white floral panicles bloom on fernlike foliage stems.

LIATRIS or BLAZING STAR

Liatris, or blazing star, blooms with fluffy rosy lilac or white flowers on slender spikes of tufted foliage.

LIGULARIA or LEOPARD PLANT

Ligularia's, or leopard plant's, outstanding features are its beautiful, enormous, deep-purple leaves with toothed edges.

LYSIMACHIA

Lysimachia are tall perennials bloom on slender spikes in reds, lemon yellows, and white. The short varieties are groundcovers with tiny yellow flowers.

PENSTEMON or BEARDTONGUE

Penstemon, or beardtongue, with their tubular funnel-like flowers, bloom in a wide array of colors.

SIDALCEA or MALLOW

Sidalcea, or mallow, adds tall graceful spikes of lilac-rose flowers on slender stems to summer gardens.

POINTERS TO KEEP THE SIZZLE IN SUMMER GARDENS

1. The first requirement for growing sumptuous summer gardens is an adequate watering system. Watering during morning hours is healthier for plants and is the most economical way to use water so the water will not evaporate in the heat. Summer rains in higher elevations are rare and sporadic so cannot be counted on for water. Most rain received in the mountains is based on a monsoon-weather pattern that moves up the Rockies from the Gulf of Mexico in late summer. Heat stress can fry foliage and pause blooming because when the temperatures move into the 80 percent, it cancels out the plants respiration or movement of water through the plant. Watering when temperatures go up will keep the garden attractive. Group perennials in watering zones so that drought-tolerant perennials are together and higher-water-need plants are planted in another spot. Container pots quickly show stress during the high sun of summer, so group these for extra daily handwatering.

2. Weeds along with flowers put on their major growth in the warmth of summertime temperatures, so consider weeding as a summer exercise program. Plug in the ear phones and "weed-out" to your favorite tunes. A layer of spring mulch is the best method of weed prevention in flowerbeds because the seeds will have no sun to help them germinate. Mulch makes the weeds easier to remove and solves heat stress for it helps the plant's roots to stay cool.

3. Plant food will give more abundant flowers to summer gardens so this is a prime time to fertilize. Fall fertilization causes lush growth on the plant that takes away from the perennial's need to promote root growth in preparation for winter so no fall fertilizing.

4. Deadheading doesn't really become a chore until July, but deadheading is the secret to keeping perennials blooming and looking sharp. Small leaf perennials like *coreopsis verticillata* and *nepeta* will quickly rebloom after deadheading by shearing. Bushy-stemmed perennials like *echinacea* or coneflower and *leucanthum* or shasta daisies maintain their naturally good looks by deadheading one spent stem at a time. Remember: less seeding, less weeding!

5. Hot dry windstorms, and occasionally a summer hailstorm caused by the clash of a low and high pressure systems over our mountains, will wreak havoc on a summer garden. Mother Nature rules in the garden, so clench your teeth, wipe your tears, and cut the flowers back after a hail storm. Healthy foliage and most flowers will regroup in no time, but the big leaves of *hosta* and hollow-stemmed perennials like *delphiniums* will take the brunt of hail. A layer of trees and shrubs around the perimeter of a yard that is prone to winds takes time but is well worth the protection it provides.

6. By summer, many of the spring perennials like *dicentra* or bleeding hearts and *doronicum* or leopard's bane go dormant in summer's high heat. Dormant perennials can leave holes in the garden. Plan to fill empty garden spots by using later-blooming plants like hibiscus, dahlias, cannas, or annual seeds like cosmos. *Chelone* or turtle head and *verbena* or vervain, *bipinnitifida* are two fall-blooming perennials that can be seeded right in the garden and will furnish huge groups of tall blooming flowers for the late season. Moving a container pot to fill in a hole left by an earlier-blooming perennial makes the spot more beautiful. Remember, many dormant plants like papaver or poppies will start to grow in August or September so prepare to move the pot before they break dormancy.

7. Finally, accept change. Your summer garden may have started out as a full-sun-favorite flower garden, but as trees fill in or another garage or fence line is added, your favorite sunny flower bed may become your favorite shade flower bed. Often a perennial will go rampant and take over an area. Remove these rogue perennials with a sharp shovel, fill the spot with amendments, and redesign. Gardens are living, breathing entities, and that means there is no such thing as a static garden—or a finished one for that matter—so just enjoy the process. It's more fun than a destination.

Helenium
(Hel-ee-nee-um)
HELEN'S FLOWER

SHAPE	Vase-shaped, sturdy stems topped with daisy-shaped flowers
HEIGHT	Big, three feet tall
WIDTH	Twenty inches wide
BLOOM TIME	Late summer
COLORS	Russets, oranges, golds, mahoganies, and yellows
SITE	Average soil or clay, likes moisture
LIGHT	Partial shade
HARDINESS	Zone four
COMMENTS	Great fall color for the back of the border

The intricate golden banding that surrounds the dark-hair like center of *Helenium*'s center disk resembles the golden headbands wore by the women of Hellenistic ancient Greece.

It's hard to ignore the fiery, robust colors of *helenium's* autumn display when it blooms to welcome fall.

The original wildflower species were not the lavishly splashed *helenium* of today but had subtle yellow coloring with brown button centers.

The vivid russet blooms of *helenium*, 'Moerheim Beauty,' are a favorite with gardeners, for even with a zone-4 hardiness rating, it grows well in Rocky Mountain gardens.

PEOPLE AND PLANTS change as they mature and develop. All too often, that nondescript little girl who sat in the back of the classroom and hidden in the background of school yearbook pictures suddenly blooms into a raging beauty. As a late "bloomer," I fit that profile, so here is my scenario. I was discovered as a wildflower species in the Northern hemisphere. As a youth, some called me Sneezeweed for my leaves were used to make snuff. I was always overlooked, for my early foliage looks like all the other elongated oval-leaf-shaped perennials in the *Asteraceae* family and was not easily recognized. Suddenly when late-summer puberty arrived, everything changed. With the blooming of my strong, robust colors on statuesque stems, I'm drop-dead gorgeous. Now I'm called *Helenium*, named for the legendary Greek beauty that triggered the ancient Trojan horse war.

Gardeners hardly know I'm around until fall arrives, then they smile and say surprised, "Oh yay! There's the *Helenium* blooming. I'm always so glad when it blooms for it always shows up just in time to welcome fall."

That is my job in the garden, to welcome fall with my glorious autumn colors of bronze, russet, orange, golds and yellows or a combination of all of them, I do it well! This is probably because of my strong-stemmed, tall height that assures an abundance of flower colors are visible so they can set the garden on fire.

I'm a steadfast, long-blooming, reliable North American native that thrived early in my life in Eastern bogs, moist meadows and as far north as Canada. In fact I was called a swamp sunflower at that time. I've been called some other names like sneezeweed because Native Americans are said to have used my dried leaves to control hay fever but then they also used me to make snuff. My powered leaves were inhaled to promote sneezing for they believed it would rid the body of evil spirits. My early wild flowers bloomed mostly yellow and suffered from gaps between their petals.

Most of today's plants are hybrids that inject life into a late season garden with their energetic, never boring, multicolored blooms. *Helenium*, 'autumnale,' is the hardiest of today's perennials with its zone-three rating. It is also the most available for it can be sold as grown from seed and I'm not easily propagated by seed. 'Autumnale' blooms in brilliant shades of both red and gold. 'Mardi Gras', *helenium*, is splashed with oranges and reds and is the most colorful of all the others but is not as hardy in high elevation gardens. *Helenium*, 'Red Jewel's' color palette is dark, rich colors of reds and oranges. 'Sahin's Earl' is an early blooming *helenium* and primarily blooms in oranges. An older, dependable version of *helenium* is the stunning 'Moerheim Beauty' with its multi shades of russet-colored blooms. All of these varieties appear similar in bloom, and it may take genetic testing to really tell us apart.

All of this hybridizing is great but I still haven't really changed from that dependable perennial that bides its time to bloom until late summer and fall arrives. I'm not really noticed

'Autumnale' with its zone-three hardiness is the best *helenium* for growing in higher elevation gardens. The yellow and gold blooms are more prevalent on 'autumnal' but who would complain at a flower as delightfully beautiful as this yellow *helenium*.

'Red Jewel' *Helenium* shines as a splash of rusty red blooms in the garden. 'Red Jewel' stands above most of the other late-summer blooming perennials and is an absolute show stopper.

until I bloom, and this is probably why I could be called an underused perennial. If gardeners could see me in bloom at spring flower sales, they would never pass me by.

One look at my delightfully different, raised center buttons and I would become a part of every garden. My leathery buttons protrude higher than most daisy-shaped perennials. They also bloom in autumn colors but often match or contrast with my petals. Each button is rimmed with an intricate edging that resembles golden chains. The hot sun of August is when my flowers will open and I'll strut my stuff for over ten weeks for I'm considered a long-blooming perennial. This is when gardeners will wish they had noticed me on the nursery shelves.

Growing in the western mountains with their arid climates is different from living in the wetter East Coast regions of my origins so there are controversial issues about the way I grow here. The first is good, even better than good, it's excellent,

The strength of *helenium's* stems holds the vase-shaped perennial, tall and straight. Fertilizing *helenium* will increase the height of the perennial causing it to flop. The lean drier soil of western gardens keeps *helenium* shorter and sturdier in gardens.

Looking closely at the rich details of the center button of a *helenium's* bloom finds gardeners asking who could have created such a marvelous creative work of art!

for I do not grow as tall as I do in warmer climates where I can get top heavy and flop. This means that I rarely need to be cutback and usually will not require staking. However, drier climates can be bad because I love a nice, moist spot for my thirsty roots. This can be successfully accomplished if I'm planted in water holding clay but a regular layer of mulch or compost every spring will also keep my roots damp and cool. The bacterial activity in the compost also guarantees that I won't be bothered by pests for in compost pests soon become organic. Go easy on the fertilizer for it will cause me to get too tall. I rarely need fertilization, for I have a tendency to really spread, especially when growing in Eastern swampy conditions. I prefer the desertlike western climate, for I stay put and I'm very well behaved in the lean, drier soils of the west.

When first planted as a young, single perennial I look okay but as I get divided and replanted I'll build a large drift of flowers that is spectacular! I have a heavy stock and a dense fibrous root system so I'm not easy to split but this is the best way to get matching perennials for forming huge garden drifts. Divisions made about every four years, in early spring, planted

immediately back into the garden, will bloom by fall. Dig and split my root ball, dividing it into smaller clumps. Replant these starts about a foot apart around the parent plant and in fall I'll dazzle the garden. Cuttings taken from the top of my stock in spring will encourage me to bush and stay shorter but what gardener prefers a shorter *Helenium*? My cuttings can be easily rooted. Test for root readiness by tugging on the start, when it refuses to release, I'm ready to be planted in the garden. Seed propagation is questionable and rarely will I seed in a garden. Should it happen I'll be far different than my Mother. It is better to allow the birds to feast on my seeds after my flowers fade.

Companion plants for me are any flower that blooms in fall. My burnt oranges, mahogany reds and golds are attractive with everything especially if it blooms in blue or purple shades like *Asters*, Spike Speedwells and Russian Sages. Some of my favorite companions are perennials that prefer wetter soils like the tall grass, 'Karl Foerster.' *Eupatorium*, Joe-Pye-Wee, *Monardo*, or *Ligularia* both bloom in late-summer and prefer a partial shaded, moist area of the garden so are excellent companions. I've been called a full-sun perennial but find I

Like all members of the *Asteraceae*, daisy-shaped flowers, *helenium* provides food for pollinators especially birds. *Helenium* stems are sturdy enough to provide a comfortable feeding spots for the birds to feast on.

Helenium is really attractive when planted with blue flowering perennials like the above Russian sage. Russian Sage is a full-sun plant, but even though *helenium* prefers a little shade, it is versatile enough to grow well in both environments. My strong, toothed, and lance-shaped stems make nice cut flowers for a fall arrangement. A variety mixture of dried flowers, grass stems, and white baby's breath creates a professional looking centerpiece. Any perennial that is long-blooming has the reputation of being a worthy cut flower, and I have that reputation. I'm also reputed to be deer resistant. All of this along with the easy-care, long-blooming color I bring to the fall garden should be plenty for any flower to accomplish.

Helenium seems immune to pests and is found to have some toxic properties that can be upsetting to goats and other small animals if they consume a great deal of it. Perhaps pests don't like it either. This toxin may cause skin irritation to some gardeners, so wear gloves when working with this plant.

grow and bloom better in the high elevations of the mountains with a little protection from the intensity of a western sun. Surprising, but I'm really adapted to both full sun and partial shade so companion choices are huge. Joe Pye's's blooms are the size of basketballs so we look nicer when used to balance each other at a distance. *Monarda*, or Bee Balm, and I love wet soils, but I start blooming as *Monarda* finishes so we are perfect companions for covering each other's backs. *Ligularia* and I are so different in our foliage that it almost is a jarring type of relationship. This brings me to my favorite companion, the ornamental grasses. We belong together, for the more water we, get the bigger and taller we grow. My foliage looks especially nice with the strap-like foliage of grasses. My bottom leaves have a tendency to dry out and curl if I don't get enough water.

UNITED HOUSE AND SITE DESIGN

CHOOSING THE RIGHT site for a home can be a mindboggling experience. Many new home builders might consider a mountain side a problem building site because it isn't a flat housing development spot. All too often problems in a piece of property usually turn out as assets when they are solved. The terrain of Rocky Mountain valley property is rarely flat but may have hills, rocky embankments, and steep slopes There may be low spots where water puddles and even some weedy native plant colonies. Study a site thoroughly before calling in big machines to level and grade or nixing it as too much work. Simply embrace the challenges and enhance the relationship of the landscape with your desired architect of the home. Successful gardens take time and are a journey not a destination. Respond to the land and build a house that suits the site and belongs to the property where it will stand. Below are samples of a union between house and site:

The charm of the gingerbread artwork of this home is enhanced by the intricacies of the Victorian wrought-iron fence. The feast of colors and cottage garden flowers that surround this vintage Victorian house add to its charm. By using the old-fashioned cottage garden type of perennials like peonies, iris, or daisies, the home and site have joined forces to present a perfect picture of a place called home.

TEAMWORK BETWEEN HOMEOWNER, HOUSE, AND SITE

In planning a residence and garden, it is very helpful to have thought through the style you really prefer. Being objective may not come easily, but you really have to ask yourself, "What is the style I really, really like? Do I feel more comfortable in a modern simplistic design with its grid of straight lines or do I belong in a more contemporary setting?"

"If we are planning on living in a rural area, will a cottage style of home and garden with its masses of colorful plants feel

The clean, uncluttered look of this modern home is accented with the clean, uncluttered look of the gardens. "When in doubt, go without," are key factors in a modern-looking landscape. Grasses, flowering shrubs, and perennials with precision foliage give a modern home a fresh, spacious look.

A Contemporary home and garden is complemented when using strong natural materials like rocks or boulders in the landscape. Perennials with perfect all season foliage like the evening primrose and striped iris shown are natural companions to a contemporary structure. Many homes are a mix of styles providing broad latitudes when it comes to landscaping.

The warmth of a cottage-style home is enhanced by larger trees and a softer informal landscape that says "welcome." Planting perennials with multi-seasonal interest like the collection of grasses, *echinacea,* and Russian sage adds color and keeps a bungalow-style of home attractive.

more like home? An unadorned Colonial style of home with its space and many bedrooms might be what our large family would be happy living in?"

All of these questions need honest answers for each style of home looks more natural with landscaping that suits the homeowner, house, and site.

The ornate architectural geometry of this stately Colonial home is unadorned. Landscaping for this type of home needs to be understated with straight lines and well-trimmed shrubs along with tulips for spring and rose gardens for summer. Plantings hug the foundation for an authentic period look.

The couple's home has captured their view by elevating the height of the house. Rocks from the property have been used to create focal points, retaining walls, and a stairway. At the lower back of the house is a low rock-walled patio, extra parking, and a water feature. All of the features the couple desired were fit into a quarter acre standard building lot.

Curb appeal happens naturally when the style of the home suits the land and landscaping where the house is sitting. For example: A couple chooses a building lot when they are enamored with the panoramic view from a rocky mountain-side property. Access is their first priority. Rather than leveling out the accumulations of rocks and steep hills, they allow the driveway to curve around the area. A curved driveway is often much more satisfying that a straight shot from the road into the garage.

Positioning the house is their second consideration. A steep hill's high spot on the property was where they decided to locate their home. Being able to gaze down over one's property is often reserved for kings, but any property owner is a king.

The next site interaction they choose to do is utilizing the rocky hillside by designing a rock garden where they can grow tough, easy-care alpine perennials.

Their forth decision is to keep a low spot on the lower back level property, where they contoured the area for a naturally shaped water feature spot.

The couple chooses to use the rocks on their property for landscaping purposes. They build retaining walls, rock steps, and flagstone patios and position the largest of the rocks in areas as focal points.

Topographical issues can be utilized by an unhurried preplanning for a seamless transition between site, house, and garden.

A list of necessities such as bringing in water and power as well as sewers or septic tank placement has to be considered. To do this, the land must be measured, well walked, and carefully observed. Then and only then can thoughtful decisions can be made. Once the cement gets poured, the house is signed in cement.

SIMPLE PLANNING BEGINS WITH:

1. Site Assessment drawing; use different colors of pencils for different levels on a new property. On an existing property a site inventory of what is there on your drawing will help make intelligent decisions about what is to stay and what is to go. A few suggestions are:

   a. Knowing the path of the sun or wind is helpful when placing a patio on your drawing.

   b. Checking the type of soil and drainage with a soil test is beneficial before- knowledge so you have a plan for using, amending or replacing the existing soil.

   c. Know how and where your water will come from.

2. Notebook for listing your important must have necessities and personal priorities.

Many garden designers have access to virtual software landscaping programs, but many property owners might prefer graph paper taped together so it's large enough to allow a square on the graph to equal each foot of property. This gives a workable, hands-on drawing board to those who prefer a visual they can draw on while on site. Photograph favorite views for planning where focal points are to be located, then plan for a huge window where the view can be enjoyed. Take pictures of problem spots like power poles or an area that you want to play up. Pictures along with your drawing are a reminder of site specifics so when you sit down to dream, all the information is in front of you so the property will become much more than a dream.

My own experience of a site assessment occurred in a landscaping class I was taking years ago. The instructor gave me the following pointers that I used to landscape our newly purchased Bear Lake property.

The site assessment was the assigned first task. Our lot had steep slopes that dropped down to the lake level and would require many retaining walls. The colored pencils, one color per level gave a quick and easy visual on the graph paper that made it simple to remember when not standing on the property. The soil was hardpan clay and the property was covered with sagebrush. The property was bathed in full sun all day and the wind came up off the lake almost every day around 5:00. However the view was so spectacular that none of this mattered and we knew the house would sit on the highest point.

The notebook held two lists; the necessary "must haves" had to be addressed first. Probably the most important was access to the property with both an entrance and exit, so the driveway curved from the state road to around the cabin's high point and out on the lower level. Next was access for water and utilities. Building codes must be approved by the city or county. Should your property be located in a Home Owners Association, or HOA, their requirements of building heights and placements plus the water and sewer system must be approved. Once these "must haves" were listed and drawn onto the graph paper, the fun part began with our lists of outdoor living desires.

PLANNING A LANDSCAPE THAT WORKED FOR OUR LIFESTYLE

1. An outdoor fire pit with an unobstructed view of the lake was a must. The family chose lawn to sit on rather than built-in benches around the fire pit. They felt it would be easier to dodge any smoke that seeks out spectators.

2. A safe play area for the grandchildren and plenty of room for sports like volleyball, touch football, and croquet were important, so we wanted as large a lawn as possible.

4. A greenhouse so I could play with plants while watching it snow outside! No, this is not my greenhouse, but if you dream, dream big.

Once the driveways, lawns, garage, cold frames, gardens, and fire pit were drawn on the graph paper, we concentrated on the house plans. Needless to say, after all the "must haves" and desires, the house ended up smaller than we wished for, but by adding porches, patios, and decks gradually for additional living space, we have room to roam and probably would not change a thing. One note of interest is that a couple of years ago when moving furniture to paint, we found the old rolled-up graph paper assignment from the landscape architecture class behind a heavy cabinet. It was interesting that our lake property design had not been changed from the original wish-list drawing. A little thoughtful planning saves a lot of mistakes and furnishes a more enjoyable space for outdoor living. An attitude that time isn't significant when creating a home and garden eases the demands of the process. Given enough time, most anything can be accomplished so only do what you have time and money for and enjoy the process. As long as the plan is there it can always be chipped away at. The important part is a plan that suits you and your site.

3. A storage that could be locked came next on the list, but my husband drew in a mammoth-sized garage on the graph paper. He figured the steepness of the slope would facilitate a double-decker garage, so there would be room for a boat as well as big boy toys. The garage was a much better choice.

5. Yes! This is our greenhouse. This is a working greenhouse and it is never heated.

If our perennials can't make it through a Bear Lake winter without heat, they are not good enough for our gardeners. The low pitch of the roof is designed for carrying a deep snow load and much stronger than an inflated plastic-covered arch. Garden areas to grow the famous Bear Lake raspberries, a strawberry patch, asparagus, fruit trees, and tomatoes around the outside perimeter.

Leucanthum x superbum

SHASTA DAISY

SHAPE	Tall, stiff-stemmed bush with daisy-shaped flowers
HEIGHT	Tall up to thirty inches, medium twenty inches, and short ten to fifteen inches
WIDTH	Usually as wide as it is tall
BLOOM TIME	Mid-summer
COLORS	Pristine white rays around a golden center
SITE	Well drained but tolerates dry and clay soils
LIGHT	Full sun to partial sun
HARDINESS	Zone four
COMMENTS	Shasta daisies are symbols of the summer garden

This colorful garden would lose its appeal without the white "pop" of the shasta daisies.

The saddest day in the life of a gardener is the day they cut back the shasta daisies. Without the attention-getting, white sparkling daisies with their big gold centers, the garden looks bare, blah, and forlorn.

One perennial shasta daisy will expand in a garden by simply dropping their seeds to mix with other flowers like the *malva*, and *achillea*, 'Coronation Gold,' in the picture.

Cold winter temperatures may be a problem for many daisies but not to the 'Alaska' shasta daisies. 'Alaska' is hardy down to a cold, zone-three winter.

GREETINGS GARDENERS! A summer garden is not a garden without the cool eye-catching "pop" my daisies add. The cheerful innocence I bring to a garden lifts spirits, and we are so loved we've been crowned as one of the birth flowers for April. I'm as easy to love as I am to grow. When my blooms open wide, they captivate gardeners everywhere. The love story between gardeners and I began when I was first bred and named in 1901 by Luther Burbank. Burbank, a famous botanist, lived in northern California under the auspices of the snow-capped Mount Shasta. I'm sure my pristine petals surrounding a sunny golden center reminded Burbank of the sunrise on the snow covered Mount Shasta peaks so now I'm known as Shasta daisies.

The genus of the *Leucanthemum x superbum* part of my name says that I'm related to the *Chrysanthemum* family. The small "x" after any flower name means I'm a cross breed or bred from several other flowers. Luther Burbank crossed four different daisies: the European oxeye daisy which is the parent I most closely resemble with field daisies, one from Japan, another Portuguese, and a chrysanthemum found on the mountain range border between France and Spain. So now gardeners are fortunate to have the simple charm of Shasta daisies to shine in their summer gardens.

My long ten-week season of bloom is suitable to every type of garden. I'm extremely appropriate for cottage gardens for I'm happy weaving my way through a mass of other flowers but my simplicity looks at home in formal or contemporary landscapes. I readily drop seeds and germinate uncovered so my daisies spread easily to fill in wild meadows gardens. The freshness of my sparkling white petals surrounding a golden disc gives me a classic look for modern settings. Even in structured English borders my generous, long blooming, simple design looks right at home.

Vigorous, stout stems hold each of my solitary flowers above dark-green, coarsely toothed, oblong leaves. Our foliage forms a tidy bushy mound with larger somewhat fleshy leaves at the bottom, with top leaves becoming sparser and smaller. My foliage stays fresh, green and keeps growing after the flowers are cut back. Often in warm winters I have a tendency to stay evergreen. The height of my foliage depends on the variety of *Leucanthemum* for some types grow to over three-feet in height while others are very compact and stay under fifteen-inches. Tall Shasta Daisies are excellent cut flowers due to the strength of their stems and are long lasting, ten days at least, in a vase. We are fine with alkaline and salty soils but our plant height in the western Rocky Mountains averages several inches shorter than in other areas but we grow thicker and denser. We are easy growers so fertilization isn't necessary to how well we perform. Well drained soil helps insure us against root-rot during winter but again the high desert western gardens rarely are wet enough for this problem. We are so comfortable in western gardens that we lift our bright faces to living in the high elevations and are thankful to grow here!

SHASTA DAISY, 'ALASKA'

'Alaska' as its name infers is hardy and grows from the chill of Alaska, to the unrelenting heat of Arizona and south to the high humidity of Alabama which pretty much covers the entire U.S.A. With its adaptability to a wide variety of environments, 'Alaska' is popular and easily available. 'Alaska', one of the oldest hybrids, is the best *Leucanthemum* for the cooler high mountain gardens of the west. I will not reach my height potential of forty-inches in the higher elevations but will bloom with abundance on thirty-inch tall and wide plants that are totally dependable. 'Alaska's flowers are typical shastas with large, three-inch golden centered discs surrounded by long single rays of snowy white that blooms from early summer to fall. Alaska re-seeds easily and the seedlings will have a colder hardiness than the mother plant but will not grow as uniform. As an older Shasta daisy, 'Alaska' is free of patents for plant patents generally last for twenty-years, meaning I'm free to be propagated so allow me to colonize. Leave my spent flowers to drop their seeds in the garden then cut back my foliage for it may want to flop towards the end of the growing season. Next spring will bring a delighted surprise for my seedlings will find all kind of spots to germinate in your garden. Alaska is long-living and will continue to bloom for years.

Note: 'Alaska' has been known to cause an allergy to sensitive skinned gardeners.

SHASTA DAISY, 'BECKY'

I'm proud to tell about a newer medium height hybrid Leucanthemum called 'Becky' that out blooms any other daisy. This shasta blooms earlier and longer with extremely floriferous, three-and-a-half-inch florets that provide excellent

The gardening world has been waiting for a sturdy, shorter shasta daisy that blooms earlier and longer and that perennial, *Leucanthum*, 'Becky,' is now available. Shown here with *Monardo*, 'Strawberry Wine,' 'Becky' is valuable in the garden for its long season of bloom, upright shorter stems that do not get lanky and its performance in both southern and northern gardens.

flower coverage and larger flowers than 'Alaska'. 'Becky' received celebrity status by receiving the Perennial Plant of the Year Award in 2003 which is well deserved. She holds her own in a storm and seems weatherproof for 'Becky's stout stems are rarely damaged by strong winds or heavy rainfall. 'Becky' is an all-around superior daisy specimen due to her robust habit with a few exceptions; her zone-five hardiness causes 'Becky' to struggle in most of the west and she is patented, not allowing propagation. Licensed growers can propagate 'Becky' vegetatively with stem cuttings, tissue culture or division but gardeners need to wait until her twenty year patent dissolves to propagate 'Becky.'

'Becky's' foliage has a tendency to crash and look terrible after blooming so will need to be deadheaded. A full pruning will improve its appearance.

DWARF SHASTA DAISIES

I'm excited to introduce the most charming of all the Shasta daisies, a compact, dwarf perennial daisy to grow at the front of a flowerbed, along a driveway, or in a container. Our dwarf daisies are famous for their abundant floral display. They are shorter with stockier stems that hold their robust heavy blooming flowers. The dwarf daisies are adaptable to a variety of climates but are not as cold hardy in high elevations, regardless of being listed in catalogs as a zone-four. They are short lived unless divided every three years, vegetatively, which gives them their uniform perfect shape. Seeded varieties of dwarf daisies are not as consistent in height and habit so stick with clones from the original plant. Dwarf shasta daisies often do not set seed for many of these hybrids are sterile so they are never invasive. This is another reason to divide plants but

The compact dwarf Shasta daisies bloom profusely from July to September. They are very similar in appearance to all daisies but they have larger flowers. Their shorter, ball-shaped mass of blooming daisies look superb as edging along the front of a flowerbed or growing in a rock garden

division also maintains the vigor of the parent plant. To divide, dig the entire plant clump, discarding any dead center parts of the perennial and use only the fresh new ones around the outside of the plant. Plant and water as soon as possible.

Care of dwarf daisies is minimal and we are very low maintenance. Removal of spent flowers is about all we require. Deadheading will prolong our blooming. We are well-behaved delights, and cutting us back to basal leaves after we finish blooming seems to preserve our energy and hopefully prolong our lives for we are short lived perennials. Like all *Leucanthemums*, the dwarfs are disease resistant, probably due to their rather stinky smell.

FRILLED OR RUFFLED SHASTA DAISIES

Doubled, frilled, or ruffled daisies make pulling the petals to find out if "he loves me or loves me not" still fun, but it may take a little more time.

Several hybrid shasta daisies with the same huge golden centers surrounded by crisp clean white petals have frilly-feathery rays around their center discs. 'T.E. Killin,' shown above, has double shorter rays that give a ruffled feel to the daisy but the biggest eye catcher of T. E. is the intricate crested center disc so take a close look. An award-winning double-frilled 'Aglaia' Shasta is delightful and indestructible and can be started with seed. 'Marconi' Shasta is also frilled and double and almost resembles a *Chrysanthemum* in the garden. Once planted these daisies are carefree just like all daisies only requiring standard deadheading. These hybrids are heavy producers with more variation in size and form but still maintain the visual portrait of a shasta daisy. Gardeners will be pleased with these terrific looks on such a traditional plant.

Shasta daisies have always exuded charm and friendliness. Many gardeners grow Shastas because of the nostalgia of remembering how charming they were in their mother's or grandmother's garden. Cutting Shasta daisies for the vase or flower arrangement will always be a tradition so whatever the reason, these delightful perennials promise to bring our own brand of charm and fresh happiness to every garden.

FRONT PORCH

Welcome Home is the delightful greeting extended from the combination of Shasta daisies and the warm invitation of this ranch-style front porch.

A PORCH'S MAIN attraction is its ability to merge indoors with outdoors so a person can still have one foot in, and the other foot out. A few years ago, we added a straightforward addition of a porch to our Bear Lake home. Our thinking was the roof would be as good for escaping as any fire escape from upstairs bedrooms and the cement slab porch floor would solve the snow melt problem of water trying to enter the basement windows during a spring thaw. The porch was built for utilitarian reasons, but it quickly taught us the real value of a porch.

First off, a porch is a covered entrance attached to the house that is the public face of your home. The roof on the porch makes it an extension of the home architecture for its part of the house. A porch invites visitors to sit without dragging them into the house which may or may not be visitor perfect. Porches offer shelter from the elements, especially in a storm, when the front door key gets stuck or when the grocery sacks are heavy, The porch is a shaded but open area where families and neighbors are comfortable interacting. Porches furnish shade for windows keeping the home cooler in the heat of hot summers. Porches do all this and more, but the best part is being outside while still as comfortably cozy as when sitting in the living room. For example Grandparents can rock in their comfy cushioned wicker chairs in the shade of the porch while interacting with Grandchildren who are racing and running off-steam across the lawn, is an example of one foot inside the house while the other one is outside.

Another example is one of our family's fondest memories. We were together, sitting on the porch in protected comfort watching the energy of a summer Monsoon storm move across the sky. Lightning flashed, cracking the sky into shards. The light show was accompanied by the faint smell of ozone filling the air. A furious rain followed. The pounding splashes exploded on the roof in a cacophony of sound. The turbulence slowed, and the rain gentled as we sat mesmerized, feeling the dampness but we were still dry. Surrounded by the fragrance

of wet gardens we knew an unforgettable experience like this could never be experienced inside a house or even looking through a window. Only outside on a porch is where you are both protected and able to fully experience nature.

Porches were a cultural, American way of life in the mid-1800s and early 1900s linking the home with its landscaping and the street. They were large areas serving as outdoor living rooms with plenty of space to have dinner, display potted plants and hang the American flag. The space gave a creative homeowner who is fortunate enough to have a big vintage porch, a place to show off their talents while adding to the appeal of the porch. Notice the patriotic themed vintage porch in the picture.

The popularity of these huge porches where people had an outdoor space that was as comfortable as an indoor space eroded with the development of technological forces like television, air conditioners and automobiles. Technology could be blamed for also eroding the traditional neighborhood camaraderie along with front porches by making the inside of the house more appealing than the outside. The family now planned an inside room or family room simply to house their technologic gadgets and watch TVs. Rather than an evening stroll, neighbors would drive past, hurrying to get somewhere making them not socially accessible.

Victorian porches with their balusters, columns, cornices, chair rails and "gingerbread" trims were built in the heyday of porches when instead of television's bombardment of the nightly news, neighbors gathered on the porch to share the news, gab, gossip and simply watch the world go by. Show-off the many intricate details of a Victorian home by keeping the landscaping in the front yard simple and short. Using smaller, tidy evergreen perennials like Helleborus and Iberis along the homes usual narrow walks and pathways will not detract from the house's architecture. Huge trees planted in the back yard will serve as a backdrop for this Queen of Homes.

Malva
(MAL-vuh)
MALLOW

SHAPE	Large, bushy shrub, cup flowers
HEIGHT	Thirty-six inches
WIDTH	Twenty-four inches
BLOOM TIME	Late June through October
COLORS	Pinks and mauves, some with stripes and streaks
SITE	Average, even alkaline clay
LIGHT	At least six hours in full sun
HARDINESS	Zones four through nine
COMMENTS	Disease and pest free

Malva fastigiata grows as a lacy-foliaged, rounded shrub. Nepeta is a soft blue spike. The yellow daylily sports trumpet blooms and strappy foliage. Together the very different perennials display drama and contrast with a variety of flower shapes, colors, and foliage.

Malva's soft-colored, funnel-shaped blooms with their soft delicate coloring mix well with every other color of perennial, like the golden *achillea* and the blue spike *veronica* in the above picture.

Malva's black seeds are edible and offer a tasty, nutty treat when dried. They can also be used as a thickening agent for soup while they are still green.

The satiny blooms of *malva* in their soft violet colors are easy companions to every summer blooming perennial like these shasta daisies and golden marguaretes.

WE LIKE TO hang out with flower friends and keep things lively in the garden. Call it mingling or social skills, but we add appealing charm to every garden for we are great companions with all the other perennials. Part of our success is there are three different sizes of us. I'm *Malva, 'fastigiata,'* the largest and resemble a bushy shrub. *Malva moschata* is shorter, with pale or white flowers and *Malva sylvestris* is the tall skinny attention getter who demands to be noticed. Between us we keep the summer garden attractive during summer meltdown when most of the other perennials are calling it quits. Now, we better back up, for it's time to get really acquainted with *malva.*

The first year I'm planted, I'm not much to look at, just a skinny kid on erect stems with no basal branching. Give me a few years and I'll fill out to my three-by-three-foot shrub size. At maturity, I often have up to thirty or forty strong stems rising from my crown-base forming an excellent shrub that will never flop or need staking. This fullness lets me hide eyesores like garbage cans or utility boxes in the garden. My size wins me a spot in the back of the garden border, but I think my unique foliage should put me up front and center for I'm an excellent hedge material. My rounded *malva* leaves of dark green start out at my crown and look a lot like hollyhock leaves at first for both of us are in the mallow family. As my flowers climb to the top of thick stems, the leaves divide into intricate lace that gives my lovely flowers a softened background to show them off. All I really require to accomplish all of these tasks are at least six hours of daily sunshine, normal moisture and regular soil, even clay. I also prefer an alkaline ph like that found in the high mountain valleys of the west for this is my soil of choice.

I put forth a lot of energy and grow fast. I'll begin blooming in late June and continue until a fall cold spell tells me it's time to rest. I've been known to almost bloom myself to death, but no worries, I'm also an amazing self-seeder. Just let my seeds scatter in the garden and I'll easily fill all the empty crooks and crannies around the garden efficiently. If I have enough time before the arrival of cold temperatures, I sometimes germinate and develop fall seedlings that will over-winter and surprisingly reappear in the spring. These infants will bloom because they were cold weather vernalized. New spring seedling starts will need to wait another year for they require a cold spell before they will bloom.

Most self-seeding perennials like *malva* lend themselves to the generous, overflowing qualities of the cottage garden. I'm so free flowering and unpretentious that I mix well with a variety of flowers, a picket fence, an old fashioned rocking chair, and treasured objects or flower pots tucked here and there in a cottage garden.

My thick, strong tap roots that grow deep in the ground give me drought tolerance but also make me difficult to divide so seeding is more successful. My roots emit a musky sort of aroma in the heat of summer that along with my hairy stems, wards off hungry deer and wildlife. The insides of my long roots are full of thick mucilage that is used to make marshmallow. By heating this with sugar it makes a sweet spongy paste, thus I'm the beginning of how marshmallows came about. My root mucilage can also be used as a substitute for egg whites. Bring the roots to a boil and let them simmer until the water thickens then whip to a froth. Other uses of my root pith is that of a binding agent in pill manufacturing and the root itself serves as an excellent toothbrush if you ever find yourself in dire need of one.

All parts—leaves, flowers, roots and seeds—of plants in the mallow family are edible. Even the common mallow weed, called buttonweed or cheeseplant, is a nutritious plant that can be foraged and eaten cooked or raw. The leaves and flowers of mallow have a mild pleasant flavor that can be added to salads or cooked as greens. The seeds with their nutty flavor are delicious and well worth the time it takes to harvest them. *Malva,* like most wild vegetables, are at their most nutritious and tastiest in early spring.

Not only is my family edible but we are used for soothing "owies" of the skin. I can be used as a natural topical lotion to soften and heal the skin by mixing my flowers with oil. Also let me mention that natural fabric dyes in cream, yellow, or green can be made from *malva* plants. I'm sure you now realize how valuable I am and that I offer much more than just a beautiful flower. It's obvious I'm talented and far too busy to be fussy about my environment, but living in the Rocky Mountains is like a shot of adrenalin. The alkaline clay, with its rich minerals, gives me shorter stems, thicker plants, and richer-colored blooms. It's interesting that by fall my blooms are no longer the soft colors of pink but are rich vibrant shades of fuchsia. The cool summers of the west are the reason I bloom longer and the wide open spaces give me plenty of room for my huge size and to spread my seed.

SISTER *MALVAS*

MALVA MOSCHATA

I'm the white version of *malva*. I'm smaller, more dainty looking, and full sun heat is just too much for my delicate disposition, so plant me in partial sun where I'll bloom mid-July to September. I'm the rarest of the *malvas* and hard to come by and I'm frequently found in older gardens where I've grown for years. A gardener fortunate enough to have a white *malva* in their landscape needs to treasure me by sharing, saving, and carefully germinating each and every seed.

Malva 'Zebrina' is more a biennial than a perennial. 'Zebrina' grows tall and thin like a miniature Hollyhock. Zebrina is a non-stop blooming machine but seems to run out of gas at frost and will succumb over winter. The plant has to reseed because 'Zebrina' seedlings do not transplant well so seed is the best alternative.

As white *Malva* reaches a certain height, its foliage will change from a rounded *Alcea* leaf to an intricate, lacy backdrop for masses of attractive flowers.

MALVA SYLVESTRIS

Malva sylvestris is our tall skinny sister 'Zebrina.' She is gorgeous with multi-colored strips in an intricate pattern of deco swirling mixtures of deep purple, pink and wine. Once 'Zebrina' has been in your garden, she will always return for her self-seeding is legendary and she blooms the same year as she germinates. Deadheading or removing the spent flowers will slow down her reseeding and may extend her life. After germination in spring she quickly sends down tenacious tap roots so if it's necessary to move her do so as early as possible for she doesn't transplant well. It's wise to leave 'Zebrina' right where she chooses to grow for she gifts the garden with a special, elegant touch of class that only she has. 'Zebrina' is a heavy producer of two-inch satiny flowers that start blooming in summer and keep blooming into fall and right through several frosts. Her swirling colored flowers march delightfully up her thirty inch stem and bloom continually. This presents a problem for she blooms so profusely she blooms herself out so 'Zebrina' could actually be considered a biennial.

We feel so comfortable growing in the high elevations of mountain gardens for we love everything about it! The higher pH, alkaline clay with its rich minerals gives us shorter stems, thicker plants and a richer color of blooms. The arid climate of the west keeps us healthy for soggy soil may lead to root rot. Our only fertilizer needs are a general purpose spring feeding for we perform better in a leaner average soil. The cool summers are an incentive to bloom longer and the wide open spaces give us plenty of room to spread to our full size and spill our seeds. Butterflies and birds enjoy our blooms and our leaves are known to ease a bee sting. Deer shy away which is surprising because we are edible but our musky smell must turn them off. Pick my spring foliage as an alternative to lettuce for I'm delicious and full of nutritious vitamins. There are tons of reasons to grow us, so we are hoping we'll be added to your perennial garden so we can hang out with other high-garden perennials.

Malva, hanging out with friends, *nepeta*, Maltese cross, daylilies, and Shasta daisies, furnishes fun for all!

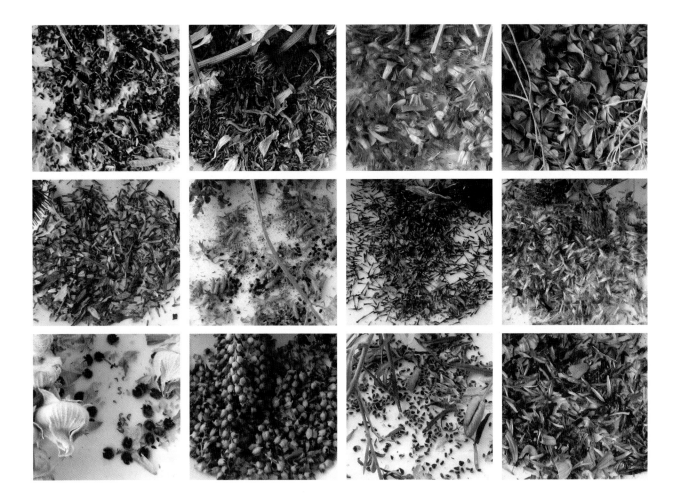

SELF-SEEDING PERENNIALS OR LET MOTHER NATURE NURTURE

WITHOUT THE SEEDS of autumn, there would be no next year's gardens. In the challenging Rocky Mountains, gardeners fight to grow. Western perennials never reach the heights or dimensions that wetter, warmer gardens do, with one exception, the self-seeding perennials. Self-seeded starts like *malva* have a vigorous hardiness and natural beauty that compliments the mountain gardens far better than many of the new pricy hybrids.

Add to this the satisfaction a gardener feels when nurturing those funny little hard brown seed nodules into the brilliant colors and breathtaking fragrances that flowers become! What a rush! Besides, it's a great deal! Few things in life are free, especially something as special as perennials!

Perennials that readily self-sow or naturally propagate themselves are the backbone of a garden. Fall dropping or sowing of seeds mimics nature by allowing plants to germinate in spring after being subjected to the cold temperatures and moisture of winter or vernalization. These seeds are so anxious to germinate they will sprout in the spring garden, eliminating any worry of hardening off or sun burn that greenhouse plants deal with.

Most seeds come from the center or end of a perennial that has finished blooming. Seed heads hold thousands of seeds within their dried blooms. Perennials with daisy-shaped blooms hold their seeds in the middle disk of a flower. Stem-type perennials form their seeds on the end of the stem.

The sowing of seeds is done in three common-sense approaches. For one, the gardener can collect, dry to ripen fully, and spread the seeds. Another option is to relax and allow the perennials to do their own sowing. Many will be lost to wind or birds, but this can be a blessing unless a garden has room for thousands of *malvas*! The usual method of sowing is a combination and has been performed since the dawn of gardening, so let's get started!

Enjoy this look at some of the easiest self-seeding perennials. They are all easy to seed, easy to germinate and easy to grow. The examples shown are just a small minority of self-sustaining perennials and know there are tons more to try.

Alcea rosea or Hollyhock seeds form round pods that are full of seeds. The seeds are large and easy to handle. They yield a high germination rate even when the seeds are not fresh. Grow seed lightly covered.

Aquilegia or Columbine seed pods form on the ends of stems and must be used immediately or it will go dormant, so fresh seed is mandatory. Seed germinated columbine will be stronger and hardier than the parent. Grow seed uncovered.

Aruncus or goatsbeard seeds true but are slow growing. Fresh seed is imperative. If seed is held, the germination rate drops by a fourth. Grow seeds uncovered.

Delphinium grandiflorum is short and bushy and could be called an annual/biennial/perennial, but whichever it is called, it's a first class self-seeder. Sow fresh seed lightly covered.

Echinacea or purple coneflower and Rudbeckia are in the same family so are seeded the same. They are easily propagated from seed either exposed or lightly covered.

Gaillardia seed forms round balls of seed. It is such a friendly seed that it can be sown anytime with excellent results. The seed needs to be exposed to light so grow uncovered.

Heliopsis or 'Summer Sun' germinates reliably at about 70 percent from a fall self-sowing. Grow seed uncovered. New seedlings will bloom the first year.

Leucanthemum superbum, or shasta daisy, form seed in their circle disk. They are easily propagated by seed. Grow seed lightly covered. Hybrid seed will not germinate successfully.

Nepeta or Catmint, almost seeds too easily, so keep the perennial deadheaded unless you choose to seed the entire United States. Grow seed uncovered.

Scabiosa caucasica, 'Fama,' or pincushion plant, is a premier perennial for western gardens but the seed and plants is not readily available so I harvest the seed carefully. Cover the seed lightly.

Allow Veronica 'Crater Lake Blue' to sow itself. As soon as the seeds are ready they will fall naturally off the stem. Leave the seed exposed.

Poppy seeds have filled this meadow with their glorious blooms without any intervention by man. The poppies may have been sown by wind dispersal or bird droppings but however it was done it is glorious!

These are just a sampling of perennials that are easy to self-sow. If you are uncertain about a plant, experiment and allow the seeds to dry and fall to the ground off the plant. If you want seedlings in your garden do not use pre-emergent herbicides for this chemical does not allow seeds to germinate.

Chemical fertilizers sprinkled around the parent plant often kill germinating seedlings.

As the mustard seed symbolizes that all things are possible, seeds have the same purpose that of replenishing the earth. Seeds are a powerful symbol for the beginning of everything.

Sedum, 'Autumn Joy'
(SEE-dum)
STONECROP AND LIVE-FOREVER

SHAPE	An almost square, strong shape, with huge heads of flat topped flowers in fall
HEIGHT	24 to 30 inches tall
WIDTH	20 to 24 inches
BLOOM TIME	Fall blooming plus other seasons have interest
COLORS	Fall blooms are pink, rusty red, and burgundy
SITE	Alkaline, poor or dry soils
LIGHT	Full sun to partial sun
HARDINESS	Zone three
COMMENTS	Excellent for xeriscapes

Sedum, 'Autumn Joy' makes a strong, dependable statement in the garden. Autumn Joy is a forever perennial and will always add stability to any garden. If you are curious how I dared make this bold statement? It was easy because it's true, and 'Autumn Joy' will prove this fact as we get acquainted.

Sedums bloom in the fall at the same time as asters. Both perennials become a hive of activity as they pleasure pollinators hurrying to prepare for winter.

Sedum with its strong silver-grey architectural consistency acts as a contrasting border or layering against the bronze-foliaged Canna Lilies. The 'Autumn Joy's' flowers are changing color, still having a trace of lime-green in their florets. *Sedum* in full bloom with its dense flower heads of russet pink will add another unique contrast between the two plants as the season passes.

The *sedum* hasn't quite colored into full bloom and is pictured here in its mid-season mode. When it shows up after winter without fail it's like an old trusted friend returning each year, better than the year before.

IT'S OFTEN COOL to be "square" for I'm as square as a flower can be both in shape and temperament and my name is *sedum*, 'Autumn Joy.' If you reside in the high western valleys, I guarantee that you will be more than pleased to make my acquaintance. The reasons are many: First of all, I'm indestructible, self-sustaining, and a hardworking, square-shaped perennial! The alkaline, rocky clay, often salty soils of the west along with the clear intense mountain sunshine give me a grand handsomeness. When planted in your garden, I'll remain as long as you wish. I suppose this is why my common names are, live-forever or stonecrop and my Latin verb name means to sit on stones for I'm tough, live as long as a stone and need about the same amount of care!

My flat-topped star-shaped flower heads give bees a custom landing strip so they can grab a quick snack. I'm a rich food source, so they flock to my flowers. Little do they know they are far more important to me than to their bee colony! Bees are the only successful hybridizer for my family. New varieties of *sedums* are not produced in plant laboratories but only by the pollination of bees. Hybridizers keep trying but I'm good as I am and have no desire to change. One word of warning, position me away from paths, walkways or children's play areas for bee stings are never enjoyable.

Another strength I bring to a garden is my unusual texture. Everything about me varies from the fussy, flamboyance of other flowers for my foliage and flowers are totally different. My flowers are such tightly packed symmetrical clusters that I stand out in the garden and can easily define one space from another. I can be used as a short hedge around an area like an herb garden or perennial flower bed.

My hardiness is legendary. I handle cold winters even when they are dry plus I handle the hottest of summer heat and dry conditions. I always look excellent in xeriscapes or other tough conditions because my waxy, succulent leaves store water. I'm related to another famous drought, water storing succulent like the house plant, Jade with it thick water filled petals. It' an interesting fact that my leaves will curl in hot dry weather as a visual reminder to water the garden so I act as a sort-of moisture monitor for the other Perennials. Wildlife, except rabbits, will shy away from me so this is another feature of my appropriateness when growing in the Rocky Mountains. Gardeners find that I can be planted where no other plant will grow; for example on a steep bank that is impossible to water or in the shade of a pine tree. I may not bloom as fully under the pine tree, but I'll still grow with attractive foliage that may be a little smaller and shorter but I'll still fill a very tough spot.

Like an old trusted friend, I return and establish instant rapport with other flowers in the garden. By fall, when so many of the earlier perennials are past their prime, I reach my prime potential and dominate borders with my unique look and stable shape.

I provide the garden with four seasons of interest. I break dormancy in a charming silvery-blue rosette groundcover form that is attractive with the spring alpines. As summer progresses, my clumps lift up their thick stems, stretching silvery spoon-shaped gray-green leaves to become the background for summer and fall bloomers. With the first cooler temperatures, my blooms start to flush to rosy pink and then age to a deep rusty burgundy finish. With a hard frost my foliage drops but my strong stems remain standing even in deep snow, so winter fails to tamper with my persistent ornamental appeal. The winter birds will visit me daily, landing on my dried blooms to pick a few seeds.

Less is more with *sedums*. Do not pamper me with lots of water for I'm not a diva. I grow much better when abused, ignored, cut in half, topped, tortured or divided. Divided

The summer shape and color of 'Autumn Joy's' rounded flower forms are often referred to as looking like broccoli, but the strong structure of sedum partners well with garden rock work.

sedums never miss a heartbeat and a division will easily reach the same size as the mother plant by the next year. Dig up the entire *sedum* root ball in spring. Split with a shovel or knife into any desired sized sections and replant at the same depth I was previously growing. Cuttings are also easy to start with a 99 percent success rate. Take my cuttings before July. Cut six inches off each *sedum* stem and stick it in a well-draining pot of soil. The biggest failure will occur with over-watering, so keep my starts comfortably dry. By late summer the new starts will be ready for the garden or as gifts to gardening friends. A point of interest is that upright *Sedums* grown in the west rarely flop unless planted in a highly amended soil and are babied!

Sedum adds a spectacular sight to fall gardens when my enormous rosy-colored blooms reach full potential. Usually my thick stalks hold them proudly upright, but occasionally the blooms are just too massive and I'll splay open. When this happens, it's time to divide me next spring. Division always invigorates me. Weak stems can also be the result of overly rich soil. I prefer lean, even sandy or rocky soils and grow really well in clay. As long as the soil causes me to struggle, I do well. The same with fertilizing, a sprinkling of the same spring feeding given lawns is more than enough for me. Excess fertilizers will cause me to grow taller, fall open and dump my flower heads in the mud so go easy on babying me with amendments and fertilizers if you want me to look my best. Low light areas like when I'm planted under a pine tree will cause me to grow spindly stems as I reach for more sun. In this situation pinch the tops off knowing I don't really bloom well in shade anyway, but the pinch will freshen and strengthen my foliage. Keeping me at my best during bloom time is easy for all that is needed is to divide, plant me in full sun conditions that require some struggling and if really necessary cut back my stem to help shorten and thickens my stalk.

When *sedums* reach their full fall bloom potential their flowers are as huge as grapefruits. The blooms can bow from the weight of these heavy clusters.

'Autumn Joy' is the standard from which all other upright *sedums* have emerged even winning the Royal Horticultural Society's Award of Garden Merit. But hybridizers keep trying, sometimes coming up with a new leaf or flower color but the end result is that these new varieties even with a new, different colored foliage will still look and act like just like 'Autumn Joy'!

'Purple Emperor' is a tall *sedum* that actually differs from 'Autumn Joy'. With its rich, satiny, plum foliage 'Purple Emperor' has dramatic eye-catching quality that stands out from the border, easily replacing any flowering plant with its dark shiny elegance. The graceful 'Purple Emperor,' unlike its blockier cousin, mingles easily with other plants without

Sedum will perform all season long and does it so low-key that there isn't a flower that doesn't look great alongside live-for-ever. Here *sedum* fronts for Russian sage and backs for stripped iris, geraniums and 'Homestead Purple' verbena.

dominating them. 'Purple Emperor' doesn't splay open if it is topped in mid-spring, becoming more appealing with age. The key to attractive 'Purple Emperors' is to give them time! In flower 'Purple Emperor' will display balls of dark pinkish-burgundy-red stars on the tip of each stem. 'Purple Emperor's stems are more delicate than I am and have a tendency to bend but are still eyecatching in any flowerbed.

Western gardeners are fortunate that I find growing in mountain gardens so pleasing. I'm a delight to observe through the seasons as I start out as a mini groundcover, stretching to a cabbage and becoming a lush green back-up foliage. Fall brings my handsome pinkish-rusty-red ball-shaped flowers. I thrive in sun, partial shade and even under a pine tree where nothing else wants to grow. The western environment with their variety of poor, rocky and even salty soils are to my liking as well as my preference for alkaline soils and water. How blessed regional gardeners are to have a perennial like 'Autumn Joy' to watch their backs wherever my help is needed.

Sedum, 'Purple Emperor', a hybrid *sedum*, with elegant dark burgundy foliage has a tendency to almost cascade (as in this picture). This splendid perennial grows more relaxed than 'Autumn Joy' but will stay more compact if topped in spring. 'Purple Emperor's plant structure improves with every year of maturity.

ROCKS GIVE GRAND GARDENS

WESTERN GARDENERS are fortunate to live where there is an abundance of rocks for their versatility as a landscaping medium is phenomenal. Our mountains are full of these timeless beauties with the integrity of the ages written in their weathered faces. Rocks are so powerfully dependable that once a gardener has a rock they will always have a rock. Rocks are so easy to use in the landscape, just dig a hole and set it in. As the old saying says, "Find a rock and pick it up! For the rest of time you will have good luck"! The following are a few of many ideas to make your yard grandeur with rocks.

Rocks are valuable, cost-effective resources when landscaping a home if you have the manpower. These rocks were already located on the homeowner's property, so he added the simple rocked ledge to give his home's entrance a grounded unity with the mountains in the background.

Water features and rocks are like bringing soul mates together. The combination adds a special ambiance to a landscape. Water features can be as small as a single stone, as seen in the picture below, or as magnificent as the waterfall in the following photo.

Rocks, no matter how they are used in landscaping, change a "ho-hum" garden into a jaw dropping, "a-ha" work of art. Acquiring rocks is not for the "faint" of heart or back. It is a hard strenuous labor of love as apparent by the above picture of my husband, Donrey, who helped me haul rocks for our Bear Lake gardens. Permission from the owner of the property where rocks are located was the first step and usually has a price tag involved. The Government, BLM lands, owns all mineral rights on mountainous BLM property, so this acreage is off limit. There are businesses now that sell rocks by the pound and they load and some even deliver.

ROCKS TO THE RESCUE

By using rocks, any yard can solve elevation problems. Rocks can be piled, edged, barricaded, or whatever a homeowner desires, but finding rocks in your local vicinity is convenient as long as they appeal to you. The Bear Lake valley, in Northeast Idaho, where we garden and collect rocks, is famous for its sandstone quarries of russet-reddish colored sandstone. In Pocatello, Idaho, black basalt lava rock is the rock of choice because the city is situated between black lava rock formations. In Montana, their rocks might contain clear or colored crystals. Local rocks look more natural and keep the cost of hauling more manageable.

The simple ambiance of a single slab of rock with cooling, relaxing sounds of running water is the center stage spotlight of this garden. The rock mulch beneath the jewel-like looking stone grounds the rock and covers the water's reservoir below.

Every type of waterfall is possible when working with rocks. The sky is the limit, as shown by this beautiful rock waterfall.

Rock can be used to build retaining walls that are primarily a soil barrier when a change of elevation is required. They help level and stabilize the ground while providing easy to reach planting areas. The rocked walls will stop erosion of valuable soil, especially when they are planted with tough-rooted perennials like alpines.

Rocked edges for flowerbeds give a tidy look to a garden, but more important, they are easy care and raise the flowerbeds so they visually show off better. Tall rocks will form a higher wall while short rocks act more as a division between two areas.

Stepping stones are a way to get from A to B in a part of the garden that gets stressed by foot traffic that has created natural yard trails. A strip of narrow property located along the side of a home is another area that will become more usable with a pathway. Choose stone that compliments your home and yard. The ideal rocks for stability in a path are the largest, flattest, most solid rocks available. Too small of rocks will tilt and lift in western winters. To build a straight rock path, use a double set of string and stakes. For a curved path, use two hoses laid in graceful curves with wider spacing at turns. Try a test run, grab a friend and stroll between the

How to access the lower house level of this home was a big problem but the rocks came to the rescue and gave the home a very unique appearance.

Tall skinny rocks planted firmly around a flowerbed edge will add a much-needed finished look, especially when planted with alpine perennials like this *sedum*.

string and hoses to check out the walking comfort for the path is easy to adjust at this time. For a more permanent path installation, excavate the sod or soil to a depth of at least five-inches. The wider the path the more usable and enjoyable it will be.

Fill the path base with at least three inches of sand, for sand is cheap and easy to shift for leveling. The frost-freeze cycles in our high valley gardens can cause the rocks to heave, so the sand is crucial. Heavier, thicker stones can be set directly on the sand. Thinner stones like flagstones will require more sand for leveling. Fit the rocks into a path jig-saw puzzle by placing a larger rock and then two smaller sizes for a balanced look. Check the rocks for stability by rocking back and forth

A garden bed may be difficult to work in due to its width. An attractive rock path or stepping stones will give easy access to a hard-to-reach area for maintenance purposes.

on each rock. If the rock wobbles adjust the sand base. Fill the cracks with sand and sweep. Your rock pathway is now ready to be enjoyed.

When purchasing property in the Rocky Mountains, unlevel foothills or mountain sides are typical building lots. Steep elevation changes increase the problems to solve in landscaping but usually add to a unique and attractive landscape. These elevation changes can usually be solved

A flat stepping stone placed in the flowerbed is an attractive focal point but also a convenient way to reach a tap or cut a flower without getting your feet wet or muddy.

by using rock for building steps. The site will decide how many steps will be needed to facilitate a safe passage in both directions. Professional rock landscapers have a measurement method to find the run or length of the stairs and the rise which is divided by seven inches, the normal height for most steps. This will tell how many tread stones will be needed.

Start with the bottom step which acts as an anchor and foundation. Stairs set in a ready mix mortar are longer lasting and safer to climb because water and ice have a tendency to shift un-cemented rocks over time. In colder climates use mortar that contains an air entrained admixture. This type of mortar uses less water so use the squeeze method to check it. Take a handful of mortar in your hand and squeeze. If the water content is correct the concrete will not crumble or ooze through your fingertips when your hand is opened.

To construct the first riser, fill the back of the bottom tread-rock with mortar and press the riser into the mortar. Patience will be needed for mortar can take one to three days to cure before being able to start the next step. A very slight tilt downward and one-inch overhang on the tread stone will accommodate water run-off. Follow this procedure one step at a time, knowing that soon the rocky march to the top will be reached.

Rocks in the Mountain West are a major player as focal points in the garden. It often seems that homeowners think the bigger the rock the better. A nesting of an odd numbers of smaller rocks may look more natural, not like something dropped from outer space, and still give a similar effect. Bury the boulders, by one-third for a natural look as well as for stability. A variety of boulder shapes from tall vertical to low massive and flat, placed creatively, become interesting focal points. Boulders are so easy-care, never needing trimming, weeding, fertilizing or watering, and they promise to never need replacing.

Stone mulch adds a crisp, clean modern look to a property but also grounds boulders. The mulch will heat-up a flowerbed earlier in spring and will cut way-back on the amount of water needed. Drought tolerant perennials in this type of area will be more successful.

The unique beauty of stone in all its shapes, sizes and colors has made it very popular as a welcoming street sign/ focal point. Huge boulders are favorites for housing developments but many are smaller and simply have the name or address of the homeowner engraved on the face of the rock.

Sandstone is composed mainly of sand-sized minerals or grains of rock. Sandstone is formed when compacted by pressure of overlying deposits that become cemented by the precipitation of minerals dripping into the pore spaces between the sand grains.

As snow and rain filter into the pores it becomes hardened and forms sandstone. Common mineral cementation agencies are silica made from weathered earthen crust materials called quartz and calcium carbonate or lime. This is why these intricately colored slabs of rock are called limestone.

The combination retaining walls and stairs has given this home a very appealing entrance. That the rock work was probably done by a professional rock layer is evident in the quality of workmanship. Sometimes a do-it-yourselfer must bite the bullet and hire help.

Rocks become focal points in any garden and are just as attractive in winter. How satisfying to never have to water, weed or trim and always have an attractive entrance like the one above.

This well-groomed entrance planting is attractive and only requires a blower to remove occasional debris. A weed barrier is usually laid beneath the rock mulch to help deter weeds. Rock mulch is very effective in drought-tolerant, xeroscape gardening.

An engraved rock is a forever address sign. This rock was given to us as a Christmas gift from our children. When opening the gift, I started to cry. My son gave me a comforting hug and explained, "There aren't any dates, Mom." We really love our engraved rock!

The sandstone appears to be growing right out of the tops of this high mountain range, or perhaps the mountain is growing out of the rocks. Actually they are both interacting and this is how.

Sidalcea, 'Party Girl'
(sy-DAL-see-uh)
PRAIRIE MALLOW

SHAPE	Tall narrow spikes with orchid petite flowers
HEIGHT	Up to thirty inches
WIDTH	Stays narrow
BLOOM TIME	July and with cut back into October
COLORS	Orchid to pink with white centers
SITE	Well-drained light soil, even sandy, with adequate water
LIGHT	Full sun
HARDINESS	Zone five
COMMENTS	*Sidalcea* is a miniature hollyhock

I'm a California girl, called *Sidalcea*, 'Party Girl.' I was first discovered as a native wildflower or "wild child" growing all along the high coastal meadows of the west coast of the United States. Now hybridized and named 'Party Girl,' I'm present and not rare in Utah, Colorado, Nevada, and Mexico. My presence is questionable in colder more northern states.

The soft orchid of my satiny flowers is a low-key tint in the gardens. My color is never brash or rowdy but mellow giving me a "playing well with others" social status.

Blooming from the bottom up is standard flowering procedure for *Sidalcea* plants. By planting 'Party Girl' in a group the bottom spent blooms never show but the top flowers will.

Total opposites, stocky 'Autumn Joy' *sedum* and tall skinny 'Party Girl' sidalcea make an attractive pairing when socializing together in the garden.

FOR A SUCCESSFUL party in the garden, add my name, *Sidalcea*, 'Party Girl', to the invitation list! I love a party for I'm a comfortable presence in the sunny summer garden. My tall spiky shape and size add a vital freshness and contrast to the roundness of most other perennials. Even my flowers are unusual for they are miniature, satiny-smooth funnels of orchid with a white splotch heart center. The low-key colors give me a comfortable mixing with other perennial colors. Plant me in a group of three to thirteen plants for I'm so skinny I could easily evaporate among the other perennials.

In mid-summer, when my delightful buds are opening I become center stage for my stocky stems hold me so straight I resemble a florist's vase of cut flowers growing right in the garden. My shape also furnishes attractive fillers and height for cut flower arrangements, and I last about ten days in a vase. I naturally belong in a cottage garden, for my seeds will germinate and randomly weave through the other flowers giving that unrestrained informal appearance cottage gardens are famous for. The hardiest, longest-living *sidalcea* plants are the self-seeding varieties that show up in meadows and along the sides of roads. Perhaps this is a genetic backtracking to my earlier wilder roots. No matter what garden I'm in, plant me in a group so I can mingle nicely for I'm better with others than in a solo situation.

As I get ready to bloom, my one-inch buds will open vertically up my stems so I bloom from the bottom up. This blooming is typical of my popular relative, the very hardy *Alcea* or hollyhocks for we are both mallows. I'm considered a native perennial but I often wonder if some weird genetic drift or multi-pollination could have changed me from the Hollyhocks for everything about me is more delicately refined. I could be called a miniature Holly hock but unlike the biennial , *Alcea* family, I'm a true perennial. Most *Alcea* other than the fig-leaf varieties are biennial so their seed germinates in spring. Their foliage develops throughout the season, with tap roots moving deeper into the ground, but *Alcea* will not bloom until the following season. This is the role of biennials. They grow the first year, bloom the second and then succumb after flowering and die. As a perennial, I return in spring, wintering well in mountain gardens with the exception of the bitter cold of the lower zoned highest elevation areas.

My foliage is classy also. I form a rich green eight inch clump of palmate or palm- shaped deeply lobed basal leaves. My stout spike stem foliage becomes more deeply lobed as it lifts up to about thirty-inches with blooms forming in mid-July. Staking is not required due to my thick fibrous roots that hold my tall stems solid and secure. As long as I get enough to drink, for remember my name is 'Party Girl', I will keep performing into fall but if I'm forced to dry out I'll refuse to bloom and move into a premature state of dormancy. With plenty to drink and a good cutback, I've been known to bloom until the end of October. These four months of blooming time places me at the top of the long blooming perennial list.

I prefer the arid mountain climates with their intense sunshine, warm days and cool nights and will not grow in the heat and humidity of southern gardens. I'm advertised as a zone-five perennial, but, surprisingly, I'm so at home in the brighter sun of the mountains I survive quite well. There will be losses for I'm a short-lived perennial. Unfortunately I'm not like the long-lived peony but enough will seed and survive to enhance the summer garden. Allowing me to reseed furnishes new seedlings to "watch my back" as insurance for future generations. Because I bloom from the bottom up, my seeds ripen and drop sporadically so it is tricky to try to save all of my seed. Removing the seed stems would eliminate fall blooming so a more simple policy is to let me do my own sowing and then weed out the seedlings in the spring. My seedlings are more robust than our parent and act more like the original wildflower before it was cultivated as a hybrid. Here's how to seed 'Party Girl.'

SEEDING 'PARTY GIRL'

1. The age of the seed determines the ease of growing. Old seed will probably require a two-week chilling treatment followed by heat for germination. They might also need scarifying the seed coat.

2. New seed germinates quickly in a week to ten days.

3. Cover very lightly. I need light to germinate.

4. Seedlings can be transplanted three weeks after sowing.

DIVISION OF *SIDALCEA*

I CAN BE DIVIDED, but like most tap-rooted perennials, I may or may not be successful. Division for me is the same standard procedure used for dividing any perennial.

1. Prepare the garden soil in full sun.

2. Add organic matter to keep me cool and moist along with good drainage.

3. Dig a deep hole and fill it with water. Let the soil soak before planting so I can adjust to my new environment.

4. Plant me at crown level twelve inches apart so I'll grow as a full clump.

5. Fertilize me in spring.

Beekeepers often seed me commercially in a meadow, because not only do I restore the area with my deep taproots but my rich pollen makes tasty honey. Beekeepers purchase me by the pound and will use a seeder or fertilizer spreader to broadcast my seed at an approximate rate of two pounds per acre in meadow gardens. Icelandic poppies for early season nectar-rich food and *sidalcea* for fall feeding is a splendid teamwork, host-home for pollinators to lay eggs and furnish all season food for bees.

Sidalcea plants are uncommon or not readily available from the American perennial trade and a gardener may need to search for them.. Looking under my other common name of Checkerbloom may help. Widespread popularity may have jumped over me probably due to my short-lived nature and preference for cool summer climates. Sometimes Eastern plant growers assume incorrectly that westerners are not in-to gardening. Other hybrid varieties of *sidalcea* offered are 'Elsie Heugh' with light lacy pink flowers. 'Brilliant' is a pale mauve pink and is the hardies of the sidalceas at a zone four, hardiness. 'William Smith' has salmon-pink flowers. These hybrid perennials are only propagated vegetatively, meaning by cuttings or divisions and not by seed.

I'm known as an easy care plant, I self-seed, grows with average requirements and most important, I'm beautiful. My nectar is of the highest quality so my "Sippy cup" is always full for humming birds and bees. As a native habitat for pollinators like bees, wasps, flies and butterflies I provide a host plant for their eggs as well as forage so I'm very valuable in the garden. All of these are valid reasons for enjoying sidalcea so hopefully I'll be on the guest list of your next garden party.

The dissimilar foliage of *Sidalcea* from the bottom rounded leaves of the basal clump compared to the lacy foliage at the top is another unusual element of this delightful perennial.

Sidalcea has a natural knack of appearing attractive with any companion plants in the garden. The pink and white tall garden *phlox* surrounding the base of *sidalcea* have the same blending, monochromatic colors as *sidalcea* so they are attractive neighbors. The clean fresh pink and white colors appear softly romantic. The small white *antimus* or golden margarita in the background also adds to the feminism feeling the colors and flowers give this garden. Companion perennials demonstrate how well I fits into the group so I certainly deserve the first invitation to the garden party.

Sidalcea, 'Party Girl,' and *Dianthus*, 'First Love,' blend so that the colors of both plants are more beautiful.

The background tall *Aconitum*, or wolfbane, also has palm-shaped foliage similar to *Sidalcea's*, but the two foliages are still attractive together. The later-blooming *Aconitum* will start flowering in deep blues as soon as the weather cools.

PERENNIAL COLOR COMBINATIONS

COLOR IS SEEN in the eye of the beholder and your location on the planet, for light is energy that moves in tiny particles or photons on wavelengths. Light moves like sound waves but are much faster and is a portion of radiation given off by the sun. Sunlight is the key factor in photosynthesis that fuels both plant and animals activities and without it there would be no flowers or no green. So what does this have to do with the color of perennials? Colors have different wave lengths and each wavelength is perceived by our eyes as a different color. The shorter wavelengths are seen as violet. Then as they start to stretch longer our visible light sees blue, then green, then yellow, and then orange. Finally, when the longest wavelengths reach us, we see red.

The primary colors; blue, yellow, and red create all the other colors we see. So now let's see how primary colors work in the flower gardens.

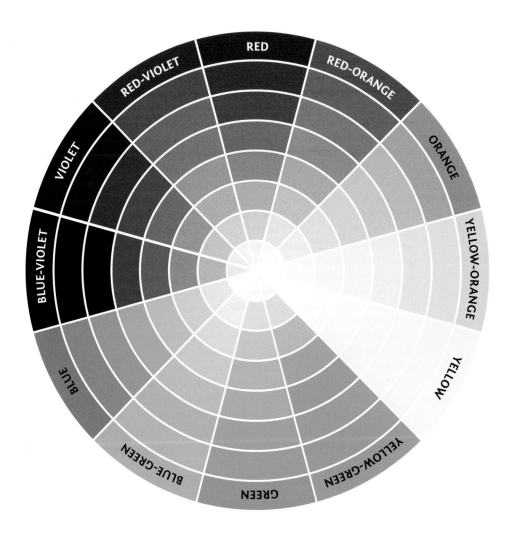

A gardener's favorite colors and flowers are a source of great satisfaction in the garden. Working these flowers and colors into the landscape requires some understanding of how colors blend or contrast. A color wheel, even though it is an abstract illustration, helps gardeners visualize these concepts. For example, *Sidalcea* is attractive with other perennials because of its mellow color and the mood of quiet beauty it brings to a garden. Not all flower colors are so subtle. Certain other flower colors like the basic primary colors of red, blue, and yellow are high-energy colors that attract attention by adding an exciting design element to the garden. Green is always a color in play, so it is not considered a primary color in gardens.

PRIMARY COLORS

Planting perennials that bloom in primary colors of red, yellow, and blue backgrounded with the green of their foliage delivers high drama to a garden giving a totally different look from a planting of the soft tones of *sidalcea*.

Note: Green in the garden is a primary color also, but it is not counted as a color but as a background. White is used as an accent with any of the other colors, so it is not a part of the color wheel. Below is another example of flowers blooming in primary colors.

Not only do these three perennials add a hardy stability to a garden but when placed as a trio they add an exciting drama. The longer I garden the more I like using a trio of primary colors for they make the garden look amazing.

COMPLEMENTARY COLORS

Any two of the primary colors mixed will create complementary colors of orange, purple, and green. These six colors are the basic color wheel. These colors bring a vibrant high energy to a garden and work well together when a gardener wants something to stand out. A glance at the color wheel will show complementary colors are red and yellow, blue and orange, yellow and violet. Complementary colors make bold statements in the garden

The bright red of the *Lychnis*, 'Molten Lava,' contrasting with the pure yellow of evening primrose is a dramatic example of complementary colors or any two of the primary colors used together.

The orange of the *papavers* are a perfect complement to the blue of *nepeta*.

Opposite colors on the color wheel are complementary colors because opposites actually complement each other. When purple and yellow are planted together, they make each other seem brighter. The pure yellow of the *lilium* contrasts nicely with the purplish spikes of the *veronica*, 'Royal Candles.' Opposites complement each other, so they are called complementary colors.

SECONDARY COLORS

Secondary colors blend subtly because they are a blend of two colors. While complimentary colors are pure colors the secondary colors are a mix. Secondary colors occur when mixed colors are blended together, for example red and yellow make reddish orange and red and blue makes violet.

The secondary colors of the red and orange *Lilium* contrast beautifully with the red and blue or violet colors of the *Salvia*. Both flowers are a blend of colors and not pure colors of the primary colors.

TERTIARY COLORS

Tertiary colors are formed by mixing a primary and a secondary color. These colors have a two-word name; yellow-orange, red-orange, red-violet, blue-purple.

So many perennials, like these *gaillardia*, have the color blends all ready for the gardener to pick their favorites. Here the tertiary colors of yellow, and orange-red, a secondary color, still shows touches of the primary red in the flowers blooms.

ANALOGOUS COLORS

Analogous colors are three colors which are side-by-side on a 12 part color wheel. They blend nicely and are often used as a vignette. Usually one color dominates in this type of color scheme. The following picture shows two sets of three analogous colors; Yellow, lime green and green and blue, blue violet and violet.

The Sweet Potato vine in the foreground is a mix of violet, violet blue and blue. Behind it are the analogous colors of yellow, lime, and green. Perhaps a gardeners instinct does not need to know they are an analogous mix but only that they are dynamic together so they like them. Liking certain color combinations is the key to design.

TINTS AND SHADES

Tints and shades are easier to picture than analogous colors. Tints of white have color values of lightness while the darker shading have values defined as darkness of a color. Adding a tint is adding white to lighten a color. Shade refers to adding black to the original color.

Light tints add freshness to a flower's color. The addition of white tinting to red turns *peonies* to a pink tint. The 'Bowl of Beauty' *peony* is a shorter, later blooming peony that does not need staking. The lighter colors stand out more from a distance and are noticeable in a garden.

SHADES

Shade refers to dark colors of flowers or foliage. Dark colors add intensity to a garden. The 'Chocolate' Eupatorium's foliage and stems are a rich dark shade of bronze that contrasts with its white lacy flowers. Excessive dark colors will almost hide in the flowerbed so Mother Nature made the *Eupatorium* stand out by covering the dark foliage with white flowers.

The secondary colors of the red and orange *Lilium* contrast beautifully with the red and blue or violet colors of the *salvia*. Both flowers are a blend of colors and not pure colors of the primary colors.

NEUTRAL COLORS

Silver or gray colors with their neutral coloring are valuable in the garden. Their three major tasks in the garden are separating colors that otherwise might clash, tying flowerbeds together, and high lighting other colors.

The silvery neutral *cerastium* has seeded into the red *sedum* giving a delightful planting for edges or rock walls. Grey foliage always acts as a highlighter or a break between two plants that may clash. Sometimes natures color schemes are just what a garden needs.

WARM AND COOL COLORS

Colors can be warm or cool. The color wheel can actually be divided in half with all of the reds through yellows called warm colors. Flowers with warm colors are vivid and energetic. They make a space seem smaller. Cool colors are the blues and greens that give the feeling of soothing calm. Cool color gardens give an impression of space.

The heat in this picture sizzles and can almost be felt when viewing this hot-colored garden. Hot colors in the garden make the space seem smaller by seeming to bring the flowers closer.

The quiet values of cool colors shown by the blue salvia and pale-pink dianthus add space to a garden for they seem to withdraw further into the background.

MONOCHROMATIC COLORS

Many gardeners prefer a monochromatic color scheme. They like to grow flowers that are in the same color shade family and blend well together.

The monochromatic colors of pale pink, rose pink, and wine bloom together on this columbine showing exactly how three shades can be blended together for an alluring look.

Many gardeners allow perennials to figure out their own color scheme and just enjoy whatever grows wherever it grows.

Perennial gardens are interesting because they are never static and never grow according to some label or the descriptions found in a catalog. Many gardeners find a natural garden of all colors to their satisfaction.

Perennials are very independent and often choose by death or seeding where they want to grow and bloom. No matter how much color scheme planning is done, Mother Nature seems to have the final say on color schemes for gardens.

The following list of several perennials to suit your favorite color scheme may be useful: Some spring flowers bloom in every color like *Aquilegia* and tulips so are listed once and many flowers are long blooming, so they cross over seasons, but this will give a gardener a chance to find a flower in their favorite color and find out when it blooms.

FLOWERING SPRING INTO JUNE

YELLOW	RED	BLUE TO LAVENDER	WHITE	PINK
Alchemilla or 'Lady's Mantle'	Aquilegia or Columbine	Ajuga or Bugleweed	Anemone or Snowdrops	Armeria or Thrift
Aurinia or Basket-of-Gold	Armeria or Thrift	Allium	Aquilegia or Columbine	Bellis or English Daisies
Corydalis lutea	Centranthus or Red Valerian	Aubrieta or Rockcress	Arabis or Rock Cress	Bergenia or Heartleaf
Doronicum or Leopard's Bane	Guem or Avens	Brunnera	Cerastium or Snow-in-Summer	Dianthus or Pinks
Daffodils	Heuchera or Coral Bells	Centaurea or Bachelor Button	Convallaria or Lily-of-the Valley	Dicentra or Bleeding Hearts
Euphorbia or Cushion Spurge	Paeonia or Peony	Iris	Galium or Sweet Woodruff	Dictamnus or Gas Plant
Lamiastrum or Yellow Archangel	Papaver or Oriental Poppies	Myositis or Forget-me-Nots	Helleborus or Lenten Rose	Saponaria or Soapwort
Thermopsis or False Lupine	Pulsatilla 'Rubra' or Pasque flower	Phlox or Creeping Phlox	Iberis or Candytuft	Thalictrum or Meadow Rue

FLOWERING SPRING INTO JUNE (CONTINUED)

YELLOW	RED	BLUE TO LAVENDER	WHITE	PINK
Trollius or Globeflower	Tanacetum or Painted Daisies, crimson	Pulmonaria or Lungwort	Lamium or Dead Nettle	Thymus or Mother of Thyme
	Tulips	Plumbago or Lungwort	Tiarella or Foam Flower	
		Salvia or Sage		

SUMMER FLOWERS INTO AUGUST

YELLOW	RED TO ORANGE	BLUE TO LAVENDER	WHITE	PINK
Achillea or 'Coronation Gold' or 'Moonshine'	Gaillardia or Blanket Flower	Campanula or Bellflower	Aruncus or Goat's beard	Alcea or Hollyhocks
Antimus or Golden Marguerite	Hemerocalis or Daylily	Cranesbill or Geranium	Filipendula or Meadowsweet	Echinacea or Cone Flower
Coreopsis or Tick seed	Hibiscus	Delphinium	Leucanthemum or Shasta Daisy	Malva
Heliopsis or Oxeye daisy	Kniphofia or Red-Hot-Poker	Lavender	Gypsophila or baby's breath	Mallow or Prairie Mallow
Ligularia or Leopard Plant	Lilium	Liatris or Blazing Star		Monarda
Lysimachia or Loosestrife	Lychnis or Maltese Cross	Nepeta or Catmint		Phlox or Tall Garden Phlox
Oenothera or Evening Primrose		Scabiosa or Pincushion Plant		
Potentilla or Cinquefoil		Veronicas		

FALL FLOWERS

YELLOW	RED TO RUSTS	BLUE TO VIOLET	PINK
Rudbeckia or Black-Eyed-Susans	Helenium or Helen's Flower	Aconitum or Monkshood	Chrysanthemum or 'Clara Curtis'
Solidago or Goldenrod		Asters	Eupatorium or Mist Flower
		Perovskia or Russian sage	Physostegia or Obedience Plant
			Sedum or Stonecrop

Color in your garden is a powerful tool. Cool colors, greens, and blues visually expand a garden. Hot or warm colors like the reds, oranges, and yellows make the space more cozy. Color creates moods like excitement when using primary and secondary colors. The cool colors are more calming. What does your favorite garden color do?

Tulipa
(TEW-lih-puh)
TULIP

SHAPE	Strap-shaped leaves with a stem topped by a flowering cup or trumpet
HEIGHT	Several inches to two feet
WIDTH	From a single stem to a two-inch clump
BLOOM TIME	Early spring
COLORS	Every color but blue
SITE	Fertile well-drained soil
LIGHT	Full sun to partial sun
HARDINESS	Zone 3, requires a winter vernalization
COMMENTS	Most hybrid tulips are not perennials

Spring bulbs look best when planted in huge drifts of colors. Their consistency of height and bloom time is especially enjoyed in community centers or park gardens where many visiting viewers will be able to enjoy them.

Red Emperor tulips open wide to welcome spring and hide the Easter Bunnies behind them. A quick gardening tip: When planting spring tulip bulbs, under-plant them beneath perennials. *Ceratostigma plumbaginoides*, for example, is a lovely groundcover with gentian-blue flowers and red-tinted fall/winter foliage that is a perfect companion plant to tulips.

The *cerastium* breaks dormancy after the tulips have finished blooming and by late summer have completely filled in above the tulips. The *cerastium* stays semi-evergreen over winter and will need removing in March to make way for the tulips to bloom again.

Last year, these Darwin tulips were three times as tall with huge, fist-sized, true-colored-copper blooms. The gardener chose to remove the spent foliage before the bulbs had filled with nutrients. Now they are puny replicas, for the bulbs have deteriorated, and it is doubtful they will return another year.

THE REWARD FOR surviving the darkest drabbest days of winter is spring's spectacular opening show starring the tulips. We make it worth the long winter's wait for no other class of flowers brings so much elation and joy for so little cost and effort.

We are spring! Yeah spring! And Yeah tulips! We are uncomplicated to grow for we grow from bulbs and they are not only the cheapest flower but the easiest ones to grow. Simply dig a hole and drop us in and you're done! Now, I'm going to share some pointers that will convince every gardener how easy we are to grow.

We grow from an inexpensive bulb that acts as our food factory. Our bulb is efficient and stores all the nutrition we'll need to bloom next year. That is if a few of our needs are met. First, our foliage needs to stay on our bulb as long as possible for this is our source of food. Wait until a slight tug will pull the ratty leaves easily from the ground, a sign that my bulb is filled to the brim. Even if the foliage has withered and toppled, don't remove it until I'm fully satisfied. Early removal will result in smaller quality and quantity of flowers for next

year and in some cases there will be nothing at all for future spring. The solution is to camouflage my spent foliage by planting my bulbs under perennials like daylilies with similar foliage as mine, or alpine perennials like *cerastium* that will creep to cover my spent foliage so the temptation to pull me is eliminated.

My bulbs are planted in the fall so it's normal to place them on the front row of a flowerbed for that is the quickest and easiest planting spot. You will enjoy the front edge color when I bloom in spring but I guarantee you will hate me after my flower and yellowed foliage have collapsed in late spring and turned the front of your flowerbed into a mess. To keep both me, the tulips and the gardener happy, plant my bulbs deeper back into the garden and deeper into the ground and stick me under perennials. Being planted under perennials will also keep me cool, insuring I'll stay uncomfortable during my long summer sleep.

My second pointer is to plant me where I'll grow best and we like to be planted where the winters are cold and the summers are hot for our origins are Turkey or central Asia. The western Rocky Mountains are so similar in climate that it's an ideal place to grow our charming flowers. Many other areas are not so blessed for I will not grow in humid southern gardens. To bloom there, I'll require at least a full six weeks of cold vernalization dormancy (or winter weather) before I will bloom. Growers in warmer areas must keep me refrigerated or have a gardener in a colder area grow my bulbs and ship them.

PERENNIAL SPECIES TULIPS

The next reason we may not bloom the second year is that not all of us are true perennials. Most new tulips are hybrid annuals and do not survive winter or multiply. To help a gardener solve this dilemma let me introduce you to the tulip varieties that still have perennial tendencies. The original perennial tulips were discovered in Asia. Their name was based on the Persian word for turban because of the turban shape their folded flower petals created. Those original tulips haven't been changed through hybridization and are still called specie tulips. We are still small, more delicate in appearance and grow to only fourteen inches. Our many colored blooms are mammoths in reference to the size of our small plants. Many of us have stripped or mottled blue-green foliage with multiple blooms per stem. We naturalize easy in the garden and are perennial.

I suggest planting species tulips in rock gardens in casual drifts of twenty bulbs or more. Remember, I'm a smaller bulb than the hybrids, so I can be tucked into smaller spaces. A planting depth of six or seven inches is deeper than growers usually recommend but will help save my blooms from early freeze/thaw cycles that are common in western gardens.

There are probably about a hundred kinds of Species Tulips left now, out of thousands of hybrid tulips. One of the first to bloom is the Fosteriana or Emperor Tulips. At twelve to fifteen inches tall, Emperors welcome spring in vibrant colors

Tulips grow so perfect with our cold winters and hot summers that they are used in public gardens where they create design perfection in flowerbeds. The downside of this gorgeous tulip display is these bulbs are hybrids an only bloom with such perfection the first year they are planted.

Species Tulips with their true colors and big black centers are an early favorite and will return spring after spring.

of red, orange, yellow apricot and white. The Fosterianas dark centers intensify the clear flower colors. Emperors spread well, are long-lived if planted deep and many of us have interesting foliage. We are so cold hardy that we are excellent container plantings. Stick us in any type of container, old galoshes, a ceramic teapot or even a watering can. Good drainage is necessary to keep our bulbs from rotting so plant us first in plastic nursery pots with holes in the bottom that will fit inside the container of your choice. We will bring such a welcome surprise when we bloom in spring that the gardener will be delighted. When I finish blooming remove the plastic pot from the container and store it outside under a shrub. Leave me there over the winter and I'll do the surprise spring blooming number again. Often in late winter, a gardener gets over anxious for spring color then I can be moved inside the house to bloom earlier. This is called forcing and the results

are pleasing. Outside, the cooler the spring the longer I bloom. A heat wave will cause my petals to droop and drop.

PERENNIAL DARWIN TULIPS

Our Darwin Tulips are long-lived and we begin our blooming performance in May around the same time as the lilacs bloom. Darwins are a large tulip, sometimes over two feet if the soil is rich. We bloom in every color but blue and the Darwin, 'Impressions,' are the most dependably perennial. Pollinators are often responsible for the streaking of colors on my petals for they are drawn to our bright open colors. Here are a few pointers that may help me survive as a returning perennial plant.

PLANTING POINTERS

Plant my bulbs at least twelve inches deep. Package directions for tulips say five times as deep as the size of the bulbs but if I'm planted deeper I'm not so readily available bait for moles, mice, rabbits, or deer. Western wildlife considers me frosting on cake and greedily browses me to the ground.

1. A deeper depth of planting stalls my blooming time, so I'm less apt to be damaged by late snowstorms or freeze frosts.
2. Another deeper planting bonus is providing insulation from the high summer heat. Consistent high temperatures results in a poor quality of blooms for the next year.
3. Deeper planting tends to encourage my bulbs to regenerate one large floriferous bulb each year and slow down the production of small offsets. This helps me stay younger and stronger and live longer.

Bulbs are easy to grow, just plant us a little deeper in the fall with our point side up. Never remove our foliage too early for it refills our pantry for next season's flowers. Gardeners will be thrilled come spring when the dark days of winter are brightened by the world's most popular plant. Oh, and one more point: the history of tulips says that giving a red tulip to someone declares your love.

Darwin Tulips are reliably perennial, so purchase the largest size of bulbs available and as many as affordable. Prepackaged bulbs may not be fresh so purchase from a garden center or nursery that ships at the right planting time and guarantees freshness. Plant the bulbs in masses or clusters for more garden impact. Impression tulips, shown here, bloom in a variety of colors: 'Apricot Impressions' are stunningly beautiful with apricot blooms, 'Pink Impressions' are a deep rich rose, 'Red Impressions' are glowing red, 'Sweet Impressions' are pink, and a new yellow 'Impressions' is named 'Conqueror.'

Pollinators are attracted to the rich nectars in the early bloom of tulips. The streaking and striping of the tulips flowers are the calling cards left by the pollinators.

ICE-BREAKERS OF SPRING

SPRING IN THE West is a season, not a date or a month, and is signaled by the sun. It is a season of excitement because both the garden and the gardener begin to breathe life again. The cheerfulness of the tulips help but it's the small, long-lived, easy-to-naturalize, early bulbs I call Ice-Breakers that really start out the season. These tough, inexpensive delights frequently bloom right through the snow and bring joy way out of proportion to their size.

Crocus blooms in full sun or partial shade, emerging just ahead of their grass-like foliage. Each flower has three petals which close during inclement weather and reopens when warm sunshine returns.

Ice-breakers are planted in fall, no earlier than six weeks before frost. Warm weather can trigger unwanted fall top growth that will drain the bulb's stored nutrition. Caution is key when purchasing small bulbs. Be aware of prepackaged offers that have been in the box too long for tiny bulbs will dry and shrivel, or desiccate, quickly losing their ability to grow. Fresh bulbs are a necessity so try to find a place that sells these in bulk. Should the bulbs look dry, soak them in water for at least twenty-four hours and plant immediately. Set the bulb in its planting hole carefully, making sure the top is up. That's easy on pointed bulbs, but many are not pointed and it will take careful examination to reveal eyes or root bumps on the bottom. Trying to use a bulb planter in rocky western soils is usually hopeless; a shovel is your best bet. Plant deeper than label directions for shallow planting invites winter damage from weather and rodents, especially in western mountain gardens. Plant small bulbs in clumps or clusters, one landscaper I know swears on his technique of throwing the bulbs over his shoulder and planting them where they land. This amusing, random planting looks as if nature planned it that way.

Once the bulb comes up in spring the plant does its own thing with the exception of removing the spent flowers. Allowing the flowers to go to seed saps valuable energy that would go to filling the bulb's food factory so remove the seed pods as they finish blooming. Do not remove the foliage. On the "smalls"(or early icebreakers) foliage usually just disappears and is not an issue after the bulbs bloom. In truth these so called minor bulbs really have no issues and are foolproof. The "smalls" icebreaker bulbs will grow anywhere a gardener would like a touch of spring color. They can be planted in every type of landscape from along rock ways or rock gardens, in turf, container pots, under flowering shrubs and perennials, even at the base of trees for the tree roots won't mind something so small, and they will bloom before the leaves branch out. Their real job is chasing away the winter blues and signaling the beginning of a new gardening season.

CROCUSES

The most popular of the minor bulbs are the crocuses, which seem to have a built-in heating element to melt the snow around their bell-shaped blooms. Crocus grows from a buttonlike corm that forms around the top of the old, or mother, corm that dies after blooming. They flower in a wide range of colors but mainly purples, blues, and yellows. Some have delicate shading with contrasting streaks and stripes. They are diminutive, only four inches tall unless they are a larger variety which may grow to nine inches. All crocuses naturalize easily when tucked under low groundcovers like sedum or rock cress.

Crocuses are readily available online and are shipped from Holland to the company from where they were ordered who in turn ships them directly to the gardener who hopes they are still viable.

CHIONODOXA LUCILIAE OR GLORY-OF-THE-SNOW

These welcoming little jewels add sparkle to the early spring garden with their one-inch, pale-blue blooms. Glory-of-the-snow's star-shaped, delicate-looking blooms are tougher than they appear. Once they are planted and their dormancy completed, they are ready for the sun to start their internal clock and the gardener need only to stand back and admire. Glory-of-the-snow is an ideal bulb for naturalizing, meaning no maintenance is needed. Planting small bulbs like *Chionodoxa* in lawns is a simple process that anyone can do.

1. Use the back of your shovel to dig a slit into the grass.
2. Lift up the sod and plant a handful of bulbs. They are small so this equates to about five or six bulbs.
3. Remove the shovel and tamp down the sod with your foot.
4. Standard lawn care of watering and fertilizing is adequate for this Ice-breaker's next step, which is dormancy.

Glory-of-the-snow is an apt description of this enchanting Ice-breaker that blooms before the snow has melted.

Glory-of-the-snow plants well in an area of lawn that is thin or weak and will conveniently die back before it is time to mow the lawn. A carpet of these blue stars planted under the equally early blooming, golden-flowered shrub of *Forsythia* is an unforgettable and carefree spring vignette.

ERANTHIS, WINTER ACONITES OR YELLOW BUTTERCUPS

Eranthis blooms in late winter. These tiny three-inchers are a sweet surprise with their upward-facing, buttercup yellow blooms for most gardeners will forget about planting them because they are so independent and carefree. Aconites origins are in woodland areas so they are at home under deciduous trees and shrubs. They thrive in the same environment as *Hosta* and will slowly naturalize to form a long-living golden carpet under and around the late blooming *hosta*. The variety

Eranthis hymalis naturalizes more quickly, especially in our western alkaline soils.

GALANTHUS OR SNOWDROPS

Eranthis grows in shade and mixes well with early blooming shade perennials. Winter Aconite's bright-yellow buttercups look especially endearing mixed in with a planting of sky-blue *Myosotis* or Forget-me-not's with their yellow and white centers.

Galanthus's exquisite blooms of teardrop-shaped white-and-green bell flowers resembles falling snowdrops. *Galanthus* produces just one flower per stalk but will create a carpet of fetching flowers by bulb offsets. Snowdrops are so anxious for spring that they totally ignore late winter storms as if they never happened. A word of caution, Snowdrops has been placed on the endangered plant list by being over harvested from the wild. Always purchase these delightful small bulbs from a reputable commercial nursery. Because they break dormancy so early and come up in the snow, plant Snowdrops where they can be seen and enjoyed like along a front porch flowerbed or a path. Snowdrop's spent foliage disappears, so they are tidy for front edges.

Galanthus, or snowdrops, like the other small spring blooming bulbs are perennials. They grow just like other perennials, multiplying, growing stronger and thicker, and becoming lovelier every year.

HYACINTHUS OR HYACINTH

The spikes of lilac-looking blossoms on hyacinths are more popular than the smaller bulbs. They are so lovely and smell so sweet that they belong in every garden. The main issue with these bulbs is their Dutch hybrid status. Holland produces bulbs for the entire world, and Hyacinths are one of their largest exports, but like most hybrids they are not like the subtle original species of the other Ice-breakers. However after the first year of blooming these hybrids will split and revert back to their original smaller species and become long-lived, more-realistic plants and still smell just as sweet. That being said, hyacinths grow to nine inches in height and bloom in rich shades of pink, coral, red, yellow, white, and even blue. They are a must-have for window boxes and planters because of their compact spike height and unmatchable fragrance that carries into the house and over the garden. For an easy no-fail spring display, plant hyacinths into a wide mouth, shallow terra-cotta planter. The shallow pot suits hyacinths for the tops of their bulbs stay above ground and they are not to be planted deep. Leave the planter outside to winter. After ten or twelve weeks of vernalization or when the gardener becomes antsy and can no longer wait for spring, bring the hyacinth container into the warmth and light of the house to bloom. Then just breathe in the amazing color and fragrance and know even though the garden is frosted over, spring is here.

Bulbs grown inside to force an early bloom are not usually salvageable. Add them to the compost.

The alluring fragrance of *hyacinth* with its floral, spicy scent smells like spring. When the *hyacinth* buds first open, the smell is soft and sweet, but as the flowers open fully, the fragrance almost becomes intoxicating. Many very well-known perfumes contain *hyacinth* oils. It's fascinating that each flower color has its own scent. This city garden planting of *hyacinths* probably fills the entire city with its enchanting fragrance.

SCILLA SIBERIAN OR WOOD HYACINTHS AND *MUSCARI* OR GRAPE HYACINTHS

When these very similar Ice-breakers bloom, the garden becomes a haze of enchanting misty blue. Their tightly packed flowers cover the stems of grassy looking foliage as they form huge colonies that color in April or May. Both Ice-breakers are dependably easy to grow and effective growing around trees, shrubs and trees. They add pleasing spring colors in both sun and shade in naturalized woodland, wild meadows and lawns but are mistakenly called *Hyacinths* for they are not hyacinths at all. They are far more vigorous than any hyacinth and seem to grow everywhere in the United States. Their origins and hardiness varies only a touch. Squill is native to southwestern Russia with zone-two hardiness and *Muscari* came from Southeastern Europe and survives easily in zone-four areas. Both bulbs have an element of toxins that make them wildlife resistant so are not good cattle grazing feed. They both are also fragrant with the *Muscari's* smell more musky thus the plants name for the word *muscari* in Greek means "musk."

The two plants' main differences are their flowers and height. *Scilla*, or Siberian squill, blooms in several colors and resembles drooping bluebells. *Scilla* grows taller, about twelve inches with strappy leaves like daffodils. Grape hyacinths' blue blends of flowers grow on small spikes covered in tight clusters reminiscent of grapes. They are shorter, only six or seven inches tall. They both spread from self-seeding, bulb off-shoots and by any roots remaining in the ground after a gardener tries to remove them. Removing them is the problem! Both bulbs have invaded our native habitats and they are outlawed as invasive species along the West Coast. They are very difficult to get rid of once they colonize for even a left-over root fragment will grow. When your gardening friend delivers a gift-box of *Scilla* or *Muscari* bulbs and bulblets for your garden, be kind and say okay or explain they are noxious weeds, and then as soon as possible put them in the garbage can, not the compost, but the garbage can for even the smallest root or seed will germinate with an unrelenting passion!

Ice-breakers are the garden delights of early spring. They are also totally self-sustaining in the garden. They all grow well in the environmental challenges of high mountain western gardens so they deserve a spot in your garden to break the ice.

Veronica
(ver-ON-ih-ka)
SPEEDWELL

SHAPE	Clumps with spikes, even short veronicas have spiky flowers
HEIGHT	Tall; *spicata*, fifteen-to-twenty-inches, med; *teucrium*, short to twelve-inches, *repens*; prostrate spreaders
WIDTH	*Spicata* and *teucrium* to around twelve inches, *reptens* low spreader
BLOOM TIME	*Reptens*, early; *Teucrium*, Mid to late summer; *spicata*, summer to fall
COLORS	*Veronicas* are noted for their variety of blue colors but also bloom in pinks and white
SITE	Not fussy and grows well in a 6.0 acidic to 7.50 alkaline as long as the soil is well-drained
LIGHT	Full sun
HARDINESS	Generally a hardy zone three or minus 40 degrees, but many of the mid-sized Veronicas are considered a zone one or two
COMMENTS	Veronicas of one type or another are flowering from spring through fall

Veronica blooms in high summer with other summer flowers like *achillea, leucanthemum, rudbeckia,* and garden *phlox.* Speedwell provides an important contrast with its eye-catching dark-blue color and spike-shaped flowers.

Crater Lake Blue, AKA 'Royal Blue', is famous for its low, zone-one hardiness that makes it at home everywhere in the higher elevations of the Rocky Mountains. The families of *austriaca tuecrium veronicas* bloom with a short spike of intense blue in late spring. The stems are so prolific with blooms that it could be called a cascading perennial. *Veronica* "aust." as I nick-named it, is blooming here with early summer flowers of *centranthus ruber.*

The stem nodules of creeping *veronicas* root easily when they touch the soil. This is how *veronica's* common name "speedwell" came about. Speedwell refers more to the spreaders that nicely carpet the ground. That being said, the name Speedwell is old fashioned, for the *Veronicas* of today are very well behaved.

The short spikes of this early blooming *veronica* add a vibrant gentian blue flower on bright green foliage that enlivens and contrasts with the many late-spring pastel colored perennials flowering at the same time.

I BRING VERTICAL interest with my upright pointed spikes to landscapes everywhere and the best part is I do it so easily. As immigrants to the North American continent, my family mimicked the behavior of other settlers and thrived once we planted our roots in the American continent. Also like most immigrants to the United States, we have spread from coast to coast and grow ideally everywhere.

The heritage of my tall spikes, grouped as *spicata*, or spike, originated in Europe and Asia. The medium height *veronicas*, exampled by the *austriaca teucrium* 'Royal Blue' are natives of Germany and the *gentianoides* such as 'Crater Lake Blue' were discovered in the Caucasus Mountains between the black and Caspian Seas in Europe. The low creeping *Veronicas* like *liwanensis* came from Turkey while many of the reptens are from the Mediterranean area. *Veronica*, 'Georgia Blue,' another mat-forming, creeping veronica is from the mountainous country of Georgia that borders the Black Sea on the west and Russia on the north, so it is quite obvious we are of a European gene pool that is well suited to our life in the western Rocky Mountains.

VERONICA REPTENS

Now that my different sizes and bloom times have been reviewed, let's check out a few more details of what a wonderful and special perennial I am for western gardens. We are handsome perennials, and some of us start blooming in early spring while others are still blooming in fall so one of our varieties will be coloring your garden the entire gardening season. In spring, the alpines and *reptens* varieties are the first *veronicas* to bloom. We smother ourselves profusely with tiny flowers of light cobalt or sapphire blue that will also bloom sporadically throughout summer. These tiny blooms may not appear as a typical *veronica* spike but a closer look will show that the flowers are a mini spike. The Latin adjective for reptile, or *reptens*, written after our name is a key to knowing we are the ground hugging perennials that grow well in rock gardens, between paving stones, or spilling over rock walls. Our waxy foliage helps us hold moisture and usually stays evergreen over the winter months. Our flowers and foliage may look fragile, but our looks are deceiving, for we are strong and stable and will rapidly cover all bare spots in either full sun or partial shade. Short species of Ice-breaker bulbs like tulips and hyacinths look delightful pushing up through our carpeting.

VERONICA AUSTRIACA

Veronica austriaca's late spring blooms color up next. We are grouped with the Austrian or Hungarian *veronicas* and are outstanding, long-lived and heavy-blooming perennials that require little effort. We grow short, only reaching twelve inches in height and never topple. As the years pass, our width increases providing more flowers that invite butterflies and bees to buzz frantically with desire. Because we are small, our size provides an attractive front for *penstemons*, *papaver*, *lysimachis*, or any other blooming perennial for our size is a perfect front for a flower's knobby knees and blue is attractive with every other flower color. After we finish blooming, shear our elongated stems into a tidy mound. We will stay this way until frost. We are so excellent we received the Royal Horticulture Societies Award for garden merit.

MID-SEASON VERONICA SPICATAS

In early summer, our spiked speedwell family starts to "strut their stuff." The earliest to bloom is a new hybrid called 'Royal Candles' or 'Glory'. 'Royal Candles' grows only fifteen inches tall but is a dense, heavy-blooming perennial with rich, dark-blue solid spikes. 'Royal Candles' is a superb accent to every perennial but is especially effective with any of the ever-blooming daylilies with their contrasting strappy leaf foliage. The low-mounding gold flowers of *coreopsis verticillata*, another long-flowering perennial, mixed with 'Royal Candles' will give the garden a snappy blue and yellow color spot through the long summer season. Cutting 'Royal Candles' back to ground level as the blooms fade or if mildew appears will encourage another flush of bloom in August. A consistent watering schedule that keeps us not too wet or too dry will help prevent mildew. Mildew will not destroy us but only causes browned foliage on our lower branches. A cover of spring or fall mulch will help prevent mildew for it locks in moisture plus will lock out weeds. My shorter, more compact height gives 'Royal Candles' priority as a perennial for planters, containers or the front of the border. As one of the longest blooming, most reliable and hardiest of any other perennials, 'Royal Candles' is in demand by gardeners of the western high mountain valleys and every place else for that matter.

'Royal Candles' is very well behaved, requiring little care except a full sun spot to grow in and a little extra fertilizer. Like an annual, it blooms all summer. This fine perennial is so long blooming and dependable, it can be planted as a replacement for annuals along the front edge of a flowerbed.

White spikes are hard to come by in the late summer to fall garden so the white spiked speedwells are doubly appreciated especially in night gardens. Hybrid, 'White Wand' with its showy, uniform flowers above a rich, darker-green foliage on a neat compact perennial are custom plants for growing along a walkway or flower border edge. Hybrid, 'White Wand' veronica grows to only twelve-inches and is a hardy zone-four perennial. 'White Icicles' is a taller, almost sixteen-inches, hybrid with spikes that add snowy, exclamation marks to a landscape.

Pink *veronica spicata* holds on to its blue origins and is more fuchsia than pink. It is similar to the blue *veronicas*, but its pointed leaf stems are topped with pink spikes. The flowers start blooming in mid-summer and keep coming into fall. Pink veronicas are hardy, a zone-four perennial like most veronicas, and have delightful names like 'Tickled Pink.' Like all *spicatas*, they gain beauty and strength with age and look more beautiful year after year.

Veronica 'Sunny Border Blue' has a spotless reputation for its long bloom time, ease of care and hardiness. It is a zone-four perennial but always returns from winter in my mountain garden. Pinch out the middle spike of 'Sunny Border's' first flower and the plant will become thicker and denser. Some of the hybrid *veronicas* struggle in my higher elevation gardens and the white speedwells are not as vigorous or as long lived, but the 'Sunny Border Blue' delivers everything a gardener could wish for: the foliage is lush, healthy, and attractive, the blooms are sturdy and their dark blue accents add a classy look to a border. This explains why it got the 1993 Perennial Plant of the Year award.

FALL *LONGIFOLIAS VERONICA*

The tallest of my *veronica* clan are the long-leaf or *longifolias*. Some like the 'Sightseeing Mix' bloom in all three colors— blue, pink, and white—and can be grown from seed. They are larger perennials often reaching twenty-five inches in height. 'Blue John' is handsome, one of the best *longifolias* and grows to thirty inches tall in bloom. 'Eveline's' foot-and-a-half spikes bloom in pinks and violet purples. Tall *veronicas* stand up well to the wind but we look more attractive supporting each other's backs when grown in a clump of three or more plants.

Veronicas bloom from the bottom up, staggering flowers for over a month or more. The taller speedwell blooms of *longifolias* fill in nicely without overpowering a flowerbed.

We may need staking with grow through supports. Due to our height and stability, we make excellent cut flowers and are long lasting in a vase. Plant us with daylilies, tall garden phlox, or shasta daisies for a pleasing combination for my tall spikes will attractively accent other shapes of perennials.

Growing *veronica* in the garden is easy because we rarely reseed. Our fibrous roots can eventually outgrow our space so will need division. In early spring dig the entire plant and slice the crowns into smaller sections containing a sturdy crown. Replant these starts knowing success will be near one-hundred percent. Stem cuttings taken in spring root easily so this and divisions are the best method of production.

A little known tidbit about our speedwell family is that we are an edible perennial and our foliage tastes similar to watercress. It's said a tea made with *veronica* will break up bronchial congestion and that may be true for I'm very rich in vitamins.

All in all, I hope you have found me interesting for our blue spikes add to the beauty of every other flower color shape and size. We are pleasing but more than that I hope you realize I'm a minimum-maintenance perennial. I'm not fussy about soils, fertilizers, water, cold temperatures, or anything else for that matter, and I don't reseed! I hope you will aid in my immigration by adding me to the high valley gardens of the western Rocky Mountains.

Veronica in a mixed flower border.

SPIKE PERENNIALS FOR DRAMA IN THE GARDEN OR VASE

SUNNY BORDER BLUE, *Veronicas* are perennials that rescue the mid-summer border with its rich color, height, and primarily the energetic spike shapes of its blooms. Spike shapes add excitement to a perennial border because of the energy radiated by their rising above so many rounded and daisy-shaped flowers. The vertical interest they bring to the garden is dramatic and spike flowers tend to be the favorites of gardeners and florists alike for their strong stems are easier to arrange. Shown in alphabetical order are a variety of spike flowering perennials that are stunning both in the garden and the vase. All are a zone-four or under, unless a notation is made.

SERIES OF STRIKING SPIKE PERENNIAL

Aconitum, or monkshood, varieties are so beautifully breathtaking when they bloom in either late summer or fall. They bloom on unflappable strong spikes two-to-three foot tall. The blooms are long lasting in the garden and have a ten-day vase life. Cut the stems just as the buds are opening and do not chill *Aconitum* with cold water. Luke warm water moves easier through every type of flower stem. Monkshood has toxic qualities so wearing gloves when working with this plant is wise.

There are some flower spikes that do not make good cut flowers. *Alcea* has been shown here because it is not a good candidate for a vase because it collapses once cut. Hollyhock's radiant blooms are in every color but blue, and there is a black hollyhock that is magnificent. I've even tried burning their ends to help preserve them but finally gave up and just enjoy them in the garden.

Delphinium, or larkspur, brings sumptuous flowers to the mid-summer garden and the vase. Like most stem flowers with multiple buds on each stem, *delphiniums* need to be gathered while only half of the florets are starting to open. If gathered too early before the buds show color, *delphiniums* will not open in a vase of water. *Delphiniums* will hold lovely for a full week of exquisite vase life. Adding delicate branches from the yard will give the hollowed-stemmed heavy blooms an attractive support.

Digitalis, or foxglove, is so elegant in the garden or vase that it is a very popular cut flower. Remember foxglove is a biennial, meaning it needs to be allowed to reseed after blooming. Only cut a few of their blooms so the splendid plant can drop seeds to propagate foxglove for next year's flowers. When cutting the thick stems of foxglove, use a sharp razor knife and cut on a forty-five degree angle. Commercial preservatives added to the water are more effective than the myths of aspirin, sodas, or pennies.

Eremurus's, or foxtail lily's, fascinating golden feathery spikes mixed with the rounded globes of purple *Allium* are a winning combination. Foxtail lilies are a zone-five bulb so must be planted deeper than suggested by the shipper and grown in the warmer areas of the West or harvested after they bloom and stored in a cool, dark storage. Cut foxtail lily stems just as the buds start to open for a full week of enchanting vase life. The *eremurus* stems are tough so use a sharp razor knife not a pair of household scissors that may crush the stem not allowing the gorgeous flowers to take take up water. A fresh cutting on each stem as it goes into the vase helps flowers absorb water.

Kniphofia, or red-hot pokers, bring thirty inches of statuesque uniqueness when they bloom. Their poker-like shapes and hot colors of red, orange, and yellow provide a striking impact outside in the garden or inside in a vase. Do not cut *Kniphofia* until the lower stems' florets start to open. Red-hot pokers last nicely for over a week in a vase if kept watered almost daily—their thick stems and huge size suck water as if through a straw.

Liatris's, or blazing star's, fuzzy spikes bloom on sturdy stems in shades of blue-violet or white in August. The very different vertical interests they add to gardens are also attractive in a vase. *Liatris* are very long lasting as a cut flower, up to two weeks, and are also an easily dried flower. This makes *Liatris* very popular in the florist trade. Do not cut until most of the blooms have started to open. Early morning cutting is beneficial for their stems are filled with water. As the day warms up, flowers gradually dehydrate.

Lilium, or lilies, bring fragrance and their alluring hot colors of high summer to the garden and vase. Their captivating trumpets bloom on strong, handsome, up-to-four-foot-tall elegant foliaged stems and stay fresh for a couple of weeks in the cut flower vase. To keep these elegant blooms attractive and increase their vase life, change their water every other day and add a floral preservative to their water.

Note: the alkaline waters of western states will reduce the life of all cut flowers, so a floral preservative is even more important for they contain an acidifier that not only preserves but will stabilize colors.

Lysimachia puncta, or yellow loosestrife, is delightful in both the garden and the vase. Their loose spikes of star-shaped flowers with red heart-like centers appear in early summer. Harvest their flowers when they are half open and remove any foliage below the flower. As with all vase arrangements the foliage is the flower's major source of carbohydrates so add a floral preservative to replace the foliage food. Yellow loosestrife will provide up to a week of long-lasting brilliant yellow blooms.

Lupinus, or lupine, bloom in summer and are fussy when choosing a place where they'll decide to grow. If *lupines* like your garden, you'll have a gorgeous three-foot flower in your choice of any color that will light up your landscape. They will also hold nicely for a week in a vase.

Add your own preservative to their water in the vase to keep your lupines looking great. The recipe is simple: mix 1 tsp. sugar as a source of energy, 2 tsp. of lemon juice to acidify the water to prolong life, and 1 tsp. of bleach as a microorganism growth inhibitor.

Penstemon, or beardtongue, brings spikes in blues, violets, pinks, samon-reds, or white to the summer garden. Their two-to-three-foot spikes will be massed in colorful blooms. Cut *Penstemon* just as the first blooms start to open, and they will look lovely for over a week. Always carry a water bucket into the garden when cutting all flowers. Once cut the blooms have been removed from a source of water and will quickly wilt, become limp, or get bent necks and have a short, unattractive vase life if not placed immediately in water.

Physostegia, or obedience plant, blooms in late summer in delicate pink or white, snapdragon-like, two-lipped flowers. *Physostegia's* erect, stiff, square-shaped, two-foot flower spikes are dynamic in every garden and vase. Obedience spikes can be permanently curled or twisted in flower arrangements, making the plant a very popular florist item. Cut the stems as the lower buds start to open for obedience blooms from the bottom up. *Physostegia* lasts lovely for a full week in a vase.

Solidago, or goldenrod, has to be the most underused flower around, which is sad because goldenrod is perfect in the garden, as a cut flower, and for dried arrangements. At a recent wedding I attended, huge bouquets of flower decorations filled the room. They were composed of dried, newly budded goldenrod as masses of fillers with a few sunflowers stuck into the goldenrod. The decorations looked spectacular. Cutting solidago for dried arrangements is better done in mid-morning after the dew has dried. Cutting for the vase is best done very early while the stems are fully hydrated. Goldenrod grows so thick that the removed stems will never be noticed from the perennial.

Veronica's spikes in a garden add drama, and from the examples above of other tall strong-stemmed spike perennials, it's obvious that all spikes add that same energetic feeling in both a landscape and a vase. Besides the examples of the spike blooms shown above, there are other sturdy perennials that are great additions to a garden or vase. *Salvia* with its long blooming whorls of small two-lipped bloom-covered stems, flowers almost nonstop, and can usually be added to arrangements. *Nepeta* and *lavender* have long seasons of bloom and will add blue spikes and silvery foliage to an arrangement. Russian sage and *Yucca* spikes are okay but drop their petals when their stems are cut. The best method is to try what is growing in your garden to find out which perennials are best for cutting.

Here are a few tips that will help cut flowers hold up longer in a vase.

1. Cut the flowers early in the morning when they are at their best.

2. Cut only those perennials with new buds that are partially starting to open.

3. Use a sharp razor knife to cut stems.

4. Clean foliage from stems to prevent rotting in the water.

5. Lukewarm water is taken into the flower stems more efficiently than cold water.

6. Recut the stems on a 45-degree angle before placing them in the vase.

7. Stems that drip sap will last longer if they are seared with a flame.

8. Flowers like *Delphiniums* and *Dahlias* with hollow stems last longer with a touch of cotton pushed into the stem.

9. Always used a floral preservative, either purchased or from the homemade recipe offered in this article.

Many gardeners find it very uncomfortable to remove flowers from their garden so they utilize an out-of-the-way section of their yard as a cutting garden. Many inexpensive annuals can be seeded in a cutting garden like snapdragons and zinnias that can be mixed with spike perennial blooms for cut-flower arrangements. There is nothing more rewarding than a bowl of fresh flowers gracing the patio, foyer, or dinner table to welcome visitors to the home and there is no better shaped flower than a spike that make the fresh flowers look spectacular!

FULL-SUN PERENNIAL SUMMARY

FULL SUN SUMMER gardens are "sun-sational" glories of colors and textures. More choices, bigger flowers, richer colors and lusher foliage are all part of a full-sun garden. No wonder gardeners adore their full-sun gardens. This summery will point out a few cautions and list all of the full-sun perennials that grow in Rocky Mountain gardens.

POINTERS FOR FULL-SUN GARDENING

Gardening in the nonfiltered light of the full summer sun of western mountain valleys is risky for the ultraviolet radiation strengthens when the sun is physically closer. Above five thousand feet is considered a high altitude but our average mountain elevation is six thousand, and many Rocky Mountain areas climb to twelve thousand. Heat stress affects perennials in the form of leaf scorch or the ends of foliage becoming crispy and brown. Plants will often wilt with their foliage and flowers falling off. Deep soak these plants, and if this doesn't help, plan to move them to a shadier spot. Plants aren't the only garden residents who may suffer from full sun and the gardener may need an arsenal of sun protection tools.

1. Layer clothing to adapt to the quick-changing mountain temperatures. Morning temperatures may be 50 degrees or less but by afternoon will reach 90 degrees and it's shorts and T-shirt time. The high temperatures in late afternoon can usher in winds that deliver rain or hail to summer gardens, so the warm clothing layers will need replacing. "Put it on or take it off" is how gardeners adapt to the changing mountain weather conditions.

2. Sunscreen with an SPF of 30 (an SPF of 15 is not adequate) is a must. Cooler temperatures actually have an increased light intensity so gardeners mistakenly thinking it's cool outside so sunscreen won't be needed are making a false assumption. Sunburn at higher altitudes happens quickly.

   Note: Some herbal supplements like St. John's Wort seems to increase sun sensitivity so check out herb labels.

3. Hats protect both the face and eyes. Wearing a gardening hat will become second nature with practice and so will wearing sunglasses if they fit. Not only does solar radiation multiply at higher elevations but the glaring light intensity increases so sunglasses are a crucial gardening tool for western gardeners.

4. Water bottles in the arid West's low precipitation areas will help keep a gardener hydrated. Lots of fluids will prevent heat stroke. Not only do plants need more water in the high valley gardens but so do gardeners.

   Note: Alcoholic beverages are stronger at higher elevations.

A great benefit of gardening in full sun is the thousands of flowers on the market. Summer flowers bloom in spikes, daisy shapes, trumpets and bells. Full-sun gardens are six to eight hours of mostly afternoon sun. Morning sun is cooler and evening sun shines angled.

That being said, the following perennials are examples of full-sun plants that tolerate the higher elevation's challenges of cold, drought, and poor soils. Many perennials grow short, medium and tall and bloom in different seasons but are only listed once. Grouping perennials is similar to grouping people for their prime season may come in between spring and summer or summer and fall ,so know that any list is a rough reference.

SPRING-TO-SUMMER-BLOOMING, FULL-SUN PERENNIALS

SHORT–MEDIUM: ALPINES

The most popular and readily available alpine perennials are profiled in the first two units of chapter two, Full Sun. Reference *Achillea* and *Aurinia* for these lists of alpines that includes pictures and descriptions. Other, not as well known, short, spring to summer full-sun bloomers are included

Achillea tomentosa

Antennaria or pussy toes

Arabis or rockcress

Arenaris or sandwort

Aubrieta or rock cress

Cerastium

Delosperma Dianthus

Draba repens

Euphorbia

Fragaria or strawberry

Gaillardia

Geum or *avens*

Lewisia or bitterroot

Lychnis or campion

Nepeta

Papaver or Iceland poppy

Phlox, creeping

Potentilla

Pulsatilla or pasque flower

Salvia

Saponaria or soapwort

Saxifraga

Sedum

Stachys or lambs ear

Veronica

MEDIUM–TALL

Allium or ornamental onion
Centaurea or Montana bluet
Centranthus or red valerian
Dictamnus or gas plant
Hesperis or dame's rocket
Iris
Paeonia or peony
Papaver or poppy
Salvia or sage
Tanacetum or painted daisy
Thermopsis or false lupine

SUMMER-TO-FALL-BLOOMING, FULL-SUN PERENNIALS

SHORT–MEDIUM

Anaphalis or pearly everlasting
Artemisia or wormwood
Bulbs
Callirhoe or winecups
Catananche or cupid's dart
Coreopsis or tickseed
Delosperma or hardy ice plant
Dianthus or pinks
Erigeron or fleabane
Gypsophila or baby's breath
Helianthemum or sun or rock rose
Oenothera or evening primrose
Scabiosa or pincushion
Sempervivum or hens-and-chicks
Thymus or thyme

MEDIUM–TALL

Achillea or yarrow
Anchusa or bugloss
Anthemis or golden marguerite
Delphinium or larkspur
Echinacea or coneflower
Echinops or globe thistle
Gaillardia or blanket flower
Heliopsis or sunflower
Hemerocallis or daylily
Leucanthemum or shasta daisy
Liatris or blazing star
Lychnis or Maltese cross
Lupinus or lupine
Lysimachia or loosestrife
Malva or mallow
Monarda or bee balm
Nepeta or catmint
Penstemon or beardtongue
Phlox paniculata or tall garden phlox
Rudbeckia or black-eyed Susan
Sidalcea, 'Party Girl' or false mallow
Veronica or speedwell
Yucca or Adam's needle

FALL-BLOOMING, FULL-SUN PERENNIALS

SHORT–MEDIUM

Asters, 'Woods Series'
Sedums or low-growing stonecrop

MEDIUM–TALL

Alcea or hollyhock
Aster
Chrysanthemum or mum
Eupatorium or 'Gateway' Joe Pye weed
Helenium or Helen's flower
Hibiscus or rose mallow
Perovskia or Russian sage
Solidago or goldenrod

This table of full-sun perennials provides a huge selection for any full-sun garden. Most are hardy in zone three, a minus 40 degrees F. and zone four, a minus 30 degrees F. A few are nudging a zone five so it is wise to not only check the label but socialize with other gardeners in your specific area to see what grows well for every garden is full of microclimates.

Shade of trees,
summer breeze
Tech time-out,
unease flees.

PARTIAL-SUN/ PARTIAL-SHADE PERENNIALS

OUTDOOR GARDENING IN PARTIAL SUN AND PARTIAL SHADE

THE TERMS "partial sun" and "partial shade" are a judgment call done by the gardener. They are interchangeable terms, for sunshine varies during seasonal changes and times of day. By mid-summer, the sun may have climbed high enough to clear the roof-line of a tall structure making the garden sunny and in spring before tree leaves open a typical shady garden may be in full-sun. There is a difference between sunshine during morning hours and afternoon hours for afternoon sun is more forgiving. The location where the garden grows also changes the sun's intensity. The elevations of western Rocky Mountain gardens have more intense sunshine than the weaker sun of lower elevation. Where the garden is physically located is also a sun exposure factor. Huge, mature deciduous trees may grow in your backyard furnishing dappled or full shady gardens in summer and fall but is sunny in early spring before their leaves unfurl. The direction of the home in relationship to the garden defines the perennials' sun or shade comfort zone. The east side of a home is an ideal garden spot because sunrise is the gentlest light and northern exposures are light without direct sun. Southern and western exposures without some type of screening to protect plants are not as desirable for partial sun and partial-shade gardens.

Lilium, phlox, and *physostegia* performs radiantly in a partial sun/shade garden in the mountain west. Growing on the east side of a home in the early morning cool of a partial-shade garden is almost a promise of eternal childhood to *lilium* and other partial-sun-loving plants for the blooms last and last. Partial sun and partial-shade gardens are the best of both worlds for flowers.

Sun exposure for plants is not an exact science. There are always variables such as cloudy days or tree growth, so clear definitions do not exist. A plant's food is produced by photosynthesis which is produced by the sun on the plants. This explains why plants grow well in different sun environments for some plants require less sun to thrive.

Partial sun and partial shade refer to a plant that prefers three to six hours of sun a day. Their differences are that a partial sun plant requires at least four hours but will do better with six. The partial-shade perennials mean the plant never gets more than six hours of sun a day and will do better with less.

Plant tags or labels are interesting with their full round circle noting a partial sun or partial-shade perennial but are still confusing. Seed packages have the same symbols to help match a perennial to its comfort zone but a gardener's observation may be a more accurate method of where to locate their perennials. The first sign of too much shade is that the stems will stretch and lean awkwardly toward the sun. The plants may grow taller but flower production will be reduced or stopped. Then it's time to move that perennial

All of the *penstemon* family of perennials are considered full-sun, drought-tolerant perennials. This superb *penstemon,* 'Husker Red,' is growing in partial sun/shade in this Idaho garden. The location deepens the maroon-red of the lovely plant's foliage. Many full-sun perennials display a preference for more shady spectrums; especially in the higher-elevation gardens.

to a sunnier spot. A perennial that wilts with curled or crispy leaves is struggling in the sun even when its label says it is a full-sun perennial so needs to be moved to a shadier area. The bottom line is that gardeners know best.

WHAT DEFINES PARTIAL SHADE?

Partial shade gives a perennial about four or five hours of shade a day. The intense sunlight of western Rocky Mountain gardens seems to give many full-sun perennials a preference for partial shade. A partial-shade garden is usually where trees are planted quite close together so the gardens receive the angled early and late afternoon sun. An area under trees may seem to be shaded all day but the sunlight will filter through the canopy of leaves throughout the day. The heavier the canopy, the less sun will reach the plants on the ground, while more-open, lacy tree foliage allows more sunlight to reach the garden.

Delphiniums have a reputation for being a full-sun perennial. These *delphiniums*, a hardy zone-three plant, prefer the cool summer temperatures of mountain gardens. The above *delphiniums*, 'Summer Skies,' have lived in this partial-shade garden for years and years. If magnificent elegance is what you crave in your garden, plant *delphiniums* in a little shade.

Anthemis tinctori
(an-THEME-is)
GOLDEN MARGUERITE

SHAPE	Branching stems, flowers with button centers and daisy-like rays
HEIGHT	About twenty-five inches
WIDTH	From fifteen to twenty inches
BLOOM TIME	Summer to frost with deadheading
COLORS	Vibrant yellow or white with golden centers
SITE	Well drained, best in poor soils
LIGHT	Partial or full sun
HARDINESS	Zones three to seven
COMMENTS	An aggressive self-seeder

Anthemis, or golden marguerite, has self-seeded to mix skillfully with other summer-blooming perennials. Give your garden a stunning summer display by allowing *Anthemis tinctori* to self-seed attractively with other summer blooming flowers like shasta daisies, *nepeta* and *malva*.

Delicate creamy white *Anthemis*, Susanna Mitchell, has sprinkled its seeds among the elegance of double white *lilium*. This delightful color scheme could only be designed by the creativeness of Mother Nature.

Anthemis is covered with newly opening blooms that are at the perfect stage to cut for drying. *Anthemis* is one of the most successful perennials to dry for flower arrangements.

Golden marguerite daisies bloom in profusion, bringing masses of bright colors to the summer garden. When using Golden Marguerite for dying wait for the blooms to open fully at the end of their bloom time before harvesting the blooms for dyes.

*A*NTHEMIS IS THE only well-known perennial growing in North America that is pulled from the garden as soon as we finish blooming! Don't hold your breath in shock! It only sounds rude and works for me! When I've finished blooming up come my flowers, root ball and all so I won't reseed and start looking lax and lanky. Besides I'm not as pretty my second year any rarely survive after that. Fresh spring germination from my previous summer's seeds will bloom next summer. Pulling me out is a big timesaver for I won't need deadheading and in the shorter seasons of high elevation gardens, I never really re-bloom after getting cut back anyway! I'm a perennial that sort-of grows like a biennial but unlike a biennial; I don't require a full year of growth before I'll bloom. My seeds stay vital, perhaps even some from previous years, so most any seed I have managed to drop will easily germinate without any gardener intervention. Charming informal drifts of my bright white, yellow or golden flowers will appear here and there in the garden. So now I hope you understand that pulling me from the garden is harder on the gardener than me for I know what a self-sustaining, reliable seeder I am and know I'll return to brighten the gardens next summer.

My blooming time from seed may be a little later in the summer season but still coincides with the shasta daisies, lilies, malva, bee balm and nepeta. Any spots these perennials leave bare will be magically filled with my flowers.

My heritage starts in the Mediterranean, and I'm a member of the much-loved, twenty-thousand-strong family called *Asteraceae,* or flowers with button centers and fringes of ray-type petals surrounding them. We are often called composites because the flowers are actually a composite of florets arranged around a head. More commonly, our family is referred to as the Aster family, for asters are the flagship for all of the delightful daisy-shaped blooms.

Another name I'm often called is golden marguerite or yellow chamomile. Chamomile has long been used as a medicinal herb for skin irritations like diaper rash or a bee sting. There is also a popular tea made from my dried flowers. Chamomile tea has been used to ease anxiety and provide restful sleep. Drinking a cup of relaxing Chamomile tea as you sit outside on the porch and watch the consistency of the stars and moons that return without fail every evening, is a sure way to know "all's-right-with-the-world" and results in a sound night's sleep.

The diminutive loveliness of my blooms is popular in the cut flower trade for I add delicate fillers around the larger blooms. I'm also a favorite flower for drying for several reasons, first, I'm a small bloom plus I'm easy to dry.

For drying, only cut stems with new buds or flowers just starting to open. Dry weather is best for all flowers have a tendency to mold or mildew, however the dry western summers are excellent for drying us, as long as we are kept out of strong sunlight that will fade our color. Next remove the leaves from my stalks, and bunch six stems together. Tie my stems together with a rubber-band that will adjust when I shrink. Hang me in a well-ventilated, dark area for about a week or until my flowers feel crisp not sticky. I'm a delight in country style homes when placed in vases, on wreaths or even in a huge old milk-can to fill a corner of the entrance.

Another little known talent I want to brag about is I'm excellent source of fabric dye. My flowering heads create varying shades of yellows, golds, oranges, and rich beige colors depending on how many blooms are used and the texture of the fabric. To dye, wait until my flowers are almost finished blooming then remove my blooms. It's good I bloom so thickly, because you will need a lot of flowers for dye. The more flower heads used, the darker the golden colors will be. Simmer the flowers for an hour, then strain. Add the fabric and simmer another hour. My warm-yellow colors come from flavonoids in my flowers. For centuries, virtually all dyes originated from plants. The more you discover about perennials, the more interesting we become.

Anthemis is a favorite of pollinators, especially bees, just like *Monarda*. It's called bee balm because bees are so fond of it.

Golden marguerites are traditional garden fillers in cottage gardens. We stand two feet tall on aromatic, bright-green, lacy foliage. Our serrated leaves are pinnate, meaning finely divided, and have velvety down on the undersides. Strolling through a fully blooming summer garden where Golden Marguerite is residing is like walking through an apple orchard for my foliage smells like apples. My companion plants benefit too for my herbal healing qualities act as a care giver, aiding an ailing perennial growing next to me. I'm valuable in the flower border for my aromatic smell chases away pests, including deer, but bees adore visiting my flower heads almost as much as they adore Monarda or Bee Balm.

Gifting sublime, graceful beauty as a filler to enhance other garden flowers is my task in life. I'm not a huge flamboyant flower but bloom in prolific masses of small-round daisies on the ends of multiple stems. My colors are the summer colors of the sunshine. Here are a few favorites:

Anthemis, 'Kelwayi,' or golden marguerite, has golden-yellow daisy-like flowers with darker-gold centers. 'Kelwayi' is an extremely prolific and vigorous bloomer in a summer border.

'Charm' blooming here in its second season is full and colorful but does not have the compactness of 'Charm' in the first year. It's sad to say but 'Charm' did not return its third year. The happy news is that 'Charm' has self-seeded its third year so now graces the garden with a start here and there unlike most hybrids that are sterile.

The flowers of *Anthemis*, 'Sauce Hollandaise,' may be small, but the intricate rounded centers contain hundreds and hundreds of seeds that will germinate when they sprinkle to the ground.

The popular hybrid cultivar 'E. C. Buxton' is a hybrid from this species and is so easy to grow they are one of the best sources of all perennials for cut flowers. 'E. C. Buxton' blooms are larger sized and creamy-white with yellow-centered flowers.

Anthemis, 'Susanna Mitchell,' grows twenty-four inches tall and the same width. Her creamy-white daises with bright-yellow centers add lacy-like fillers around other perennials, showing them off to an advantage.

Anthemis, 'sancti-johannis,' or sometimes called St. John's Chamomile, blooms with single orange flowers and darker orange button discs and is the only orange colored anthemis. Sancti is longer blooming, almost all summer, and has overly bushy feathery foliage with larger flowers. 'Sancti-johannis' is not readily available in nurseries and may have to be ordered from a seed-exchange or specialty nursery growers.

Anthemis, 'Sauce Hollandaise' or hardy marguerite has a small daisy with yellow centers on branching knee-high stems. Hollandaise has darker, finer foliage and is lovely as a cut flower.

A shorter, highly acclaimed hybrid cultivar of *Anthemis*, 'Charm', has been introduced in the nursery trade.. 'Charm' grows such a consistent, compact mound that it is suitable for the front or middle sections of the garden. 'Charm' is a more costly hybrid so is not up-rooted from the garden after blooming but is deadheaded. With a longer, warmer fall it may rebloom. 'Charm' grows smaller and tighter the first year but will decide to do its own thing and may or may not come back the next year. 'Charm' covers its self with masses of golden blooms that reach about fifteen inches in both height and width and is spectacular in bud and bloom. The hybridizing of *Anthemis*, 'Charm', has hindered the usual zone-three hardiness of golden marguerites, so it is labeled a zone five and in higher elevations will often winter kill. This charming perennial is available at most nurseries now. Unlike many hybrids, 'Charm' will drop a few seeds that may germinate in spring but they do not have the consistency of 'Charm' its first year.

'Charm' has petite blooms that cover every inch of the perennial and blooms most of the summer. Its consistent rounded clump looks delightful in a full-sun garden. Surprisingly, hybridized 'Charm' does drop seeds that will germinate the next spring.

Summer's favorite colors of yellow and white light up gardens, and *Anthemis* does this superbly. With my famous zone-three hardness, the northern areas of the American continent are my ideal growing environment. I grow in every type of soil—poor, alkaline, acidic, dry, rocky—and in any growing condition. In the higher elevations, I bloom more beautifully in a partial-shade garden, but I adapt easily to any place where I can reseed.

I germinate from either a self-sowing from my summer blooms that will reach maturity the following summer or from a seed that can be started in the garden after all frosts are over in the spring. I can be divided and moved to another area of the garden if too many of my aggressive seeds have germinated. Moving will set me back, timewise, but I'll recover better with the top section of my plant trimmed to help me salvage my energy. Other than my reseeding abilities, I'm not aggressive in any way and can be pulled from the flower border with a simple tug on my stems and moved to the compost pile. I rarely break. I'm just a plain old flower patiently waiting to be noticed. My special gift is adding glamour to every other perennial like many golden medallions surrounding another flower.

The sweet softness of the lacy-stemmed *Anthemis* holding an adorable tiny daisy on its tip is sublime gardening design.

TIMESAVING GARDENING TIPS

MULTITASKING IS THE middle name for most gardeners for they are juggling family, home, and careers. The main reason they do such a great job in their gardens is because they would much rather be outside in the sunshine than doing mundane, inside tasks. So here are a few timesaving tips dedicated to the hardworking multitaskers who make our earth more exalted by their gardening.

TIMESAVING FLOWERBED TIPS

1. Invest in a piece of garden art as a year-round focal point. Art objects made of metal or cement are the best outdoor materials for high-mountain gardens because they are maintenance free and just may hide an eyesore in the garden.

   a. Convince yourself that vigorous out-of-control spreaders that can't be mowed, like mint, need not grow in your garden (even if it was a gift from your cousin). Get rid of the time-takers that leave spent foliage to be deadheaded and high-maintenance chemical-users like roses that take way too much time.

   b. Select perennials that find their comfort zone in your garden. Never assume that all plants sold locally will thrive, for often new hybrid plants have not passed a maturity test of living in Rocky Mountain gardens. A stroll through your own neighborhood to see what grows well is always more accurate than labels. To remember the plants names, make your own labels with paint stirring sticks. If they have paint on they are even better.

The only requirement of candytuft is one shearing of the spent blooms when it finishes blooming. The perennial will hold its perfect shape and foliage throughout the season and will still look lovely as the snow melts around it. Plants like candytuft are so attractive and easy-care that they are very timesaving.

   c. Avoid fussy, finicky perennials. Planting easy-care perennials like those in the daisy families or sedums and veronicas in full sun are always dependable. Easy care hosta, bleeding hearts, or ferns will survive forever in a shady garden. Staking tall, floppy perennials like delphiniums and dahlias takes a lot of time unless it is an act of love.

   d. Focus clumps of one type of perennials in several spots for a big flower color display per season. Having too many types of flowers blooming at the same time of year can appear chaotic. Massed plantings of perennials are the most eyecatching and can be easily divided to increase the color display.

   e. Choose perennials with excellent foliage for your garden. These perennials usually grow in compact shapes with foliage that stays pleasing all season like all of the Alpines, striped iris, artemisia's and sedums. Try out perennials with year around interest like the

A gigantic metal sunflower graces this flowerbed. The sculpture is attractive in deep snow and really draws pleasing applause in the summertime. Invest in a piece of garden art as a year-round focal point. These focal points may draw the viewer's eye away from a garden spot that is just not up to the gardener's usual standards.

ornamental grasses that only need a spring haircut. Bergenia, Helleborus and Iberis perform well in shade and have all-season interest with their remarkable evergreen foliage.

f. Cut fertilization time for perennial beds to a one-time, spring slow release, pelleted fertilizer with or without pre-emergent herbicides. Applying pre-emergent in early spring about the same time as daffodils bloom will prevent weed seeds from germinating. Many fertilizers have both pre-emergent and slow-release pellets so one spring treatment will be all the flowers need.

TIMESAVING HELPERS

2. High-use gardening helpers placed in convenient locations can save tons of time.

Aprons are convenient to slip over gardener's clothes for protection. The deep apron pockets also hold a gardener's most-needed items like a cell phone, gloves, or favorite trowel.

a. Wearing a gardening apron that holds favorite tools, gloves or cell phone is my best personal timesaver. Cell phones stuffed in the back pocket of jeans make butt-calls when the gardener takes a break to sit down. They often fall into the toilet and get wet when the gardener has rushed into the house to potty, but a gardening apron will hold the phone, an energy bar, or whatever the gardener needs, safe and secure. When the phone rings, it's easy to answer so the gardener doesn't have to "run a mile" to answer it. An apron also protects clothing from the mud of a messy job. A spring-clothespin-type of clip hooked to the apron's edge will keep gloves from disappearing.

b. A tote or tray for muddy shoes at the back door saves tons of time. The gardener or kids know where to find their shoes (unless the dog finds them first). A sturdy plastic laundry basket not only will hold shoes but can act as a strainer so the shoes can be squirted clean with the hose.

c. Frustration! Where is my trowel or weeding knife? A handy shelf attached right to the wall outside the back door for storing common use items is invaluable when a gardener wants to do a quick job. Use the shelf to hold common, much-used garden tools like gloves, a hat, scissors, a trowel, and a trimmer or watering sprayers. A hook on or by the shelf to hold a gardening apron is also very convenient. More gardening time is wasted searching for tools than any other gardening practice.

Half of a westerner's outside time is spent in imperfect weather. Early season mud and watering tasks require the investment of a good pair of rubber or waterproof boots.

TIMESAVING TOOLS

3. Invest in tools that are big timesavers like a long-handled pruning pole, watering wand, and lawn edger. Shovels with measurement markings, battery-operated tools, and a garden wagon save lots of time and energy.

a. Finding the ladder to cut an unreachable limb and setting it to balance level in a garden is a disaster about to happen. Keeping your feet planted firmly on the ground saves time and perhaps evades other problems, so add long-handled pruners to a want list.

b. A long-handled watering wand on the end of a new stretchy hose is a godsend for watering container pots. Lugging a full watering can or bucket to containers is backbreaking.

c. Sharply trimmed lawn edges add the final classic touch to a yard. Two ways to keep edges trim are to install a mowing strip and keep it trimmed with a string trimmer before each mowing. If the string on your trimmer jams, spray with a vegetable oil like those used to keep cooking pans from sticking.

This small shelf attached solidly to a brick wall just outside the homeowner's door holds the gardener's favorite gardening tools.

d. The directions say plant one foot apart, so the gardener lays down the shovel, runs to the house, takes off their shoes and opens every drawer to find a ruler and then wouldn't you know the phone rings and your bare root plants are lying in the sun. A timesaving tip is to spray paint foot measurements on your planting tools. Simply lay the measured and marked shovel or hoe down, and place the plant in its correct spacing and plant. No plant deserves to lie in the sun. Put that shovel or hoe away in a garbage can on wheels that is filled with sand. The sand will sharpen the tools and prevent rust. The gardener will always also know where to find them.

e. Electric or rechargeable battery-operated tools are big timesavers. Electric tools will require an extension cord for power and unfailingly a three-pronged ground plug. The cord may not reach, so another cord will need to be found, and the search goes on and on. Battery-operated trimmers are more efficient and can deadhead an entire perennial garden area in relatively little time. Buying an extra battery for rechargeable tools is an excellent timesaver for when the batteries on the first tool is exhausted switch batteries and get the job done.

f. Let a wagon do the heavy lifting. Wheel barrels are "ok" if a gardener is pouring cement on a level surface but for regular gardening use a wagon. The size of the wagon fits a bale of mulch or peat moss that can be cut open with scissors and be rolled to the exact garden spot for spreading. Shovel the amendments right from the bag and the mulch is spread without the gardener having to lift the cubit foot or two of dirt. Wagons can be pulled for convenient placing of heavy container pots, another back-breaking job the gardener should avoid for the gardener must live to garden another day. Filled tubs of yard clean-up are easy to manage for a wagon can be pulled to the compost or green waste can rather than carrying a bundle at a time. Many wagons are equipped with side panels so the yard waste can be piled high. Wagons are also convenient in the gardening off-season for groceries can be moved from the car to the door in one easy load. A gardening wagon will prove useful for many lifting jobs.

Colored one-foot increments on a hoe or shovel handle will give the gardener an instant measurement to use when planting. A garbage container filled with sand keeps long-handled tools like shovels and hoes not only organized but sharp and rust free. The garbage can sits inside a roll-around metal frame on wheels so it can be moved to any location.

TIMESAVING MISCELLANEOUS GARDENING JOBS

4. Gardeners usually have timesaving things they do to make gardening easier. Here are a couple of mine.

Fall clean-up and harvest are a cinch with a wagon. Garden wagons are easy to pull and save gardeners from over-lifting back- strains.

a. Spraying to get rid of bindweed or morning glory in the fall when the hated weed is pulling all nutrition down to their roots is the most successful time. By gathering the vines and placing them on a paper plate, the spray stays on the leaves longer, for weedkillers usually neutralize when touching the ground. Herbicides become a gas and will damage other plants in its vicinity, so spraying an herbicide will do more damage to the perennial plants around than the weed. Solution: Wait until fall when all plants are taking in any nutrients to prepare for winter. To protect other flowers, wait until they have been cut back for winter so there will not be worries about spray kill. Using a paper plate sliced with one cut to the center, fit the plate around the bindweed's base and pull any tendrils up and into the paper plate. Spray

Wagons are so much more than a gardening tool. To these young kids, a wagon can be a train, a snowmobile, or a take-turns ride. My wagon is more fun to the kids than a swing set or sandbox, and they never get tired of it.

the vines with the strongest herbicide available. Many weedkillers lose their potency when touching soil, so the paper plate prevents this and the weed killer will actually puddle in the plate. Spray several times as long as there are sixty-degree daytime temperatures and next spring there will be less bindweed.

b. Hoses and extension cords when thrown in a tool shed are not only irritating but can cause tripping. Keep different lengths of twist ties in a jar so these messy items can be wrapped and stored safely.

c. Has your hose ever snapped flowers when being moved around a corner of the yard? Plant heavy clay pipes in the ground, leaving five inches of pipe above ground on these critical spots. The hose will slip around the bed instead of being a hazard to plants.

The most disheartening job to a gardener in the west is an attempt to remove bindweed or morning glory from their flowerbeds. This obnoxious weed sends a taproot sometimes nine feet down that will stubbornly stay alive and keep coming back. The top of bindweed twists and winds around.

d. Many gardeners swear that they prefer to plant their flowers bare-handed or without gloves. They maintain there is an energy transfer between the gardener and earth so the flowers grow better. Several studies are saying that soils are a natural energizer and have been shown to act as a natural antidepressant that activates brain cells improving a gardener's mood. So by all means, gardeners, plant those flowers bare-handed, but scrape your nails over a softened bar of soap so the dirt will wash out when you are through planting.

e. Last but not least, hire help for jobs that are difficult or not what you choose to do. A lawn-mowing service or tree removal may be more than you physically handle. Professional help makes your gardening time more enjoyable.

Gardening tips are helpful but are all based on organizing plants, tools, and the gardener. So the real timesaving tip is to get you organized!

Aruncus
(ah-RUN-kuss)
GOATSBEARD

SHAPE	Tall, shrub-like with spiky flower plumes
DWARF	Shrub-like with tightly packed flower plumes
HEIGHT	Tall, grows spires to a sturdy five feet
DWARF	Eight inches of fine lacy foliage
WIDTH	Tall, two feet
DWARF	One foot
BLOOM TIME	Mid-summer
COLORS	Male plants are creamy white and females are creamy with a green tinge
SITE	Clay with consistent moisture and organic amendments
LIGHT	Partial shade
HARDINESS	Zone two or a minus 50 degrees F
COMMENTS	Nonaggressive and noninvasive

Tall *Aruncus dioicus* with its lovely creamy-white plumes on five-foot strong-stemmed foliage adds a shrub-like, architectural structure to a partial-shade garden. *Dioicus* is the prime species of *Aruncus* and is a native throughout northern regions.

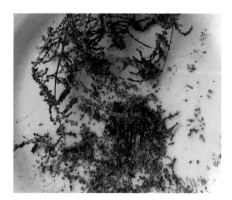

Both male and female plants are required for seeds to germinate, but only the female produces seed. Freshly harvested seeds are the best method for starting *Aruncus*. Goatsbeard may pollinate and self-seed if both male and female plants are present, but this happens rarely. This is probably why aruncus does not spread. The seeds from *aruncus* have been reported as being poisonous.

The huge creamy-white sprays of *aruncus* are so distinctive and eyecatching, especially in partial shade, that attention is always drawn to the part of the garden where they grow. The compounded leaves are large, but overall the perennial looks airy and lacy.

Goatsbeard can reach a height of five feet in western gardens, making them bold, shrub-shaped, herbaceous perennials that will grow as a privacy fence or a specimen planting or will simply add their sparkling white fern-like flowers to the back of a partial-shade garden.

GREETINGS. IN THE last plant profile you met *Anthemis,* or golden marguerite, a perennial that performs well in partial sun. In this profile you will get acquainted with two partial shade flowers; tall *aruncus dioicus* and dwarf *aruncus aethusifolius*. Chapter three perennials are introducing both partial sun and partial-shade gardens.

I'm one of the nicest plants you will ever meet. I'm a hardy-hardy zone-two perennial and need the cold to do my best. I'm so trouble free that I take the place of shrubs in the garden but I'm better than a shrub, for I die down in winter and never require a trim. I can be deadheaded after blooming, but my flowers stems hold nicely and my foliage continues to develop and stay green, so deadheading isn't necessary. I'm also noninvasive and nonaggressive; I stay right where I'm planted and resent being moved. Division is never necessary and it's a good thing, for my creeping rhizomes form a tough, woody stalk that grows a root similar to an ancient sage brush's root. It's best if I stay right where I'm planted and perform year after year without maintenance. There I'll simply grow bigger and better as I mature. I'm one of those slow-starter perennials, like peonies, so I take several years to mature. Giving me a little extra time to get my roots under me will pay off in big flower dividends.

My shrub-like stature and huge compound pinnate foliage are commendable, but it is my flowers that steal the show! My tiny white five-petaled blooms mass on fifteen-inch-long sprays, bringing light into the partial-shade garden with my feathery plums. *Aruncus* with its frosted florets may be female or male but it's hard to tell. It's said the male goat's beard have showier flowers with more florets but the female seedpods are more attractive.

In the coolness of mountains gardens we bloom longer, to over four weeks. After flowering, our sprays will persist and dry to a soft beige color, adding a nice texture contrast in the garden. Our autumn tints of golden leaves and orange-red berries add another season of color, so in reality we are an all-warm-season perennial. The sturdiness of our plumes holds and can be used for long-lasting dried flowers. Using our tall fluffy white stems in a cut flower arrangement makes a magnificent floral display.

Tall perennials like *Aruncus dioicus* add dramatic impact to a garden and can be planted as easy-care shrubs that go dormant and underground in winter. This means I will not need trimming or be ruined by deep snow and winter burn like many of the shrub families. I will fill the background of a flowerbed, or I can stand alone to make a focal point statement. Your choice of how to use this perennial will dictate how many plants will be needed. For a hedge or privacy border, figure the length of the area divided by four to tell how many *aruncus* to plant. My foliage and flowers grow almost five feet tall and three feet wide with maturity, so plant me in a permanent spot. Transplanting me isn't for the weak or short-of-time gardener. A single *aruncus* will be adequate for a focal point ,for I have a handsome presence. When planted in shade, I grow adequately but will usually refuse to bloom. Moist soils like the water-holding clay of intermountain gardens provide me a comfortable stability where I'll never slump. Clay's constant moisture will not allow me to dry out and scorch my leaf edges when the temperatures get really hot. I also grow well in wet woodlands with acidic soils so amending the clay, rocky or poor soils of the west with generous amounts of organic mulch will actually increase my blooming potential.

Companion plants for me are other part-shade loving perennials like *aconitum* or monkshood, *aquilegia* or Columbine, and *polemonium* or Jacob's ladder. The early white blooms of snowdrop *anemone* planted around my feet add a spring woodland garden feeling to the flowerbed. Wild geraniums grow in partial shade with delightful ground-hugging accents that weave softly around my feet and so do the silver foliaged lamiums. Keep my garden focal point strong by not planting other tall perennials in too close of a vicinity to me.

Dwarf Aruncus aethusifolius
DWARF GOATSBEARD

SHAPE	Tall, shrub-like with spiky flower plumes
DWARF	Shrub-like with tightly packed flower plumes
HEIGHT	Tall, grows spires to a sturdy five feet
DWARF	Eight inches of fine lacy foliage
WIDTH	Tall, two feet
DWARF	One foot
BLOOM TIME	Mid-summer
COLORS	Male plants are creamy white and females are creamy with a green tinge
SITE	Clay with consistent moisture and organic amendments
LIGHT	Partial shade
HARDINESS	Zone two or a minus 50 degrees F
COMMENTS	Nonaggressive and noninvasive

Everything about dwarf *Aruncus aethusifolius* is finer, smaller, and more delicate looking, for it stays short, not growing over ten inches. Dwarf *aruncus* with their creamy-white spikes with star-shaped flowers on reddish stems are charmers at the front of a part shade border. I was delighted to find dwarf *aruncus* growing in a huge commercial planting at a local hospital.

The name goatsbeard can cause confusion between tall aruncus, dioicus, or short aruncus, aethusifolius and salisfy and could possibly lead to consuming the poisonous perennial. This shows the importance of knowing the Latin name of perennials, for common names are used for several different plants.

ARUNCUS AETHUSIFOLIUS IS the only naturally occurring dwarf goat's beard and I'm often referred to as Korean goatsbeard. I'm a miniature version with the same traits as dioicus goat's beard except my foliage is ferny. Due to my petite, compact size and zone-two hardiness, I perform excellently in planters or container pots. Several named cultivars of dwarf aruncus are being bred and are taller. 'Kneiffii' stands about three feet tall and 'Child of Both Worlds' grows to almost four feet. Any of these *aruncus* will be trouble free and add a fine, fluffy foliage clump to the edge of ponds, woodland paths, or fronts of flowerbeds.

My family has a long history of external herbal healing and makes a great soak for poor aching feet but hopefully I'm not one of the highly sought-after perennials that are gaining popularity as edible green vegetables. In early spring, foragers seeking organic greens move into meadows around ponds and roadside dirt disturbances to gather newly breaking, tender, edible wild plants. *Aruncus* is often a look-alike plant mistaken for wild asparagus and is edible as a young shoot, but as it matures, it should not be used for culinary purposes for it develops toxins. Plants are difficult to identify in early spring and a blooming flower is often the only sure identification. Part of the problem with identification is the confusion over plants with the same name.

Aruncus's common name, goatsbeard, is derived from its Greek name, *Tragopogon*, and is not an attractive name for a very attractive perennial. The Greek word for "goat" is *tragos* and *pogon* means "beard." The words translated to English are "goat's beard." The weed yellow salsify also goes by the name of goatsbeard and is a popular edible plant. Salsify blooms in either purple or yellow, but only very old salsify plants are purple, so I'll refer to the yellow salsify. The salsify or goatsbeard is becoming very popular as a green vegetable, for the entire plant is edible. The roots are long taproots and resemble parsnips. When cooked salsify can be substituted for artichoke hearts for the textures and tastes are similar. To prepare goat's beard or salsify, first clean the root, peel, cut it into short pieces and simmer until they are tender. Grated roots and all parts of this nutritious plant are delicious and a little unusual when added to salads.

The yellow-flowered goat's beard grows wild and has naturalized from Europe and is now found over the entire Northern U.S. and Canada and is the most common goat's beard for the Rocky Mountains. They grow everywhere in the west for there is neither a soil so poor and compacted nor a sun too bright for their seeds to not establish themselves and take root. The foliage of the salsify plant is slender like a grass and appears most notably in July with a yellow daisy shaped, spiked ray flower. Harvest salsify in the morning when it is easy to spot for the flowers close their eyes at noon. After pollination, the closed flower heads will start to swell and form a puffball of seed resembling dandelions that the wind will disperse. Every part of this goat's beard is edible.

A few of the other edible wild plants are asparagus, wild spinach, chickweed, mallow, water cress, sweet woodruff, and dandelion. Timing and plant identification is all important

Aruncus 'Misty Lace' is one of the new shorter goat's beards bred for smaller gardens or to grow in containers in partial-shade gardens. The dwarf aruncus have autumnal tints of excellent fall foliage.

when foraging plants so risking an emergency ride to the ER isn't worth the risk. One known chemical found in my leaves is cyanogenic glycosides. When mixed by chewing with the enzymes in the mouth it changes the chemical to hydrogen cyanide. Cyanide is a rapidly acting poison that is toxic to animals and humans. Both birds and deer stay away from me so that is a good indicator. The matured seeds of aruncus are also known to be poisonous. Instead of wanting to eat *aruncus*, enjoy my unique beauty and do some research before seeking vitamins in unknown wild vegetables.

Cyanogenic glycosides information taken from Plants for a Future, no date, copy used: naturalmedicinalherbs.net/herbs/a/ aruncus-dioicus=goat's-beard.php

LAYERING FOR PRIVACY

A layered garden with a combination of distinctive shapes and a variety of colorful foliage not only adds an element of privacy but its attractiveness lasts all season.

NATURE, THE ULTIMATE landscaper, grows plants in layers. The layers add a three-dimensional feeling that nature does so skillfully a gardener may never notice. Gaze up at our high mountains toward the ridge or skyline. The top layer planting is a bold planting of dark-foliaged pine trees. A drift of quaking aspen trees usually follows and skillfully softens the starkness of the pines with their white-barked beauty and trembling leaves. A creekbed of red-stemmed willows may be merging with the quakes and act as the bottom layer of the landscape. Each layer has added a completely different texture and foliage color to the vignette. In reality, all gardening is trying to mimic the rightness of how nature plants. Layering plants is a first step.

Time-tested techniques like planting tall plants at the back, medium-sized plants in the middle sections, and finishing with short plants as edgings provides enclosure, but mixing it up is more natural. Perimeter layered planting with hedges and shrubs may be an easy design but hedges are high maintenance, requiring constant trimming or they become overgrown and unattractive. Using a combination of these along with a variety of perennials is an easier way to go. A privacy fence layered with lush greenery that blocks a prime use area like a patio, children's play yard or swimming pool may create a backyard paradise for a homeowner. Layering plants blocks noise pollution as well as giving the gardener a sense of being in their own isolated space. Landscape layering around the foundation of the home can ground the home and make it more lush and attractive. Now let's take a look at the following suggestions for layering in your garden:

USING SHRUBS FOR LAYERING

Shrubs add structure, screening, and value to any property. When planting shrubs in high mountain gardens, the hardiness or ability of the shrub to withstand not only cold but also heat, wildlife, and other adverse conditions is the first consideration. A brief overview of shrubs with the reputation of being hardy in Rocky Mountain gardens follows, but the most efficient way of choosing shrubs for your own garden is to drive around your community and see the shrubs that look great.

1. EVERGREEN SHRUBS

Well-trimmed evergreens are layered down from tall at the back followed by medium and short for an attractive screen from the street. The contrast of foliage, bronze through golden or green adds to the handsomeness of this landscaping.

2. FORSYTHIA SHRUBS

Forsythia is the first shrub to bloom, and its brilliant blooms welcome spring. Shrubs like forsythia can be planted and trimmed as hedges for a solid perimeter screen, but because they are herbaceous their winter appearance may not be as pleasing as they are in early spring bloom. A general rule for the trimming of shrubs is to remove one third of a shrub per year. Trimming wood from the base of a shrub hedge will thin the base to the point where the shrub will look ragged and top heavy. Sheared hedges are work intensive.

Forsythia planted as a screening against a metal railing lends itself to a layering of other perennials around it and they work together to screen a front porch. Trimming the shrub will be based on the room the shrub has to develop, but untrimmed forsythia is more attractive than a sheared hedge. A late-season pruning will diminish next spring's blooms, so any pruning needs to be done right after the flowers finish blooming.

3. SPIRAEA X VANHOUTTEI

The natural vase shape of *spiraea*, or bridalwreath, creates a solid privacy fence using only mature plant material. It took years to build this privacy layer and spiraea never falters; year after year, these dependable shrubs return, fuller and more beautiful than the year before.

4. POTENTILLA SHRUB

The function of *potentilla* in this garden is a long-blooming summer attraction. Shrubs can be used in multiple ways with screening and layering. *Potentilla* actually is a native wild flower, but with hybridizing, it now is a long-blooming, long-living, easy-care shrub.

5. VIBURNUMS OR SNOWBALL BUSHES

Viburnum as a specimen planting in front of a picket fence still furnishes inclusion and privacy. The snowball bush's important traits of zone-two hardiness, elegant creamy-white blooms, and fall interest with colorful berries and foliage always remain true.

6. LILAC OR SYRINGE

Lilacs are classic garden shrubs that fill the air every spring with their heavenly scent. Lilacs are long lived, lasting for decades. Liliacs can be used for layering, as hedges for privacy, or as a specimen focal point. However they are planted in a garden, they are one of the most beautiful of the flowering shrubs.

7. DAPHNE 'CAROL MACKIE'

Daphne is one of the best shrubs for colder regions and prefers alkaline soils, so it belongs in our western gardens. 'Carol Mackie' is the best of the Daphnes with its compact, rounded trim size, semi-evergreen and variegated foliage, 'Carol Mackie' is highly ornamental wherever it is planted in a yard, and the late spring fragrance from its white-and-pink blooms is intoxicating.

Shrubs furnish the height and structure for layering a fence line or foundation of a home. They furnish enclosure and privacy but also add their special traits of flowers, fragrance and form. Other fine shrubs hardy enough for high mountain gardens are as follows:

1. Almond, *Prunus*
2. Barberry, *Berberis*
3. Broom, *Genista*
4. Dogwood, *Cornus*
5. Mock Orange, *Philadelphus*
6. Privet, *Ligustrum*
7. Quince, *Chaenomeles japonica*

USE TALL-FOLIAGED PERENNIALS FOR LAYERING

Layering your garden with shrub-like perennials adds easy-care lushness to a garden that no other planting achieves for they bloom longer and do not require the trimming that shrubs require and most disappear in winter. *Aruncus* is an excellent example for layering but the bold foliage of Hardy *Hibiscus* and *Ligularia* are even better. *Ligularia* adds the bronzed color of rounded leaves to the border while Hibiscus adds huge elegantly colored flowers and foliage in late summer. *Clematises'* bold flowers scrambling on trellises or arches gives height and layering plus they cover themselves with charming long blooming trumpets in unique patterns and colors. Vines are one of the best plants to create a sound barrier from highway sounds. Shrub-sized perennials furnish the top layer of height to flower beds or can blend the higher and lower level, as well as adding seasonal colors. Ornamental Grasses are fool-proof bold foliaged perennials that give a certain modernistic edge and are attractive in winter. *Alcea*, *allium*, *anthemis*, tall asters, *delphinium*, *eupatorium*, *heliopsis*, *malva* and Russian sage are a few of these tall perennials for layering. Canna lilies with their bold many colored leaves are actually bulbs that have to be harvested in the cold of western winters but they enrich a border and add an elegant seclusion.

Ornamental grasses always provide a privacy barrier simply because of their size and dramatic foliage. Some grasses reach six feet in height, plus the foliage reaches its peak of beauty in winter.

USE MID-SIZED PERENNIALS FOR LAYERING THE MIDDLE OF A PARTIAL SHADE FLOWERBED

Medium-tall perennials make up the second layer in a partial-shade garden. Choose one perennial per season and mass it for color. *Dicentra*, or bleeding hearts, is one of the first perennials to bloom and their thirty-by-thirty-inch sizes will jazz up a section of the layered flowerbed. For late spring add in tanacetum or painted daisies if red is a favorite color and trollius or globeflower for orange/gold and allium for purple. Summer brings on the golden *achillea* or yarrow, *anthemis* and the brilliant colors of lilium. *Aruncus* and *physostegia* bloom next with *aconitum* or wolfsbane filling in with fall color. Plant clumps of three or more of each of these perennials mixed in with a few shrubs and your privacy through layering will always have a flower in bloom.

SHORT PERENNIALS ADD THE FINISHING TOUCHES TO A LAYERED FLOWERBED

Bleeding hearts bloom before the trees have leafed out, so they will really brighten a layered garden. They are timeless perennials with their curving branches weighed down with hearts and ferny foliage. In extra hot summers, *dicentra* will go dormant, so plan to cover the spot with a later-blooming perennial like hibiscus.

Plant short perennials along the front of a layered garden bed for a finishing touch. Adding variegated, silvery or bronze foliage plants will stand out in all of the green and are as colorful as flowers. Evergreen perennials like *Iberis* or candytuft, *Bergenia* or heartleaf, and *Helleborus* or lenten rose all bloom in spring but maintain gorgeous foliage through the rest of the months, including winter.

Bergenia with its heart-shaped leaves maintains beautiful shiny foliage all of the growing season. When snow arrives, *bergenia's* foliage turns bronze and this fine perennial simply hunkers down. With the melting of the snow, *bergenia* is still in full beautiful leaf getting ready to push up its rosy blooms.

The bottom or front layers of the flowerbed are the finishing touches to a garden and weave the components together. They merge and mingle with the other layers giving the garden a feeling of being whole. The shorter perennials here are long-blooming *hemerocallis*, 'Apricot Sparkles' and *veronica*, 'Royal Candles.' The mid-section perennials are *sedum*, 'T Rex' surrounding the tallest plant, dark-foliaged canna lilies.

LAYERING FOR PRIVACY USING PLANTS AND WALLS AS A SOUND BARRIER

Enclosing your yard with full-perimeter fencing is expensive and as such is the homeowner's choice, but adding a privacy fence or wall surrounded with a wide space for flowers can be very satisfying to layer. A patio or sitting retreat like a gazebo located in the midst of beds of shrubs and perennials provides a refuge from the world. Small ornamental trees give the area even more enclosure plus some shade. A chainlink fence is a great start for layering, especially when draped with the fantastic blooms of vines like *clematis* or honeysuckle.

Sound absorption is done by all parts of the plants, from leaves to stems to trunks, so the thicker the layering the more sound is absorbed. It's fortunate that sleeping with open windows is during the months when there is more foliage. In winter months when plant foliage is dropped, the plant-created

The Gazebo offers privacy, but the layering around the gazebo offers seclusion. Both of these are a result of middle of the yard layering.

sound barrier loses its effectiveness. Masonry walls and other tall, solidly built fences can reduce the noise levels and are even more effective when layered with plants.

Layering trees, shrubs, and perennials in a yard gives a homeowner a sense of isolated privacy that is hard to find in our stress-filled lives. A thick layer of plants creates a lush and colorful secluded space that deflects street noises.

Walls are natural canvases to create a painting of plants. Small trees, shrubs, and perennials mesh into a lush area of privacy where a homeowner can feel free in their own yards. Not all walls need to surround a perimeter of the property. Some walls may block noise from a busy street. Green screening, using a combination of shrubs, perennials, and fencelines, offers the privacy so necessary in our yards.

This rock wall can lower the street noises by almost 10 to 15 decibels because the rock causes the noise to be bounced away. Some plants, like the vines crawling up the trellis on the wall, absorb more sound than others, and the wind whistling through the pine tree will create what is called white noise or a sound that masks the undesirable noise.

Campanula
(kam-PAN-yew-luh)
BELLFLOWER

SHAPE	Tall, topped with bell-shaped flowers; Medium, bells cluster into a tight bloom at the top of the stem; Short are groundcovers with bell, cup-shaped, or star-shaped blooms
HEIGHT	Tall, 20-to-25-inch spikes Medium, 12 to 15 inches tall, spreads Groundcover to 6 inches, spreads
WIDTH	Tall, narrow spikes; Medium, spreads to two-feet; Short, forms a tidy ball then sprawls outward
BLOOM TIME	June thru July
COLORS	Famous for blue shades, but also blooms in white and pinks
SITE	Sandy, alkaline-type soils with good drainage
LIGHT	Partial shade
HARDINESS	Zone three
COMMENTS	Many campanulas are biennials so need to be allowed to self-seed

Takion Blue F1, campanulas look too perfect to be real. This could be because of the F1 breeding where two pure lines are crossed and the plant carries the desirable traits of both parents. Seeds are collected and sown in a controlled environment such as a greenhouse. This breeding takes years of hand pollinating from one pure line to another. These crosses must be controlled without a risk of insect pollination.

The old-fashioned peach-leaved bellflowers like 'Alba' are white for *Alba* means white in floral Latin. Their leaves resemble peach tree leaves and their bells are single hanging. Tall bellflowers resemble butterflies and can seem to be nodding gently to each other.

Clustered bellflower has up to 15 tiny bells packed together on top of each stem so it is called clustered bellflower. Spreading easily by both seeds and rhizomes many gardeners call it a nuisance but not in the challenges of high country gardening where its hardiness is appreciated. The rich purple colors of clustered bellflowers stand out by the sheer intensity of their dramatic colors.

Author's note: Today is October twenty-ninth and I just strolled through my garden and snapped this picture of 'Blue Waterfall'. This campanula is the most eye-catching perennial in the flowerbeds for it is still in full bloom. The pure, rich-blue of the star-shaped, carefree flowers is enduring in both my heart and in garden.

MY NAME SHOULD BE charming for everything about my delightful blue bells is charming. The Latin meaning of my name is "Little Bell" and even that is charming! I'm a traditional, old-fashioned cottage-garden perennial that is native to Asia Minor and the Swiss Alps, so I thrive in Rocky Mountain gardens. I know you will be happy to get better acquainted and add my romantic charm to your gardens.

Tall bellflowers bloom on a sturdy clump of erect but relaxed stems. My flowers open at the leaf axles with five lobed, distinctively curved petals that bloom in traditional shades of blue (not a true blue but softened with a touch of lavender) or white colors. My bells or cups face outward, creating an appealing group of open inviting flowers.

Medium sized *campanula* stands about twelve inches tall, and most of these blooms are clustered on the ends of their stems.

Shorter *campanulas* are actually alpine perennials that spread, mound or cascade and have the tough hardiness that alpines are known for.

I'll introduce the best varieties in each size. These will be the hardiest and best-behaved of the bellflowers and can be counted on to perform best in the cold climates and difficult soils of high Rocky Mountain's gardens.

TALL BELLFLOWERS

Peach-leaved *campanula* grows taller on stronger stems that make excellent long lasting cut flowers. Peach-leaved bellflowers shoot up-ward from a basal rosette forming a relaxed clump of stems. This looser stance looks very natural in cottage gardens. Our lance-like rough-toothed leaves are alternate, broader at the base than at the top and often stay evergreen. We bloom heaviest June through July with large delicate looking outward facing bells or cups. A snip of any dried blooms will keep my flowers blooming longer. A new hybrid named 'Telham Beauty' blooms in both blue and white has larger, more-profuse flowers that face upward but is shorter than peach-leaf and not as long lived. Many hybrid bellflowers would fit more comfortably in an annual classification for seldom do they make it into their second year. Adding the common peach-leaved bellflowers to a partial-shade garden promises years of soft summer surprises when the bells open.

MEDIUM BELLFLOWERS

We are called clustered bellflower, or glomerations 'Superba,' and grow medium tall. We are a hardy, easy-to-grow group and spread enthusiastically by rhizomes or seeds. If we really like the spot we are planted in, we have the reputation of being invasive spreaders but do not have that problem in western gardens where every plant has to struggle. However, it would be a wise precaution to cut me back when I'm through blooming to my basal foliage to prevent self-seeding. We bloom in deep purple, lighter purple or white. Our flowers are bells but are packed so tightly into a single bloom on the terminal or top raceme they appear as a cluster on the end of our stems. I'm very talented at filling any spot where a medium sized perennial is needed. Difficult spots don't slow me a bit and I've been known to carpet an area around a pine tree. I'm so unfussy that I preform in sunny or shady garden areas and any soil that drains well is fine. In fact I like the chalky, calcium carbonate or alkaline soils in western gardens. This makes me a keeper.

I break dormancy as tight rosettes. As the season progress my stems elongate to about fifteen-inches where my bloom will perch perfectly. Our toothed, lance shaped leaves are hairy, an indicator that we are quite drought tolerant. My leaves as well as my flowers and roots are edible if you like bland tasting food.

SHORT CAMPANULA

'White Clips' or 'Blue Clips' are low-growing *campanulas*. *Carpatica* is Latin for "carpet," so we grow like a spreading carpet. Blue and white clips are a very cold hardy, zone three perennial and are salt tolerant. So many of the rock garden alpines are spring flowering so by summer they are through blooming. It's nice I'm around to finish up the season with color. Mounding clips grow nicely on retaining walls or in rock gardens where many perennials would suffer. We furnish a nice tidy edge along beds and are excellent when under-planted beneath taller perennials or shrubs. My delicate-looking flowers are held above my foliage and start opening in July. Keep me fresh looking by an occasional pinching of my dried blooms to encourage continued blooming. Our clip flowers are attractive but it's the bright-green, heart-shaped, curly-toothed foliage that is really splendid.

I'm the perfect hybrid *campanula,* and I'm appropriately named 'Blue Waterfall.' Serbian *pascharskyana* or 'Blue Waterfall' has all of the commendable traits of our low-growing family plus I will cascade over rock walls and edges of containers and have none of the invasiveness of *campanula rapunculoides* which I resemble. *Rapunculoides campanulas* do not belong in your garden, for they are impossible to eradicate and spread by seeds and running taproots. Serbian *campanula* is so bad that many states have

We are *Campanula catpatica*, nicknamed clips. We can be planted anywhere a small tidy dwarf clumping perennial that blooms in blue or white would give a special finishing touch. A profusion of exquisite upward-facing cups explodes over compact mounds of bright-green heart-shaped leaves. We are long blooming, starting after most of the spring alpines are spent, and will continue flowering into fall. Clips are easy fillers, for their small tidy size makes them tuckable almost anywhere in a partial-shade garden.

it on their invasive plant list for eradication. Even round-up spray will only damage the leaves, leaving the roots to live to sprout another day.

It's always interesting to find how members from the same family can be so different. I'm glad I'm so well-behaved and dependable. I'm also a long-blooming perennial for I start flowering in June and flower again right into winter. I'm not a spreader, but my flower sprays spill gracefully from a mound and I bloom more abundantly as I mature. As my flower-filled stems bloom, they soften any hard rock garden or the edges of containers with dark-green, shiny, clumps of curled leaves and blue stars. I'm exquisite to the last detail and once planted become a very valuable perennial. As a hybrid, 'Blue Waterfall's' hardiness has changed, but I'm still considered a zone-four perennial that performs nicely everywhere but in the far northern areas of the Rockies or in dense clay. Many winters I stay evergreen.

Campanulas are all disease and deer resistant, plus we prefer cooler nighttime temperatures so we thrive when growing in the higher elevations of the mountains. We bloom heaviest in June but are apt to rebloom with a cutback of our spent flowers. Pollinators love our nectar and flock around us. We are famous for being so care free, delightfully charming, and bringing our pure clean-looking blue and white colors to partial-sun gardens.

Bellflowers are still used as traditional medicine, and in Korea, my edible roots are used in cooking.

Caring for bellflowers is simple. If the ground is not well-drained, add grit or sand. We love rich soils so fertilizers are appreciated, especially in the form of well-rotted manures or homemade composts which improves drainage. We really appreciate the cool nights and bright intenseness of the days found in higher elevations. Cut us back if we start looking ragged for we will bloom again. Keep it simple, for this is who I am!

To propagate *campanula*, spring is the best time for dividing. Cut me back to ground level. Insert the spade deep to avoid cutting the roots. I develop rhizomes that are thickened underground branches of storage stems that grow laterally. Sever the rhizomes from the parent plant and bury them in the new planting hole. Keep moist, not wet until new growth occurs.

Seeds are so tiny they must be handled carefully. Sprinkling them outside I can be easily lost. A flat of potting soil is the best method. Sprinkle seeds over the flat, leaving them uncovered. Place the flat outside eight weeks before danger of frost has passed so they get some vernalization. Keep them moderately moist and allow them to germinate. Plant the seedlings when they have three leaves and sized big enough to handle.

Campanula's bells are delightful and add softness to gardens. Short campanulas perform well in rock gardens, edges and containers, They bloom mid-summer after many short perennials have finished. We are easy care and long-blooming perennials that make gardens easy care and more beautiful!

Between a rock wall and a hard spot of cement is the only place suitable for growing the invasive rapunculoides. It has made the invasive list in many of states in the United States. Its deep taproots that resemble parsnips and self-seeding make it a tough plant to eradicate. The foliage of rapunculoides is a light green compared to 'Blue Waterfall's' curly dark-green leaves.

COTTAGE GARDENS: WHERE FLOWERS GROW

Design elements of cottage gardens are always made from natural elements of wood or stone massed with informal flowers. These colorful cosmos are annuals that self-seed year after year.

CAMPANULAS WITH THEIR amiable simplicity are a traditional Cottage garden perennial. Cottage gardens with their naturalness of informal design have become idealized in modern gardens and are often dubbed "Country Garden Style." These types of gardens are perfectly suited to the rural, high mountain areas of the USA. Spring bulbs, herbs, vines, fruits and vegetables will also be crammed into the casual mix of a cottage garden. The plants will be allowed to scramble and germinate wherever they choose and every available square inch will be packed with flowers that in turn reduce watering and weeding. Country gardens grow flowers, and in truth, this is really what gardening is about. Where flowers grow, so do people.

ELEMENTS THAT IDENTIFY A COTTAGE GARDEN

- Cottage gardens grow flowers with natural grace and charm rather than the grandeur of formal structures with manicured lawns and clipped hedges. Cottage gardens are not surrounded in cement or hardscape like so many of the west coast gardens shown in glossy magazines. They are filled with people, children, families and pets or animals. Have you ever seen kids playing in the glossy design spread of west coast gardens? It's doubtful, for some of these garden designers have forgotten that gardens are where flowers and people grow.

- Gardeners filled the foundation of their cottage gardens homes with flowers. Homeowners are delighted to open a door to be greeted with the fragrance and beauty of flowers. Many of these homeowners use this convenient area to grow kitchen herbs.

- The richness of a Thomas Kincade garden painting where flowers grow in abundance around the home are portrayals of cottage gardening. Flowers are massed in drifts of soft colors: the blues of delphiniums, the fat round heads of pink peonies and the spicy smell from pinks.

A foundation planting of perennials, coreopsis, and clematis massed against the house of this cottage garden is a typical element of a cottage garden.

- Medicinal or cooking herbs for the home mixed within the flowerbeds is typical of a cottage garden.

- A fence to protect the fruits and flowers from animals is usually a low, white picket fence covered with a wealth of flowering plants.

- Cottage Gardens will have stacked, rustic stone walls from rocks gleaned from the fields. The walls will be softened with alpine perennials and vines of clematis or honeysuckle then backed with self-seeding hollyhocks. Apple fruit trees and raspberry bushes will find a home behind the wall.

White picket fences are a tradition of cottage gardens and are used as fence barriers but here it is used as both a design element and staking to hold the herb red valerian.

- Traditional shrubs, planted for their hardiness and fragrance like lilacs, add structure and privacy to cottage gardens. Forsythia blooms early spring, potentilla blooms all summer, and rose of Sharon adds its flat funnel flowers to the garden in fall.

Flowers are filling every inch of this splendid cottage fall garden. In spring, the columbine, iris, and primrose fill the area with enchanting flowers. In summer, the delphiniums, daisies, and gaillardia are a mass of color, but the fall show is dedicated to the gardener's favorite flower: dahlias.

Herbs and other edibles define cottage gardens. Mints, garlics, chives and asparagus growing along a paver pathway intermingle nicely with alpine perennials.

underlying, long-lived garden structure. Plants will soften any structure, adding an unplanned naturalness to flowerbeds. Use nature's materials for rock walls, gravel paths, and picket fences. Install trellises or arches for vines to scramble over

Way back when, a white picket fence was stick built and painted when possible. Now we have picket fences made of man-made materials that are maintenance free, only needing a mass of flowers to call the yard a cottage garden.

Stand still and breathe deep for you are in the midst of an old-fashioned cottage garden with its myriad flowers, fruit trees, fragrances, and joy.

- A wide curving gravel walkway says welcome! This path moves through an out of the garden to eliminate any chaos. All elements in cottage gardens are from the earth, crushed gravel, flagstone, sand, or lawn furnish pathways. These wider paths are easier to maintain as well as getting the gardener and a wheelbarrow from point A to B.

- Arches, trellises, and arbors furnish spots for flowers to scramble as well as adding a vertical interest. Traditional trees like apples and pears also add height.

- Whimsical or found items like antique water knobs, weather vanes, rusted wheelbarrows, a child's toy, or a bike with its basket filled with flowers add simple appeal in cottage gardens. Old wrought-iron chairs to hold tubs or pots of flowers or an ancient wheelbarrow spilling with annuals are touches that add informal whimsy to any garden.

A variety of traditional plants are used in a cottage garden, but exotics or hard-to-grow plants are ignored. Self-seeding annuals provide seasonal color while perennials provide an

A stacked rock wall using rocks gleaned from the fields are typical elements of a cottage garden. Using any available natural material to its best advantage is how cottage gardens are built.

Flowering shrubs like this magnificent lilac bush add height, structure, fragrance, and background to cottage garden.

and around while adding height and eyecatching views. Herbs and perennial vegetables are traditional plants for mixing in, but think in terms of adding barriers to spreaders like mint. Planting smaller flowering trees like crab apples or apple and peach trees that can be easily trimmed and will not shade the sun loving flowers are sound choices. Huge shade trees will eventually eliminate a sunny garden, changing the garden's inviting personality. Birds and bees will naturally be garden visitors, so add in a bird bath or bird house painted in bright colors. Last but not least, add a soft cushioned chair where you can rest and enjoy the lushness of your resplendent cottage garden.

Vines like *clematis* and honeysuckle are right at home in cottage gardens with their untamed scrambling and delightful flowers.

The unstructured freedom of cottage garden plants may look somewhat unruly to an unpracticed eye but the gravel path gives an underlying structure to the garden.

Rusty items are charming décor for cottage gardens for they add a sense of nostalgia. An old wheel placed among flowers looks as if it belongs and that it has always been in that spot.

Planter boxes, vintage flower-filled containers, wooden bird houses, and bee hives are accessories that give a garden the cottage look. Most any found treasures that will hold flowers add the casual element that is part of a cottage garden.

Many of these ideas can be incorporated into to any garden to make it friendlier! But remember to add *campanula*, for everything about this old-fashioned traditional perennial shouts out cottage gardening!

Antique found items bring a touch of authenticity to a cottage garden. Flea markets, yard sales, thrift stores, or a grandparent's garage or basement might be places to check out first. They may think you are weird, but secretly they will probably be pleased that you like their junk. Place the items in the midst of flowers and voila, you have a cottage garden.

An ancient handcart adds cottage-garden appeal to a colorful flower bed.

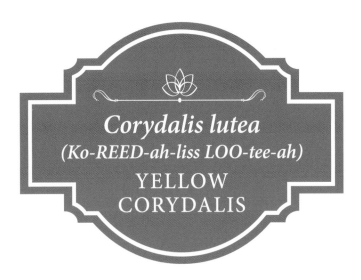

Corydalis lutea
(Ko-REED-ah-liss LOO-tee-ah)
YELLOW CORYDALIS

SHAPE	Rounded clump with tubular blooms
HEIGHT	Twelve to fifteen inches
WIDTH	Twelve to fifteen inches
BLOOM TIME	May to September
COLORS	Yellow
SITE	Any alkaline site with rocks and good drainage
LIGHT	Partial sun to partial shade
HARDINESS	Zone four
COMMENTS	Longest-blooming perennial

Corydalis has seeded and snugged itself tightly under a shade tree in the garden. The yellow blooms of *corydalis* will bloom all summer and drop seeds along the way.

This charming lacy blue-green, deeply divided foliage that stays in a rounded compact size and blooms from late spring thru early fall is the perennial called *corydalis lutea*.

The heart shaped flowers of bleeding hearts are so easily recognized that even children know their names but *corydalis* is not as well known. The two plants are related through the fumitory flower family and are easily recognized by their peculiar flowers. My name is Greek meaning crested lark for my yellow spurred rear resembles a larks head

HELLO, I'M THAT graceful little perennial every gardener has been wishing for: a partial-sun or -shade plant that never stops blooming. My enchanting one-inch yellow spurs or tubes hang down over a tight mounded ball of lacy blue-green foliage My foliage resembles my relative's, *Dicentra* or bleeding hearts, only I'm a smaller version. We are alike in that we both have very uncommon-looking flowers, but I do not have the tendency to go dormant in summer like bleeding hearts. Another difference is that bleeding hearts are very difficult to seed but not me! Self-seeding is in my nature! Bleeding hearts and I prefer a cool moist garden spot in part sun or part shade, and neither of us will survive in the hot humid conditions of the deep south. Our main differences are that *Dicentra* is a hardier zone-three perennial while I'm considered a zone four or no colder than a minus thirty degrees. I feel our most important difference is that I hold the honor of being the number-one long blooming perennial It's sad but bleeding hearts are through blooming and often collapse in the heat of July. My performance begins in May with the Darwin tulips and I continue flowering until the fall *asters* bloom.

My peculiar flowers like most fumitory flower members are unique. My dissimilar spurred outer petals flare but my inner petals are connected. Every detail about me, size, leaf or flower appears delicate but my looks are deceiving for I'm totally maintenance free and undemanding. I'm small about a fifteen-inch round ball of refined divided foliage that will stay in this same perfect shape all year. To make the foliage even more attractive I dot it with pale yellow clusters of elongated, spurred, tubular-shaped flowers that start blooming in spring and will keep blooming all season The rareness of my looks and long-bloom time gives me priority as a front of the border flower that will always look pristine. Usual shady garden pests like snails and slugs tend to ignore me so I stay undamaged. If a garden's shade area has a slug and snail problem changing out snail-bate flowers for *corydalis* would be a logical solution for I grow fine in shade. Plant me where I will show so I can reward the garden with perfect foliage and golden flowers from spring through frost.

Like most long-blooming low-maintenance perennials, I'm slow getting established in a pot. A gardener may be turned off when seeing me in the spring garden center for I may look small and forlorn. I have an aversion at being grown in a pot, probably due to my wildflower native origins. All I need is Mother Earth, for once I'm planted, I'll develop fast.

I'm completely pest free and disease resistant, but if I'm happy where I'm growing, I'll start to reseed, so some gardeners call me aggressive. The reason I'm a seeder is because the shape of my flowers are impossible to deadhead. Besides, what gardener is going to deadhead a blooming perennial? Also my spent flowers curve inward, out of sight so they aren't noticed. They form capsules with seams that will naturally break open when they are ready. This allows me to drop seeds from my flower tubes all summer. It's very important that I reseed because I'm a short-lived perennial, usually lasting only about three or four years, and you would miss not having my delightful foliage and flowers in your garden. My tiny starts seed thickly but are easily transplanted when they are small. Transplanting as I mature is not too successful for I form little teeth-like bulbs that make planting difficult. My seedlings will show up in surprising places like cracks in rock walls, stepping stones, or most anyplace where there are limestone rocks or gravel mulch. Transplant my seedlings in early spring and I'll start to bloom even when I'm small. Mother Nature's seeding provides the surest method of reproducing me, for division is all but impossible and usually unsuccessful. Trying to greenhouse germinate my seeds is erratic for I have the same complex germination requirements

My native origins began as a wildflower in the Southern Alps of Italy and Switzerland, so I grow comfortably in higher elevations. However I'm a little touchy about really cold winters so I do better in the warmer areas of the Rockies like Colorado's front range, Montana's and Idaho's western sides and Utah's Wasatch Front. An extremely hot dry summer may push me into an early hibernation but this rarely happens in the cooler high valley gardens. As long as I have a shady, well-drained, moist spot, I'll never slow my blooming until snow falls.

Notice how early in the season *corydalis* starts to bloom. Look carefully at the background and see spring bleeding hearts in bloom. Along the right side of the picture are the early blooming snowdrop *anemones*.

Nov. 3, and temperatures have dropped into the thirties. No problem, *corydalis* is still blooming, and its foliage is still just as beautiful. Notice the fall-blooming *'Chocolate' eupatorium* in the upper corner. What an amazing perennial *corydalis* is!

as bleeding hearts: 70 degree temperatures for six weeks and near freezing conditions for another six weeks. Just relax and let the real expert do the self-seeding, and if I end up too thick or in the wrong places, simply weed me out and gift me to a friend or fellow gardener.

I've been told that people use my roots as a mild antidepressant, but I know it's dangerous because if I invade pastures I'm toxic to horses. Deer and smaller wildlife also avoid me, so I would feel safer not being used as an herb or food before more information and testing is researched.

We occasionally will bloom white without any hybridizing and look lovely in the garden. Other companion plants are any of the part-shade and part-sun plants from this chapter, especially the tall soft blue spikes of campanula. I really look great when planted in front of spike flowers just because of my roundness. *Digitalis* or foxglove and the elegant *lilium* appreciate me being planted in front of them so I can camouflage any bare knees. I am also a good companion in a shade garden for I chase away slugs and snails from their favorite food, *hosta* leaves, so plant me next to *hosta* and I'll try to detour the snails. Plant me as the colorful front of the border garden plant where a full season of carefree shade loving flowers is needed. My compact rounded size is nice in planters

Corydalis seeds happened to find a spot beneath this *yucca* plant to reseed. The two plants look lovely together because of their contrasting textures. Not many gardeners would consider planting *corydalis* under *yucca*. Seedlings seem longer lived and more vigorous than their parents, so if possible leave them where they choose to grow for they will bloom earlier than transplants.

How yellow *corydalis* became white *corydalis* is a mystery. Sometimes seeds are not pollinated or simply revert, change, or simply do their own thing. Gardening seems to always bring a new adventure.

or container pots but I may not winter as well in a pot so use me as a container annual. Collecting seeds pods and placing them where a yellow lark is needed to brighten the garden next year is apt to work as long as nature does the hot and cold treatments to trigger germination. It will prove interesting for the wind and birds are efficient at seed dispersement so plan to be surprised at where I come up in the spring.

SURVIVAL OF THE FITTEST IN THE FLOWER GARDEN

I bloom continually and reseed the same way. These are the reasons I'm not a long-lived perennial. It's common

Dianthus, 'First Love,' has bloomed all summer and is still blooming in this October picture. Constant blooming takes a toll on perennials and shortens their lives.

for heavy-seeders like *antimus* or golden marguerite, and aquilegia, or columbine, to burn out by blooming themselves to death with their prolific seeding. The constant blooming and reseeding shortens their lives and I'm a member of this group. Some of the other long blooming perennials like *malva*, 'Zebrina' and *centranthus* red *valerium* don't know when to quit and just keep blooming and blooming thus shortening their lives. Allowing these perennials to reseed will give them a spot in the garden for next year.

Unlike *corydalis*, other long-blooming perennials may be sterile hybrids and bloom non-stop because they are not able to set seeds. Hybrids like *dianthus* 'First Love' never get a time to rest—they flower from spring through fall—so this shortens their life. Breeders are frantically working to place these hybrids on nursery shelves, for gardeners want a long season of bloom without deadheading but breeders probably want to replace these flowers to up sales.

Other long-blooming perennials will stop blooming without deadheading. When plants start to set seeds, a message is sent for the plant to stop blooming for it's time to put their energy into seed production. This is why deadheading is important. Removing the bloom before it starts to seed will stimulate continued bloom. After all the plant needs the flowers first before setting seeds and nature has programed survival skills in every one of her specie plants.

Long-blooming perennials add stability to a garden, so plant clumps of them in crucial garden spots where it is important to have color. Add favorites like daisies that have a shorter bloom time for more variety. Just be aware that constant color like that of *corydalis* really adds a designed look with a minimum of care and cost.

LONG-BLOOMING GARDEN COLOR

A STANDARD FIRST REQUEST always stated by a gardener shopping for perennials is, "I want a flower that blooms all summer." I find I often have to curb a sassy retort of, "Then plant petunias and marigolds!" There is nothing wrong with adding the nonstop static effect of annuals to a garden, but do you really want that kind of cost and boredom in your garden? A better solution is to plant a core of long-blooming perennials like *Corydalis*. Picking a group of five or six from the following examples of long-blooming perennials and placing a large group here and there around the yard will not only furnish all-season color but will unify and simplify the garden. Choices are varied for many are full sun and others like a shadier part of the yard. Some of the long-blooming perennials are tall; others are medium height or short, so with a little planning, your yard will overflow with color throughout the seasons. Perennials shown are in alphabetical order.

Armeria with its grassy foliage and "foxy" pink or red flower balls is a short evergreen perennial that when deadheaded keeps blooming.

Hybrid *achillea* blooms from June through Labor Day. There are two *achilleas* that are hybrids, and they are both sterile so will not spread or set seeds. 'Coronation Gold' is bigger with golden, flat-topped flowers. The smaller *achillea*, 'Moonshine', pictured above, is more delicate looking with lemon-yellow blooms. Planting *achillea* or yarrow with other full-sun perennials like *Veronica*, 'Sunny Border Blue,' shown blooming with 'Moonshine,' will give a full summer of color.

Centranthus, or Red Valerian, is a full-sun, long-blooming perennial that blooms from June through frost. *Centranthus* blooms longer in cooler summer areas so is partial to mountain gardens. Removing the puff balls of seeds along with the top six inches of the plant around the end of June will prevent seeding and reward the garden with a long second round of color. *Centranthus* blooms in both red and white flowers.

The golden flowers nestled in beautiful ferny foliage are 'Zangreb,' threadleaf *Coreopsis*. 'Zangreb,' like all threadleaf *coreopsis*, does not break dormancy until outside temperatures reach stable warmth. For this reason, they bloom the late shift in gardens, or mid-June through Labor Day. Their delicate-looking blooms and needle-like foliage are distinct and beautiful. *Coreopsis* is a full-sun perennial that shows off best on the front of a flowerbed. 'Zangreb' is hardier in colder climates so is the best *coreopsis* for western gardens.

The delicate small size of *Heuchera* will add six weeks or more of color to the front edge of a partial-shade garden. To give Coral Bells a longer flowering period, trim its thin stalks to the foliage and they will start to bloom again. *Heuchera* has gained fame with hybridizing, and its evergreen foliage is now available in shades of bronze, silver, lime, and peach to only name a few. The superb colors of the leaves look like flowers in a garden

Dianthus, 'First Love,' is a hybrid that starts blooming in May. Its fascinating flower colors are mainly pastel when it starts blooming in May but darken to a deep magenta mix over the summer. Should 'First Love's' blooming slow down due to excessive heat or lack of water, trim the plant back to about five-inches. 'First Love' will soon be in bloom again, having no idea it may be time to quit. The season-long flowering shortens 'First Love's' life.

Malva fastigata blooms from early to late summer with open funnel-shaped pale pink flowers. *Malva* grows big and shrub-like, making it an excellent filler for the back row or where height is needed in a garden. *Malva's* taproot is long and tough and almost impossible to transplant, so allowing *Malva* to set seed will furnish an endless supply of these carefree shrubs.

The soft blue spikes of *nepeta*, 'Walker's Low,' adds a clean, fragrant, fresh feeling to a garden all summer. With a late-July shearing before the perennial is allowed to set seeds, *nepeta* will bloom again from August to frost. 'Walker's Low' is a full-sun, easy-care, hybrid perennial that will not have time to reseed if it gets the July trim.

The *Hemerocallis* daylily in front of the *nepeta* is the long-blooming 'Stella de Oro'. 'Stella' is a gold miniature that starts flowering in June to July, rests awhile, and then resumes flowering sporadically in August and September.

Evening primrose opens their fragrant pale-yellow, tissue-thin petals every sunny afternoon from early summer into fall. The sprawling red stems hold elegant narrow leaves that cascade gracefully over edges or rock walls. Removing the curious-looking seedpods from *oneothera* will curtail seed production and lengthen bloom time.

Rudbeckia, 'Goldstrum,' or black-eyed Susan, fills a hot sunny garden with twenty-inch cone flowers from mid-summer through fall, leaving little time for self-seeding. Their prominent eye-catching cones are brown with a purple tinting that enhances the golden rays of this long-lasting dependable perennial. Five or more *rudbeckia* planted together creates a huge eye-catching color spot in a garden.

Salvia, or sage, flowers early summer and will continue blooming all season if it gets one deadheading. Cutting *salvia* back before it sets seeds is crucial, for once *salvia* starts seeding, it stops blooming, knowing it has fulfilled its propagation role in life, and will collapse. A deadheaded *salvia* will color a garden with its royal-blue spikes into frost.

Other long-blooming perennials not shown above are *centaurea,* or Montana bluet, which blooms and seeds prolifically both spring and fall and if the conditions are right will do a repeat performance again in June. Blue and white *campanula* carpaticas along with hot colored *gaillardia* do not start blooming until June but continue into late September, giving four months of garden color.

Many late-season-blooming perennials are not famous as self-seeders. It could be due to shorter summers not giving them time to set seed. Wild Geraniums decorate part-shade gardens with color from May through July. *Heliopsis,* 'Summer Sun,' flowers over seven weeks in cooler mountain gardens and will need a good Labor Day deadheading to curtail seed production. *Perovskia,* or Russian sage, starts blooming mid-summer. The blue spikes of Russian sage will hang on through several winter storms, allowing frost to glisten on their handsome stems, so their seeds won't germinate until spring. *Veronica* blooms from June through August for three full months so gardeners can enjoy their deep-blue spikes.

Long-blooming perennials can easily guarantee all the color a garden needs, spring through fall.

TRAITS OF LONG-BLOOMING PERENNIALS

Long-blooming perennials seem to fall into categories: the early self-seeders that require deadheading, the hybrid perennials that are sterile, or those who die young because they overextend themselves by nonstop blooming. Other methods of extending all-season color in gardens is planting bulbs, perennials with excellent foliage and perennials with persistent blooms. The small species, nonhybridized bulbs are long living, like crocus and daffodils are the most dependable in high elevation gardens. *Bergenia, sedums, hosta,* and *artemisias* are a few of perennials having foliage as nice as any blooming flower. Some perennials have blooms that persist or dry nicely where they bloomed. *Helleborus* is a good example for they bloom in March and the flowers hold nicely until the weather heats up and dries them but it takes a very close look to tell the blooms are dried flowers that have persisted. Some alpines hold on to their blooms like the short *Sedums.* Often gardeners think that annuals are the only way to keep their yards colorful, but showcasing clumps of these long-performing perennials will unify and simplify any garden.

Scabiosa flowers bloom continuously from late spring through fall, needing only an occasional snipping of a spent bloom. Pincushions are short, sun-loving perennials that bloom on sturdy single stems with blue three-inch flowers. They are prone to a short life due to their long bloom time.

Filipendula
(fil-i-PEN-dew-la)
QUEEN OF THE MEADOW
AND MEADOWSWEET

Filipendula ulmaria or Queen of the Meadow

SHAPE	Big, shrublike with clusters of pearl-shaped to lace flowers
HEIGHT	Three to four feet
WIDTH	Upright and erect
BLOOM TIME	Late summer
COLORS	Creamy white
SITE	Alkaline with added fertile organic
LIGHT	Partial shade
HARDINESS	Zone three, not frost tender
COMMENTS	Used as a medicinal herb

Vulgaris or Meadowsweet

SHAPE	Clump of ferny foliage with white lacey flowers
HEIGHT	Foliage fifteen inches, in flower twenty-four
WIDTH	Fifteen inches
BLOOM TIME	Late spring
COLORS	Ivory to white clusters
SITE	Alkaline limestone
LIGHT	Partial shade
HARDINESS	Zone three
COMMENTS	Long-lived, tidy, and carefree

FILIPENDULA OR QUEEN OF THE MEADOW

I'M QUEEN, SO MY STORY WILL BE FIRST

I'M CALLED THE Queen of the Meadow and deserve to be treated as such. I'm a magnificent, bold and erect specimen for a damp shady garden spot so queen is an appropriate name. Everything about me is queenlike. I stand straight and tall on strong sturdy stems. My stems may become furrowed with age but will always hold me upright and vertical. I'm too proud to ever need staking! I'm long lived and easy to grow, especially when my home is in the alkaline or limestone soils and the cooler temperatures of the mountains. My dark-green serrated leaves are slightly wrinkled with the undersides being a lighter green. They exude the clean fresh smell of wintergreen and have no toxins. My height and shrublike size gives me the ability to grow as a focal point or a hedge for a seasonal privacy barrier in the garden. The shape, size and density of my growth are reasons that I'm chosen for foundation plantings on east or north exteriors. Not many perennials have my regal, queenly proportions and demeanor that adds dominance to a partial shade garden.

Queen of the meadow is a showy, vigorous perennial with a strong sturdy stem that guarantees to keep the plant looking regal. Many gardeners confuse queen of the meadow's foliage with that of boysenberries because of their similar leaves.

My regal bearing is commendable, but more important is that I light up a spot dappled in shade with my exquisite dense heads of creamy panicles. My flowers have an appealing light fragrance that will fill an entire room. My fragrance intensifies when dried, so I'm used as an herb flavoring or sweetener in beer and tea. In earlier times, I was used as a strewing herb to cover floors and the smells on those floors. Now I'm used to scent linens. I dry so well that I'm used as decorations for weddings and as a sturdy form to shape bridal wreaths. My flowers dry into attractive lime-green round fruits. Placing the seed stem in a vase of glycerin will preserve their dense shape-holding sprays that can be used in modernistic floral arrangements or crafts.

The uses of queen of the meadow's dried seeds are many. Boiling the seeds makes a clear chartreuse dye, and their color and almond scent add uniqueness to potpourri.

The bright-lime color of my round, dried seed heads not only smells good but is striking when added to potpourri. My numerous other skills are boiling the dried seeds for a chartreuse-colored dye. Surprising, my leaf and stems when boiled create a blue dye and my roots produce a dark brown color so who would consider I'd be a plant that delivers not one but three different dyes. My roots contain sapions which are natural cleansing agents, so I can be used as an excellent all-natural soap. My young leaves, like most of me, are edible and can be used as a sweetener in tea. I've always been considered an herbal healer and was held sacred to the Druids. We now know that my flower buds are a good source of salicylic acid from which aspirin is made so a tea made from my flower buds can be used as a mild sedative and pain reliever. It's said that I can also alleviate heartburn, feverish colds, and mild diarrhea. As royalty, I certainly have many down-to-earth talents.

Crescent-shaped seeds will eventually fall from my drying flower sprays. These seeds will sporadically self-germinate for I'm fortunate to have both male and female organs so we are called hermaphrodites. Germination is done by insect pollinators for they are strongly attracted to my fragrant flowers and foliage. Sorry, but I'm rather slow and inconsistent at germination so gathering my seeds and sowing them in a germination tray placed in a cold frame will give a higher number of starts than a self-sowing in the garden. I germinate better in the cooler temperatures of fall but my new starts will need some winter protection. Next spring, as soon as my seedlings are large enough, pot them up. By summer, I'll be ready to plant into the garden.

Division of queen of the meadow will require a shovel and pruner for I form a strong root network to support my height. The huge-sized roots can be dug and, with a little help from the pruner, can be pulled from the root ball. These larger reddish roots can be planted directly into the garden. Smaller root subjects will need to be potted up to spend the winter in a cold frame and can be planted out into the garden in spring. If a strong visual element adds to the appearance of the garden, leave me in place—dividing isn't that necessary for I'm long lived and will colonize comfortably, Over the years I'll form large clumps of shrubbery and flowers.

Queen of the meadow *ruba* or 'Venusta' is a massive, up-to-six-foot-tall sister of mine and blooms with soft pink or reddish flowers. Many gardeners feel 'Venusta' is almost too large and has a tendency to revert back to the wild species. They are rougher appearing than my pristine creamy blooms and comfortable size.

I enjoy companion perennials as long as they are vigorous enough to hold their own beside my boldness for they must understand that I am the queen! For spring, plant the short but beautiful foliaged *Pulmonaria* or lungwort, Wild Geranium or Cranesbill, and Lamium to front for me for we both love partial shade garden. *Pulmonaria* blooms early with delicate blue to pink flowers, but it's the foliage with its bright spots or silvery leaves that stays attractive until the first frost.

Statuesque describes this naturalized perennial with its toothed leaflets. The generous ten-inch flower plumes are spectacular as well as fragrant. What could be more attractive in a shady garden area than these sparkling white, fragrant clusters of flowers?

Filipendula form good-sized root clumps that hold the plant erect and provide enough nutrition for a perennial the size of queen of the meadow. Pull the root ball into smaller sections and replant the larger ones. Smaller plants should be potted and wintered in the protection of a cold frame. My suggestion: leave this fine plant alone and allow it to become bigger and more beautiful, year after year—it really doesn't like being divided.

The low silver foliage of *pulmonaria*, 'Diana Claire,' has the longest leaves of any other *pulmonaria* or lungwort and grows well around queen of the meadow. 'Diana Claire' shines like a light around the fine shrub.

FILIPENDULA OR MEADOWSWEET

Wow! My big Sister, the Queen, really got up on her throne and hardly left any of my vitals undescribed, so I guess I'll just tell you my name, "Meadowsweet" or sometimes I'm called *hexepetala*. It's a good name for everything about me is sweet. My small rounded shape with its ferny leaves that grow from a central rosette is just as pretty and sweet as my white and pink, lacy-looking panicules. I bloom in June, earlier than the queen, and my foliage stays flawless throughout the entire season including mild winters for I'm a frost tolerant perennial. My flower stems are not as strong as my sisters so removing them so they won't flop with the heaviness of my flowers is often a gardener's option. My fifteen inch height and width makes me a fine flowerbed edger. My elegant bright green fernlike leaves look flawless against the hard lines of paths or walkways. No matter where I'm planted in the garden I add a softness and sweetness to the flowerbed.

A fall garden photo: Meadowsweet or *hexepetala* has remained perfect throughout a hot season of summer and is now adding contrast to these striking bronze-purple foliaged plantings of 'Chocolate' *Eupatorium*.

Meadowsweet is not only sweet but is exquisitely beautiful planted next to a walkway where it can be admired. Contrary to gossip that claims Meadow sweet spreads, My plant was given me over forty years ago by our Grandmother and has stayed put, right here in this same spot where it was first planted.

I'm a good companion plant to flat growing ground covers like *ajuga* but taller groundcovers will look chaotic and detract from the finesse of my ferny foliage. Taller perennials become more attractive with me placed to conceal their leggy feet. I complement the dark foliaged *Penstemon*, 'Mystica', in late spring, elegant *Lilium* in early summer and tall Garden *Phlox* later in the season. *Aconitum* and 'Chocolate' *Eubatorium* are excellent companions for fall. All of these fine perennials flourish in the same cool moist environment that I like but I'm not limited to these. I'm comfortable in most any garden spot; even the aridness and bright sunshine of the Mountains and average water amounts are fine with me. I'm not as fussy as the Queen and thrive most anywhere.

I'm sweet, but tough, often called a cold hardy zone-two perennial even though I'm usually noted as being a zone three. I'm an ideal perennial for the higher, cooler elevations of the mountains for I thrive in the limey soils of the west. I'm more flexible than the queen and will grow well in dryer soils and will even grow in sandy or clay soils as long as they are not acidic. I rarely suffer from any insect or disease issues and I am attractive to bees and wildlife.

My root stocks are composed of two-to-three-inch tubers that can be dug and easily pulled from the root ball and propagated to other areas of the garden. When these rooted starts are planted closely, I grow as a lovely lacy groundcover under the dappled light of trees. I can be divided and moved most of the growing season as long as three to five of my tubers along with a top stem are included. Not only will I look delightful all season but I will be there in perfect form for as long as a gardener wishes for I'm extremely long lived and dependable. I'm so long lived that I was considered a sacred herb in the time of the ancient Druids.

Here are a few traits I have that the queen forgot about. All parts of me are considered edible but I'm bitter. Deer don't like me. I'm consistently given high medicinal ratings for everything from inflammation and bronchitis to astringent and contain high levels of salicylic acid or the component of asprin. We are both members of the rose family and are often classified as a herb.

Geranium sanguineum
(Jer-AY-nee-um)
LITTLE LEAF HARDY OR CRANESBILL

SHAPE	Tidy mound with funnel-shaped flowers
HEIGHT	Small, twelve inches
WIDTH	Grows wider than taller
BLOOM TIME	June to July
COLORS	Pink, white, blue, purple, violet, and magenta
SITE	Unfussy plants like average, well-drained, even moist soils and alkaline
LIGHT	Full sun, partial sun, shade
HARDINESS	Zones three to five
COMMENTS	*When in doubt, don't go without, Plant a little leaf small geranium*

Geranium sanguineum, or little leaf wild geraniums, are so pleasing with their small rounded forms and lacy leaves that any spot in the garden becomes more appealing with its petite presence.

Small, little leaf *geranium sanguineum*, 'Vision Violet,' has delicate flowers that dance over the soft lace-like foliage, adding texture and a winning contrast to the solid rock accent, rock mulch, and cement mowing strip in this garden.

Small *Geraniums* planted in this parking lot look lovely even in the hot, cement-surrounded environment where few flowers will survive. As a commercial planting, small geranium are adaptable and dependable perennials that require only a minimum amount of care.

Perennial *Geraniums* will grow anywhere in the Western Rocky Mountains. They are not bothered by any pests like deer and or rabbits for their fragrant foliage smells like a mix of mint and antiseptic and is disliked by wildlife.

"NO SPLASH! NO flash!" I heard the flower shopper rudely say as they passed over me. This happens a lot to me for I fit the old proverbial saying, "Don't judge a book by its cover." I admit my cover isn't that colorfully classy looking especially when I'm in a pot, but inside I'm the most pleasing and valuable flower in the garden.

First, I'm flexible for I'm not fussy about growing conditions. I do best in partial shade/sun but will even perform in sun or full-shade gardens. Next is my adaptability to any type of soil or conditions. I grow in alkaline clay or loam, on sand dunes or beaches. I'm an excellent groundcover on rocky slopes and an edger along limestone pavements or for spilling over walls but I also grow in acidic or neutral soils. I'm comfortable in average, moist, well-drained soils, but surprisingly, I'm also planted extensively in xeriscape drought gardens. I accept low-moderate well-balanced fertilization which really isn't necessary for my sturdy roots and bushy habit establish easily and are effective against soil erosion and weed control, all without fertilizers.

The casualness of my small fine-textured mound looks excellent as an alpine in rock or woodland gardens or a lax bloomer in a cottage garden, but the tidiness of my shape also adds a sleek, modern look to contemporary gardens and the front of borders. I'm an attractive ornamental perennial for city park gardens or containers where I may get babied but will even perform in the most difficult of garden spots like roof gardens, under pine trees or beneath an extended roofline on a house where there is no chance of being babied. I may not have the "splash" of big bloomed perennials or the "flash" of tall focal point perennials that need spent flower removal or cutting back to look decent but I add simplicity and the stability of an attractive fresh-green foliaged perennial all summer. My fall leaves and stems turn a bright red or orange when they get touched by the first frost adding another season of color. In short, Geranium sanguineun called Cranesbill is pleasing in any place, any spot, in any garden for a full ten months of good looks per year.

Hardy *geranium*, little leaf *geranium* or short wild *geranium*; whatever I'm called is fine because I'll grow wherever my services are needed. I was named my botanic name by the father of flowers, *linnaeus*, when I was discovered in Europe and Asia. *Geranos* is a Greek word meaning "crane," refering to the shape of the seed or fruit capsule my flower forms after blooming. The adjective or specific Latin name *sanguineum*

refers to the red stems and leaves of my winter foliage, this explains my common name, bloody cranesbill, but we are usually just called cranesbills.

I'm gaining popularity for my 300 plus family members have spread over every continent of the earth. There is a hardy *geranium* that will even grow in western gardens with their bipolar-like climate conditions. Unlike perennials with hundreds of varieties such as daylilies, *Geranium* choices are fewer but I promise the *sanguineums*, are the hardiest of the crew. We enjoy the cold temperatures of zone-three

The precision, rounded shape of these wild *geraniums* appears as having been accomplished by shearing but they have not been sheared; this is there natural full, compact shape. Not many perennials could look this lovely growing side-by-side and looking like twins.

environments that can drop to a minus thirty or forty degrees below zero, so winter survival in the west is easy with one exception, container wintered cranesbills. We are hardy herbaceous perennials often staying evergreen but our buds remain close to the soil surface so it's best to remove me from the pot and stick me in the ground for winter. Then my buds are more deeply protected and I get watered by the snow.

Our flowers are delightful, not bold and flamboyant just steady and dependable. We only bloom at about 30 percent coverage and this is the reason we are not a plant that gets rave reviews. That being said, my blooms are beautiful in their own delicate way. Each small bloom is funnel-shaped with five equal-sized petals and contain both male and female sex organs making it easy for the bees and insects to pollinate. Our flowers open in pastel jewel-toned shades of pink, white, blue, lavender, and violet, and some have intricate striations or centers of contrasting colors. Our laid-back crop time of flowers starts in June and lasts until the end of July. We usually bloom sporadically after July so there are always a few dots of color spotting our foliage.

Patented hybrid wild *geranium*, 'Orkney Cherry's' bronzed foliage spreads and cascades rather than clumping. Its vivid star-shaped flowers bloom from June to first frost. 'Orkney's' hardiness is more in the zone-five realm due to its hybridization.

Wild *Geranium*, 'Orkney Cherry,' also has a unique personality. 'Orkney' has diminutive deeply cut bronzed foliage with contrasting hot pink flowers. The foliage starts in spring as a small mound and by fall will be cascading over edges. The combination of colors on this different looking wild geranium is stunning so show it off along a front edge where it can be noticed.

Wild *Geranium* 'Rozanne' is a new patented hybrid that is so improved that gardeners everywhere have added it to their gardens. The larger flowers and longer blooming season shows what improvements hybridizing can do for a wild geranium and it even won the Perennial Plant of the Year for 2008.

Hybrid wild *geranium*, 'Samobor', has deep-wine flowers that match the wine splotches on its maple-shaped leaves. 'Samobor' is nicknamed mourning widow, probably because the colors of the blossoms are so dark.

Many gardeners consider our lacy-lobed, palm-shaped foliage with its long season of interest as more attractive than our flowers because I'm just as pretty when I'm not blooming. Some of us have quilting, veining or blotching on our finely dissected leaves so we give valuable textures in the flowerbed. A hybrid *geranium*, 'Samobor,' has wine flowers that match splotches on its foliage. 'Samobor' is taller growing, to sixteen inches, and is not as hardy being a zone-five perennial, but if your garden spot is warmer then add this engaging, eyecatching wild *geranium* to your border. The soft stems on many of the taller wild geraniums may need a trim after the first flush of blooming fades.

'Rozanna's' big, true blue flowers with white-striped centers have grabbed hold of my affection. It never stops blooming, and the foliage is slightly marbled so it is very desirable for it is showier in the garden than most wild *geraniums*.

As with most hybrids, Rocky Mountain gardeners may need to be cautious for the perennial is a zone five.

'Biokovo' *cantabrigiense* is an outstanding geranium because it is short and grows flat like a ground cover. 'Biokovo's foliage spreads nicely with lovely rounded, palmately or palm-shaped divided leaves, that stay evergreen all winter. 'Biokovo won the

Cranesbill 'Biokovo' flowers are white, flushed delicately with opalescent pink. 'Biokovo' spreads as a groundcover mat of flowers that expands every year into larger more scrumptious carpeting. 'Biokovo' is easily propagated for as it spreads the center may start looking woody. Lift the entire root ball. Compost or discard the woody center and divide the rest. For a ground cover appearance plant each division about six-inches apart to encourage the plant to form a solid mat. 'Biokovo' is a valuable asset to a garden with its lacy carpet look.

Perennial Plant of the Year Award for the year 2015 and is a zone five.

The new hybrids are lovely but there are a lot of us who are hardier in western gardens. 'Album' is a Royal Horticulture Society winner with sparkling white blooms while 'Max Frei' and Alpenglow are a rosy-red. 'Max Frei' knits their deeply cut leaves together covering the soil like carpet. The very affordable 'Vision' bloody cranesbills are seed-propagated *sanguineums* that bloom in a luminescent pure pink or hot-fuchsia violet. The 'New Hampshire Purple' is a clear true purple and 'Elke' is a neon pink. The *sanguineas* started out life as wild flowers and can be found in our mountain canyons and snow fields, thus we are called wild *geraniums* and are the hardiest.

Seed propagation of little leaf Bloody Cranesbill rarely happens and is better done by the plant catapulting my beaked seed pods which look just like a crane's bill than by a gardener trying to seed. Sheared wild *geraniums* also do not set seed and even if they did it would take fifteen weeks of cold vernalization for the germinated seeds to.

A more successful method of propagation of wild geranium is by division in spring while the rhizome roots are short. First soak the *geranium* to be divided the day before. The best time for dividing perennials is a cool or rainy day. Dig and add mulch or manure to the new planting spot before removing the *geranium* from its original location. Dig the plant and divide the rhizome roots making sure every start has a solid crown. Plant the cranesbill in the newly amended soil and compact the soil around the plant. Water well.

We make excellent ground covers that will never become invasive. Our rounded small scale size gives us priority when used as commercial plants and we can act as spillers in a perennial planter or container. We are so drought tolerant when established that we are in demand for roof-top gardens and shopping mall xerioscapes. Our good looks are always needed for the front of the border in formal, contemporary, and cottage garden settings. Wherever we are planted we just keep going and keep on giving!

A FULL SEASON OF
SELF-SOWING ANNUALS/PERENNIALS

SELF-SEEDING ANNUALS

An outdoor wedding the first of June sounds delightful unless your garden is located in the high cold mountain valleys of the west. When the invitation arrived I wondered how the gardens with our cooler than normal late spring weather would look? Would there be a possibility of having the traditional blooming flowers? The week of the wedding, temperatures warmed and I was in for an eye opening experience for the gardens were absolutely lovely! Among every bulb and up-thrusting perennial were glorious clumps of a divine deep blue annual flower called *Nigella* or Love-in-a-mist. I was mystified at how any garden, especially with the cold temperatures, could be so densely decorated with an annual at this time of year. Each of the hundreds of blooming flowers looked as if a crown of thread like bracts around the flowers were a misty wedding veil surrounding their blooms. Even the ring of lacy foliage that supported the plant was charming. I knew I needed a nice conversation with the bride's mother later to learn more about one of the loveliest flowers I've ever seen blooming! This is how she grows Love-in-a-mist.

NIGELLA OR LOVE-IN-A-MIST

"Love-in-a-mist is an annual that blooms in cool spring weather. I harvest *Nigella's* seed pods, let them dry in a paper sack and sprinkle them in summer," The bride's mother explained. "They germinate easily and miraculously over winter in the garden as seedlings. Some of them won't make it to spring but enough will that we had plenty of blue flowers for that was my daughter's color choice for the wedding," she added. "My first experience with *Nigella* was from a package of wildflower seed that I tried. Fortunately, most of those plants died but the *Nigella* is a keeper! The plant's seeds usually drop right around the base of the parent plant, so they self-seed close to the same spot. The seeds I harvested were sprinkled to make sure that our spring gardens are full of color no matter what the weather is doing. Love-in-a-mist blooms early and dries up when weather gets hot. It's the simplest spring plant growing in my garden." The eye-opening experience with the self-seeding perfection of *Nigella* caused me to ponder on my fixation with Perennials especially due to early frost-freeze spring cycles in our mountain gardens. *Nigella's* bloom power and carefree adaptability was as dependable and beautiful as any flower growing so I questioned if there are other annuals as talented as Love-in-a-mist? The answer is a resounding yes and here is a set of self-seeding annuals (often labeled as perennials) that bloom for every season.

PAPAVER OR POPPY

Poppies nudicaule and Iceland Poppies are often called perennials but allowing the poppy flowers to drop their seeds is a better guarantee that a garden will have these bright blooms for the next spring. Poppies bloom about the time that *Nigella* finishes.

These delightful poppies bloom just as the spring bulbs are fading. They add their amazing colors of flaming orange, red, salmon, pink, rose, gold, pale yellow, and white to cover the bulbs' spent foliage left behind, and they do it with their self-sown seeds from the year before. Their luscious crepe-paper-looking satin petals open on top of twelve to fifteen

Nigella is an old-fashioned annual that once established will readily self-seed. The seeds germinate in fall and over-winter to bloom the next June.

inch stems of finely cut foliage. Their flowers bloom wide open and upward facing. Often listed as a hardy zone-three perennial, the poppies should winter but they don't in our high mountain valleys. Gardeners will find that allowing these widely-used popular poppies to reseed is a better guarantee of blooming poppies for the next year rather than hoping the perennial comes back. Alpine poppies are a native wildflower, and during the bloom season, mountain sides and fields of poppies shine red, setting a stage for a doting grandmother to prop her grandchild in the middle of the brilliant blooms for a photoshoot!

Most poppy gardens are better viewed from a distance as a mass planting due to the flower's tendency to close-up on overcast days and at night. Also, after flowering, their foliage turns to straw so poppies are perfect for cultivated farm fields. Their seed can be allowed to drop and often the flower color reverts to a brilliant scarlet-orange. Seed can also be sown in fall with the hope of a wet, snow packed winter. Snow cover also protects the seeds from birds attracted to it. A wet spring guarantees that cultivated fields will be a mass of blooming poppies. To broadcast large scale plantings, poppy seed can be purchased by the pound. Three to four pounds of seed will cover an acre.

NASTURTIUM

Nasturtiums are a carefree, old-fashioned annual flower that will start blooming as the poppies finish. Their well-known circular lily-pad shaped leaves contrast vividly with their bright red-orange funnel-shaped flowers making

Nasturiums grow as a compact vine or a trailing plant. They are great for edging a vegetable patch or will trail over a rock wall with a two-to-three-foot vine.

them a delightful addition to a garden. *Nasturtiums* grow well in cool summer areas and tolerate poor soils so are very comfortable growing in our high mountain valleys. The leaves of *nasturtiums* are edible and add a peppery taste that is rich in vitamin C when added to salads. Their taste has been likened to that of watercress, dubbing them water cress flowers. Because nasturtiums are edible with large seeds Children can easily press them into the ground. This annual thrives on neglect, poor soils and germinates quickly. If the seeds are purchased or harvested rather than a fall self-seeding they will probably need to be nicked and soaked in warm water overnight before planting.

ANTIRRHINUM MAJUS OR SNAPDRAGONS

Snapdragons reseed themselves in the garden bringing a rainbow of colors for months on end. Gardeners and children love snapdragons mainly for their non-stop incandescent colors but also for the individual flowers that have a mouth that opens when the sides are squeezed. Thus the name of snapdragon for when the dragon's jaw is open and a view of the dragon's hairy throat can be seen. Not only is the throat of the snapdragon hairy but the entire inside of the bloom is too. In fact the inside of the flower is the exact size and shape of a bumblebee's body so that when the bee enters the pollen covers the entire bee.

Snapdragons prefer a cool setting so are their most spectacular in the coolness of late spring. When days reach eighty degrees or over, snapdragons may pout a little and refuse to bloom. This is the point that a gardener removes the spent stems of seed pods and places them anywhere in the garden that could use bright colors next year. Simply lay the stem and seed-pods on the soil not bothering to first remove the seeds for they will drop automatically. No worries, as temperatures cool during fall's Indian Summer these magnificent spikes of color will come back with the brightest show in the garden. Snapdragons bloom until Thanksgiving and seem to handle frost or light snow but not the deer that browse them. It's a good thing the seeds were harvested before the deer visited.

COSMOS

Cosmos are late-summer-through-fall-blooming annuals that produce open, evenly placed, daisy-shaped flowers in many colors. The cosmos foliage has bright thread-like ferny leaves on tall stems that hold the bowl-shaped blooms on their tip ends. Cosmos add a soft frilly texture to the garden and provide nutrients for pollinators getting ready for winter.

Use cosmos to fill in garden areas where early blooming perennials have finished blooming. An *iris* bed with its tired foliage will become an eye-catching focal point by planting Cosmos seeds in spots around the spent iris. Papaver, Oriental Poppies, leave a blank hole in the garden

Snapdragons grow in several sizes; the tallest are the 'Rockets' at almost three feet in height, 'Liberties' are a medium-tall spike at two feet, and the 'Sonnet' series are shorter at about a foot. A few types of snapdragons even cascade and spill delightfully over edges of rocks walls or curbing.

Cosmos *bipinnatus* bloom in red, pink, rose, lavender, and crimson flowers with a tufted center. Cosmos *sulphureus* bloom in hot colors of yellows, golds, and oranges and are more robust, reaching heights of six feet and may look unruly. Chocolate cosmos, *atrosanguineus*, are actually tuberous perennials that can be dug and harvested before freezing.

due to their mid-summer period of dormancy but the bare spots will shine when filled with blooming cosmos. Top soil sprinkled where the seed will be spread is helpful for germination then sow the seed on the top soil. Cosmos seeds need light, so press the seeds down just enough that they will not blow away. The seed of cosmos require hot summer heat to germinate, so this makes it easy to wait until summer to

sow them. Cosmos will self-sow for years after their initial planting but fall-germinated/sprouted seedlings will not survive a western winter.

DATURA OR ANGEL TRUMPET

Angel trumpets look so pure in bloom with their luminous elongated trumpets shaded deliciously with halos of pale lavender or blue, but like vampires, they come alive and bloom at night then fade during the day. In full bloom, their sweet fragrance is intoxicating, but when the trumpets close at mid-day, their smell is disgusting. Angel trumpet's four-foot-tall and wide spread has bold, appealing, elongated leaves of soft green-gray with a fine down on the undersides. The lovely, long-blooming angel trumpet flowers from mid-summer through November, and from each angelic flower a spiny, walnut-sized ball is produced to ensure next year's crop of flowers. Angel trumpet grows everywhere in the west for it thrives in hot sun, high elevations and deserts. If allowed to reseed on farmland, the name changes to Jimson Weed that causes erratic behavior or fatal poison if ingested by cattle. If the hurtful spiny seed balls are forming they should be removed otherwise they will split, dropping hundreds of flat translucent, fly-away seeds. Use caution and wear leather gloves when removing not only the prickly

seed balls but also when removing datura for the entire plant and seeds are poison. Hallucinations and dark visions are known to result if consumed by humans. Angel or Devil, You decide? This enticing beauty is an attention getter and easy to grow but be aware of its dark side before allowing it to beautify your garden.

These are only a few of the annual/perennials that reseed nicely. Other so-called perennials like *delphinium grandiflorum* winter kill in the Rocky Mountains but will return from seeds that are allowed to fall. Love-lies-bleeding adds a dynamic, dark burgundy-red weeping spike to the fall garden. The eyecatching spikes are stunning, but it reseeds with an abandonment that makes a gardener sure it is related to the weed called red root. Experimenting with any of these fascinating plants will not only be entertaining but will add a full season of color to the garden.

Datura, or angel trumpet, is an exquisite beauty that draws attention in a garden. Angel trumpet is just a little weird for the common name of this plant, for *Datura* has a dark side. My first plant of angel trumpet had to be a seed dispersed by wind. I was so surprised that such a gorgeous plant had magically appeared in my garden that before I found out more about its dark side, I harvested and propagated the spiny seed pods and shared with gardening friends. Now I still love to grow the gorgeous plant but before I share seeds I warn them about its dark side.

Heuchera
(HEW-ker-a)
CORAL BELLS

x Heucherella
(hew-ke-REL-la)
FOAMY BELLS

Tiarella
(tee-uh-REL-uh)
FOAM FLOWER

Heuchera sanguinea, 'Ruby Bells,' has been brightening early summer gardens across the Northern Hemisphere forever for it is a native perennial. *Heuchera*, usually called Coral Bells is usually planted along a front edge of a flower bed because of its petite size, long bloom time, and evergreen foliage. 'Ruby Bells' is a seed propagated perennial that has provided the basic genetic source for creating many new varieties of coral bells.

SHAPE	Small clump with flower sprays of tiny trumpets
HEIGHT	Twelve to fifteen inches
WIDTH	Close to the same width as the height
BLOOM TIME	Early summer
COLORS	Mainly hues of red but also pink and cream
SITE	Well-drained, alkaline to a neutral or 7.0 ph. Good soil
LIGHT	Adaptable, but flowers and foliage stay nicer in partial shade
HARDINESS	Zone three
COMMENTS	Known for its colorful foliage

X Heucherella is a genetic cross from *Heuchera* and *Tiarella*. The X before *heucherella's* name is a universal symbol that signals a hybrid cross between two different plants and explains the combination of the *heuchera* and *tiarella* names. *Heucherella* is sterile and doesn't produce seeds but is very valuable to shady gardens for it will grow under trees adding an all-season splash of color.

Tiarella is an early spring-blooming, petite member of a shaded garden. As the seasons progress, tiarella's distinctive-shaped leaves become more suede-like and feel like velvet. There are two varieties of *tiarella—cordifolia* and *wherryi*—and some clump and others run, forming a solid groundcover. *Tiarella* is the female parent of many *heucherella* and the groundcover, *wherryi*, is a seed-grown perennial.

SHAPE	Small clumps with foamy-textured flower spikes
HEIGHT	Eight-inch foliage, spikes reach about twelve inches
WIDTH	Clump will widen to twelve inches with maturity
BLOOM TIME	Springtime
COLORS	Known for colorful foliage, flowers are pink or creamy white
SITE	Not fussy, average, alkaline, or acidic
LIGHT	Partial shade to full shade
HARDINESS	Zone four
COMMENTS	Stunning foliage

SHAPE	Some grow as a rounded clump while others spread as a creeping groundcover. They both have bottlebrush sort of fuzzy short spikes.
HEIGHT	Short, only six to seven inches tall
WIDTH	*Cordifolia*, six-inch spread; *Wherryi* sends out runners to form groundcover
BLOOM TIME	Spring but in the coolness of mountain gardens often blooms all year
COLORS	White or frosted pink
SITE	Well-drained but moist soils
LIGHT	Dappled or full shade
HARDINESS	Zone three
COMMENTS	Grows in dry shade, even under a pine tree

HEUCHERA

Welcome to the golden age of *heuchera*! I'm the number-one perennial with the most introductions of new varieties on the market today. I have been eclipsing *Echinacea* in sales and hybridize so readily that I'm coming close to the hundreds of *hosta* types now available.

Now before you meet the colorful foliage array of my new introductions, I want you to know the real *heuchera* by sharing some of my background and please, just call me coral bells.

I'm an original native perennial discovered by early settlers in this country. I was found along rocky, well-drained ledges or growing in crevasses in mountains and was called "Alum Root" for my astringent qualities make the mouth pucker. I suppose they puckered wildlife's mouths too, for I'm repellent to deer and, believe it or not, snails and slugs. This gives me an edge on *hosta*, a plant that snails and slugs consume readily, so I make a good substitute.

This famous coral bell with its purplish maple leaves fades to a bronze in the heat of summer. 'Palace Purple' is seed grown and can be propagated.

I grow in a small rounded clump with delightful leaves. In late spring, I send up wiry, hairy stems that are topped with hundreds of trumpet-shaped bells. I look so fragile that many gardeners try to plant me where I'm protected, but I'm easy to care for and quite drought tolerant, so plant me anywhere I'll be able to show off my colorful foliage and blooms.

My only problem is my shallow root structure that has a tendency to heave out of the ground in winter or late spring when temperatures fluctuate from one day a freeze and the

Like several of the new coral bell cultivars, 'Christa' is a smaller more compact plant with ruffled leaves. And like many of the new hybrids, 'Christa' changes from its rosy spring emerging colors, fading to green peach by mid-summer. My sister asked me when visiting my garden why I had dead plants around the fountain. The plant was coral bells 'Christa' and the foliage only appeared dead from a distance.

'Citronelle's' bright-yellow, maple-like leaves turn more chartreuse in heavy shade. Even with all the hybridizing, there is still a sameness in the coral bells that doesn't really leave a gardener overly excited, for they find it almost impossible to choose a favorite from the glut of new varieties. But with the new *heucherella* hybrids, excitement is contagious!

'Marmalade' is larger and one of the best fancy foliaged coral bells of the new hybrids. Its leaves are ruffled and of heavy substance so the plant makes a decent statement in the garden as long as a gardener is happy with fall colors all season. The blooms are a reddish brown without a lot of substance. Coral bells due to the thin wiry stems of its flowers, needs to be planted in mass to really make a statement but 'Marmalade' does not mesh well with other 'Marmalades' or other colors of *heuchera* but looks well as a specimen.

a licensed perennial nursery. Parents, *heuchera* and *tiarella*, of *heucherella* are in the saxifrage family, so fortunately we share the same chromosome and similar DNA, but a cross of two different plants never happens so *heucherella* is somewhat of a miracle. Foamy bells or *heucherella*, coral bells or *heuchera,* and foam flowers or *tiarella* are almost identical in their growth patterns and environmental needs, but due to the hybridizing, foamy bells are not as hardy as their zone-three parents. Foamy bells differ from coral bells because they grow wonderfully in areas that not many perennials will survive, in a dry shade garden, under trees and competing with tree roots. Our roots are quite shallow, so we do not need to compete with tree roots. A covering of mulch in fall will keep us at our outstanding best.

Heuchera, *heucherella*, and *tiarella* with our compact sizes and beautiful foliage are perfect container perennials. Planting us in a pot will fill the pot with stunning foliage. If you don't believe me look at the potted tiarella in the picture below.

next a thaw. Mulch placed around me in fall will help keep me from heaving. Planting these up-thrust plants back in the ground as soon as possible will help them survive such crazy weather. If my mid-center dies out as I age, divide me in the spring. Replant the healthy plants and throw the dead center in the compost pile. *Heuchera* seed is generally sterile so planting the rooted offsets will give the best success.

Today's colorful hybrids are mainly due to the parentage of three native *heuchera* core plants; *Heuchera*, Americana, a larger plant with silver markings, *heuchera sanguinea* the source of red flowers and *heuchera micrantha* for ruffled leaves and burgundy foliage. The first big breakthrough in purple foliage was *heuchera* 'Palace Purple'. Besides being hugely popular, 'Palace Purple' was awarded the Perennial Plant of the Year Award in 1991 and the award of Garden Merit from the Royal Horticultural Society.

This success started the explosion that led not only to the deep purple/burgundy foliage but many with a silvery sheen or veins. Some are green, chartreuse, or lime. Even the leaf and plant size have changed.

HEUCHERELLA

It's sad that I'm sterile and cannot set seed and can only be produced by tissue culture. Hybridizers have me patented so the only way to add me to your garden is to purchase me from

WOW! What an explosion! Gold Zebra with its mound of bright leaves with bold red markings in the center is breathtaking. Never before has a hardy, gorgeous perennial groundcover for shade been available. Foamy bells have the best traits of both parents, coral bells and foam flowers.

TIARELLA

I find it hard to believe that a low-maintenance, long-blooming groundcover perennial for shade like me has been ignored for so long. I never even need deadheading unless it's an act of rejuvenation.

'Jade Peacock' foam flower, with its chartreuse and maroon center markings, is compact and clumps nicely in a container. This hardy zone-four, low-maintenance shade perennials stays evergreen, so the planter is attractive in a protected winter garden.

My flowers are show stoppers with abundant ten-inch spikes of pinkish-white feathery blooms that brighten a shady garden for over a month. Watch for the words "clump" or "spreading" on my label when you purchase me for this

'Cinnamon Curls' completely fills this attractive container with its unique blends of orange-, red-, and purple-toned foliage with magenta undersides. The flowers are insignificant, but with such classy foliage, who needs flowers? 'Cinnamon Curls' is very desirable but it is both patented and trademarked so it doesn't matter that you are only sharing a start with a friend it is illegal to propagate. Trademarks are issued by the United States Patent and Trademark Office for protection of the hybridizer.

may make a difference where I'll be planted. If the label name says "*Wherryi*," I'm a seeded plant and can be direct sown in a fall garden where winter's vernalization will help me germinate. The *cordifolia* types are pretty much patented so can't be propagated.

All three of us are appropriate for planters and add eye-stopping focal points in spring shady gardens. We look attractive in pots and are new "hot number" on early spring garden center shelves. Watch for us for our new found popularity will cause us to sell out fast. Just look at the stunning look of *heuchera* or coral bells in the glazed organic-looking container below.

'Sugar and Spice', *tiarella*, with its beautiful pinkish fluffy spikes and dramatically marked foliage has become very popular with native plant lovers as well as those who garden in shade. 'Sugar and Spice' is a mounding foam flower that claims a zone-three hardiness

The stunning new hybrids all have a little variation like frosting or a silver patina wash over their leaves or their leaves may change color as the season progresses. Leaf edges differ as well as the leaf size. In most of the *heuchera*, *heucherella*, and *tiarella*, their foliage is far more spectacular than the flowers. They are all little different, but there is one trait they all have in common, that of the capital PP and numbers behind their names telling a gardener that this plant is patented and cannot be propagated without paying a patent holder fee. Gardeners respond to the hyped marketing and status symbol of these new perennials and buy them unaware of the patent restrictions. A better alternative is to stick with the older cultivars that are propagated by seed. The *sanguineas* with their red shades of flowers like 'Ruby Bells' and 'Firefly' and the *micrantha* like 'Palace Purple' known for their ruffled and purple foliage plus the Americana with its silver markings are all sown from seed so if you love seeding and dividing flowers and don't want the Patent Police knocking at your door stick to these varieties.

TREE ROOT COMPETITION IN SHADE GARDENS

JOYFUL CHILDHOOD MEMORIES are always remembered as happening under the friendly shade of the huge trees that encircled our yard. The enormous homemade teeter-totter where we sang made-up nonsense songs as we teetered up and down would never have been as enjoyable sitting out in a full sun spot. The thick rope tire swings and nailed board ladder to reach "I dare you spots" in the trees were the best toys imaginable. Not only are trees where children play but beneath them is where families hang out for relaxing time or picnics. Trees are valuable! They perform as a protective barrier from the outside world while they provide air conditioning, homes for birds, fresh oxygen in the air and mainly shade in the garden. Whatever is done in a garden, the first priority is to be gentle with trees for they are the basis for all enjoyable outdoor living.

Gardeners often blame tree shade for ruining their flowerbeds. But the culprit may not be the shade but the masses of tree roots beneath the ground that support the tree. Perennials, *heuchera*, though it prefers more sun, *heucherella*, and *tiarella* are comfortable growing in the shade of trees because of their shallow root systems, but they grow better under trees that do not have shallow roots. In other words, if a shady perennial flowerbed is viewed as a problem in your landscape, grow shallow-rooted plants under deep-rooted trees. Blaming shade for having a wimpy-looking shade garden could be because the soil is jammed full of tree roots that hog all the moisture and minerals, leaving nothing for the plants. All that it takes to grow shallow-root perennials under trees is to add a layer of mulch or topsoil and get them planted and established before the tree roots have time to move and refill the new mulch.

SHALLOW-ROOTED TREES

Undesirable trees because of shallow root systems are probably members of the Populus tree family for they have found the western mountains their favorite place to grow. This family includes cottonwoods with their shallow aggressive roots, and aspens that sprout new sucker trees as they invade surrounding areas. Another family of shallow root tree is the Weeping Willows or salix. Willows are invasive by the sheer volume of roots they produce. These types of trees expand their root systems into the top layers of garden topsoil and in their relentless search for water are infamous for damaging septic systems. These trees are fast growing trees for a homeowner who is overly anxious for shade.

Early settlers planted popular trees for quick shade and as a wind break, not knowing they were susceptible to many diseases and would invade septic systems

It's said that whoever plants these types of trees are planting only for themselves. The deep-rooted, slower-growing trees are planted for the individual and their grandchildren.

DEEP-ROOTED TREES FOR THE ROCKY MOUNTAINS (ONLY A FEW MENTIONED AND ALL ARE LARGE SHADE TREES)

There are many deep-rooted, low-zoned trees that are superior in providing shade in a garden, so never choose a tree just from a visual glance at the tree or the lowered sale-price on the tag. Trees are permanent structures that require research and thoughtful choices before purchasing. Here are a few deep-rooted trees for consideration: pine trees are very popular in mountain landscapes and anchor themselves with a strong taproot. Deep-rooted trees like green ash or fraxinus

Weeping willows are fast growing but very dirty trees for in every wind their soft-wood, weak branches snap off and litter the yard.

We grow male green mountain ash at our Idaho home. They have been planted along the highway for privacy because of their dense, well-shaped foliage. This is one of four we planted and all are growing beautifully. The male mountain ash is fruitless and fall clean-up is a breeze for the entire tree will turn a brilliant yellow with the first frost and within a week the leaves have fallen and can be raked.

A conifer's root structure consists of a permanent primary root that extends as deep as the height of the tree. A pine tree's secondary roots sit in the top twelve-inches of soil. Pine trees are like an iceberg with their drip line reaching a distance of two to four times the height of the tree. Loses of perennials planted under pine trees are mainly during winter when they do not get water. Their dense foliage does not allow winter snow to melt through to the ground so any plant in a pine trees drip line suffers from lack of water.

are excellent alternatives to popular maples and oaks for they are extremely cold hardy. Linden trees with their perfect umbrella-shaped foliage are dependable and hardy and are adaptable for smaller yards. Before purchasing shade trees for your yard, check local extension services to help make the best choices for your area.

These are only samples of the deep-rooted trees that will provide a shady place for relaxation and their roots will not give plants too much competition if the following tips are used. Planting the right plant in the right place is first, as usual, so plant partial or shade plants under trees. Partial-shade or shade perennials bloom readily in a shady garden as well as full-sun perennials will bloom in a hot sunny garden. Excellent foliage plants are more important in a shady area than flowers. Light-colored flowers show up better in shade gardens than dark-colored plants that seem to melt into the shade. Raised flowerbeds for maximum soil and drainage give

the best success for growing flowers in shady gardens. Many shady gardens rely on the wonderful alpine groundcovers that grow well in shade and stay evergreen like *ajuga*.

AJUGA OR BUGLEWEED

Ajuga reptens is a useful and adaptable groundcover that is attractive year around for it is evergreen to semi evergreen. *Ajuga*, 'Bronze Beauty' and 'Burgundy Glow' are the hardiest (zone three) of the bugleweeds and will fill a western shady flowerbed under trees nicely.

Ajuga is famous for its vigorous variegated foliage of bluish-bronze and rich deep greens. Flowering spikes of deep blue peak in May and June but will continue blooming into July. Leaving the spikes uncut may result in self-seeding which is an excellent method of germination over tree roots for the seedlings will find their own niche, be stronger and more root tolerant. Bugleweed's rhizomes spread by runners, quickly

Ajuga reptans usually called by its common name of bugleweed is suitable for growing under trees. Caution is advised when planting beneath mature trees to avoid damaging their roots. By adding in a top layer of mulch for planting, *ajuga* will send out runners to carpet this area into a lovely easy care garden.

filling in a garden spot with a thick carpet of foliage. In Rocky Mountain gardens ajuga is not as aggressive for our soils are a little more alkaline than it prefers and our winters a little colder but it still performs well but without its usual vigorous tendencies. *Ajuga* spreads by sending out runners on top of the soil mulch. These runners can be harvested any time of the year and replanted. Once *ajuga* grows in a garden, new starts will always be available. The runners never compete with or damage tree roots. The best time to propagate the runners is when the mother plant is still young. Lift the rooted runners of *ajuga* and plant them immediately. Pruning and fertilizing are not necessary, but if the plants become entangled, simply mow or cut them down to keep the plant contained. A tree's root system greedily takes all moisture available, so even though *ajuga* is a dry, shade perennial, occasional watering will keep it healthier.

LAMIUM MACULATUM OR DEAD NETTLE

Lamium is another shallow-rooted, drought-tolerant perennial that does a remarkable job of growing under the challenge of shade trees. *Lamium's* appearance with its silvery foliage adds light and sparkle to a shady area. My personal favorite is 'Beacon Silver' with its silver with a green margin.

'Shell Pink' is also an excellent ground cover for shade. The leaves of 'Shell Pink' are green with a middle silver stripe with pale pink flowers, almost opposite of 'Silver Beacon.' Both of these fine groundcovers will carpet a continuous silver mat of foliage without holes, especially in a raised bed with added mulch or compost. Both are hybrid perennials but show no susceptibility to winter's cold and are deer resistant. (Although, occasionally, deer will eat off the blooms of any spring-blooming perennial much to the disappointment of a gardener.) *Lamium* is not fussy about soils and will grow without fertilizers. Avoid planting *lamium* in perennial borders for it may spread too vigorously and crowd out the other flowers. Allowing *lamium* to set-seed usually results in a plant different from the parent and this is usually green with a stripe in the mid-section of the leaf. These reverted seedlings are extremely hardy and will gradually take over the entire shade bed.

Ajuga and *Lamiums* are only a couple of perennials that will perform well in the challenges of a shaded area under trees. Spring flowering bulbs grow naturally well in this environment for they are able to absorb enough sunshine before the trees leaf out. *Alchemilla* or lady's mantle with its graceful pleated foliage and bright yellow-lime lacy sprays is delightful under trees and so is *convallaria* or lily-of-the-valley. Wild *Geraniums*, especially the big leaf varieties and *periwinkle* are good choices as well as *Hosta* which is surprisingly drought tolerant.

The bottom line is being careful not to damage tree roots when digging and planting. Very often a nice shade tree can offer a higher evaluation dollar and more appeal than a newly remodeled kitchen just because of the welcoming feeling they give a home.

Hybrid *Lamiums* will revert to the original species which is superior in health, spreading abilities and wintering. To keep the silver-leafed varieties in a garden, *lamium* may have to be cut back after its initial big bloom push to prevent seeding and/or the reverted plants weeded out. Many gardeners prefer the original species in their gardens due to it hardiness and spreading abilities.

Lilium
(LIL-ee-um)
ASIATIC AND TIGER *LILIUM*

SHAPE	Tall and elegant with trumpet-shaped flowers
HEIGHT	*Asiatics* average thirty inches and Tigers grow about five feet tall
WIDTH	*Lilium* stays tall and lean but underground bulbs multiply, gradually filling out into a clump
BLOOM TIME	*Asiatics* are the earliest *Lilium* to bloom and Tiger Lilies bloom late summer
COLORS	*Liliums* are known for their rich colors of deep reds, scarlet reds, pure reds, coral reds, and inky reds, plus every shade of orange, yellow, and pure white.
SITE	Average loamy soil that is well drained
LIGHT	Full sun or partial sun
HARDINESS	Zones three or four
COMMENTS	*Lilium* with their tall magnificent flowers rise above other perennials for they are the high fashion runway models of the garden.

Asiatic lilium's magnificent flowers bloom in every color but blue. A strange occurrence in the world of perennial varieties is that flower families that bloom in red colors, never bloom in blues. Perennial groups that bloom in blue never have red varieties of flowers. Red shades of flowers are rare and very important in the garden's sea of yellows and lavenders making the red colors of *lilium* very much in demand.

The original Tiger Lily is popular due to its long, long, garden life. Its height and showy orange colors and whimsical black freckles give it presence. The classification of Tiger Lilies has recently been changed to *lancifolium*. This occurred because *lancifolium* is an older name and botany rules say the older name takes precedence. Now Tiger Lily *lancifolium* and its hybrids are available in many fine colors of red, pink, and yellow.

Asiatic Lilies are a very popular item for shoppers at Secrist Gardens, so every year we grow several thousand. They are wintered outside in cold frames and thrive with the exception of the last two years. Voles found a way into the cold frames and devoured every Asiatic lily bulb. Our nursery pots were empty along with a neatly tunneled hole in the middle of the pot where the Asiatic lily bulb had been eaten. So now we only grow the hybridized Asiatic lilies called an LA lily and the critter-repellent Tiger Lilies that remained untouched by the vole population!

The distinct trumpet-shaped flowers of LA hybrids are the first clue to the exciting breakthrough of this variety. Other traits are the robust, ever expanding growth rate for they multiply quickly, huge sturdy stems and a slight fragrance that gives deer and critter resistance. Deer resistance is a logical reason to choose LA hybrids when gardening in higher elevations.

W E HAVE EVERY right to blow our own trumpets because of our elegant, serene beauty, rich colors, and easy-to-grow bulbs. We have become a melting pot of the original Asian *lilium* species for we are easy to hybridize. This causes a great deal of confusion when trying to group us according to parentage for every group has upward, outward, and even downward facing flowers and similar traits.

We are popular across the Northern Hemisphere for we add elegant distinction to summer gardens, but not all *lilium* perform in western environments. The best *lilium* for Rocky Mountain gardens are the *Asiatic lilium* and tiger *lilium* for we are the only lilies that really thrive in these environments. Other varieties, like the oriental lilies, require an acidic soil and will gradually waste away when planted in the high mineral content soil of the mountains but *Asiatic* and tiger *liliums* are alkaline soil and water tolerant. Another bonus for growing the tiger types is their resistance to deer, rabbits, and even voles for tiger lilies have retained their original fragrance and pests stay away from perennials with a strong scent. The massive hybridizing that has been done to *Asiatic liliums* to achieve our remarkable colors and variety of blooms has left us scentless, so we are deer candy. We are so spectacular that gardeners gamble and plant us anyway. One thing they do for our protection is to plant a defensive perimeter of daffodils around and among us. Daffodills are poison to wildlife and chase away browsing deer. Another defense is planting *Asiatic lilium* deeper than suggested and add a thick layer of mulch so we break dormancy later in spring when the animals are not as hungry. Our bulbs are true bulbs meaning they grow layers of skin and never really go dormant. The mulch assists in three ways: it delays freezing, allowing our roots to continue growing over winter; the extra depth means we will not come up as early in spring; and the mulch traps in moisture to keep us well hydrated.

LA LILIUM

LA hybrids are a mix of *Asiatic* and *Longiflorum liliums* and do quite well in high valleys gardens. The L in the name LA stands for *longiflorum* or Easter Lily, and the A of course means Asiatic. Our larger blooms are breathtaking! Our colors are as brilliantly rich as any asiatic but we have larger, more trumpet like blooms and wider leaves. We bloom longer so have become the favorite in the cut flower or florist trade. Our highly scented fragrance is probably why we repel animals or it could be due to the strength of our thick tough stems. Each stem easily produces up to twenty flowers and when grasped by the hand of a gardener, you can actually feel the pulsing of our life force through the stem.

ASIATIC BORDER LILIES

Asiatic border lilies are shorter versions of Asiatic lilies. They have been bred in all of the fantastic Asiatic colors, are easily available and can be planted most anywhere in a garden.

LA hybrids seem to have genetically gotten their height, fragrance, and deep trumpet shape from their Easter lily or *longiflorum* parent. The variety of flower colors with plain or speckled brush strokes and eyecatching color-contrasting stamens along with their hardiness had to come from the Asiatic side of the family for Easter Lilies are not hardy in the west

LA hybrids are the superstars of the mid-summer garden. Their prolific hardiness produces larger bulblets that will develop into golf-ball-sized bulbs that can be dug in early spring and moved to another spot. LA hybrids are long-lived perennials, becoming thicker and more beautiful with maturity.

SPECIE TIGER LILIES

Tiger lilies, often called Martagon lilies in the nursery trade, are different from *Asiatic lilium* in that we are much taller, bloom into late summer, are slower to establish, and live longer. We are the hardiest of the lilies, surviving cold zone-three winter temperatures. A mature clump of show-stopping tiger lily blooms will produce masses of downward-facing blooms that never need dividing. Because we stay for a long, long time

153

'Bridget' is a brilliant yellow Asiatic border lily that is so attractive along the front or middle of a flowerbed. The smaller size of twelve to fifteen inches in height is often easier to work with in a garden for shorter plants with brilliant colors are hard to find as edging plants unless they are annuals. Border lilies retain all of the characteristics of their taller relative only on a shorter plant.

'Black Out' a short Asiatic lily is a favorite perennial for along sidewalks or pathways due mainly to the dark richness of its color.

where we are planted, add huge quantities of amendments to our planting hole and plant us twelve to fifteen inches deep. We bloom in white, pink, yellow, mauve, and dark reds, plus our original colors of orange. Our flowers are so fragrant we fill the summer garden with an intoxicating scent so we are never bothered by critters. Be aware when bending to smell our fragrance that specie lilies will brush freckles and golden pollen on your nose. Our tall stems with their elegant whorled leaves are self-supporting, not ever needing staking. If our height seems to have bare knees, "skirt" them with medium-sized perennials like tall garden *phlox*. Tiger lilies are one of a small group that produces aerial bulbils on the stem in the leaf joint. The bulbils, tiny dark colored bulbs, can be harvested to propagate new bulbs for this is our only method of propagation for we are sterile and do not produce seeds.

HYBRID TIGER LILIES

Tiger hybrids are handsome plants that bloom just as the *asiatics* are finished. We are more attractive planted in groups of three, five or nine because we are so tall and narrow. We tolerate more shade than the *asiatics* so prefer partial sunshine but will not grow in the hot humidity of Southern gardens. Our showy blooms are down facing but more open than the specie tiger lilies. We tower to over five feet in height, and if planted as a clump will spread to form a nice almost shrub-like perennial. We have medicinal value, and have been used to ease aggressive tendencies and for holistic healing. Our buds are edible, and our baked bulbs taste similar to potatoes.

Genetically, we still have our wild specie growing nature and require no special care. Fertilizers aren't really a requirement unless the soil is really poor. To plant us, just dig the hole deep, throw in a handful of gravel for drainage, add amendments and plant me pointy side up. Space six or more bulbs about nine inches apart to give the effect of a huge clump.

CARE OF LILIUM

Asiatic, tigers and their hybrids like all lilies have a few requirements to perform at peak performance. First off we require well-drained soil. The heavy alkaline clay soils of most Rocky Mountain gardens are not to our liking for it holds water. Too much water or water trapped beneath the bulb's scales will cause the bulb to rot. This problem can be easily solved by digging a larger and deeper hole when planting the bulbs. A shovel full of gravel along with compost placed in the bottom of the hole will help with drainage for well-rotted compost encourages good draining. Adding organic matter to create a raised flower bed also improves drainage. Mulch delays soil freezing and insulates the soil against fluctuating temperatures. Lilies planted as the high focal point of a raised flower bed are tremendous garden performers for center stage is where they belong.

Sunlight for around six hours, or partial shade, gives us our best flowers. A hot, full-sun garden seems to bake the color from my blooms. Planted in shade, my stems grow spindly as they try to reach for the sun. In a partial-shade garden, my foliage stays fresher and holds its green color into late fall. Leave my foliage intact as long as possible, for this foliage is the food that fills my storage bulb for next year's flowers.

Henrii was discovered growing in limestone rock gorges in China. *Henrii's* origins explain how adaptable tiger lilies are to the limestone soils of the Rocky Mountains. The tall gracefulness of *Henrii* grows to about five-feet in height on strong arching stems. It is disease resistant and is more attractive in a shady garden. The flowers are an artistic mix of delicate boldness with curved petals, sprinkled with darker spots and elongated raised stamens, all adding to the delicious orange sherbet color of this specie lily. *Henrii* is a parent to practically all of today's tiger lilies. *Henryii* won the prestigious Award of Garden Merit from the Royal Horticultural Society in 1993.

The glorious 'Red Velvet' *lilium* is a great example of the confusion that occurs when trying to classify these wonderful perennials into groups. 'Red Velvet' looks like a tiger lily with its erect height and reflexed petals. The plant's twelve flowers per stem also hints at tiger lily genes, but 'Red Velvet' has no fragrance and does not form bulblets along its stem so many sources call it an Asiatic lily hybrid. 'Red Velvet' is so lovely it won the North American Lily Society Hall of Fame so why worry about classifying it? Simply **enjoy its dramatic show**.

Snipping faded flowers also saves my energy. Plant perennial companion plants at my feet to camouflage bare stems. Flowers like tall garden *phlox* and snapdragons with their later bloom time, similar foliage, and environment needs are excellent feet friends.

Lilies are starring focal points in any garden, especially in a center-placed raised flower bed where they strut their beauty as well as show off their amazing foliage and colors.

In Western gardens, plant my bulbs deep. Deep planting encourages my developing stem to send out roots that stabilize my tall stems and eliminates a need for staking. Deep planting reduces the amount of bulb division, keeping my bulbs larger and healthier. It also keeps us cooler in the heat of the high temperatures of western summers. Fall or spring is typical planting time but potted lilies can be planted anytime. LA hybrids and *asiatics* bulbs can be lifted and divided into smaller clumps in spring. Use plenty of compost when replanting.

Lilium's reliability and endless variety of colors enriches any garden. Their exotic form, foliage, and fragrance are icing on any flowerbed.

TRUMPET-SHAPED FLOWER BLOOMS

Breathtaking to man and bird, the trumpet-shaped profile of *lilium* is a precision arrangement that guides a hummingbird's bill to find its sweet rewards and pollinate at the same time. The long center stem filaments or antlers plus the different colored wine stamen are the male parts of the flower. The female parts are located deeper inside the trumpet and called the pistil.

BECAUSE OF THEIR exquisite beauty, *lilium* sit at the top of a gardener's favorite perennials. Everything about the plant is so attractive and perfect—from its elegant foliage to the unique trumpet shape of its unsurpassable blooms—that when blooming, *lilium* takes your breath away!

FULL-SUN-BLOOMING TRUMPET-SHAPED FLOWERS

The symbolic shape of a trumpet has always been a mighty call to spiritual action, and perhaps this is why lilium blooms are so enchanting. The verb "trumpet" means to proclaim, herald, and celebrate. As a typical biblical symbol, the trumpet was blown to receive both God's spirit and message. The trumpet also is a strong symbol for resurrection, so this explains why so many early spring flowers like tulips,

crocuses, and the centers of daffodils symbolize renewal and rebirth.

As gardeners we recognize that it's not a coincidence that hummingbirds are ideally suited to drink and pollinate from the long throat or tube of trumpet-shaped blooms. Hummingbirds are attracted by the warm section of the color wheel so it's also not a coincidence that so many of trumpet-shaped flowers bloom in oranges, reds, and scarlets. Below are a few hot-colored trumpet-shaped favorites.

New ever-blooming daylilies grow shorter with finer foliage and narrower-shaped flowers that are truer trumpets. Daylilies bloom in hot colors but never blue. All Hemerocallis requires to "toot" their matchless trumpets is full sun and well-drained soils.

Foxgloves are pit-stops for pollinators as well as fairies. Most foxgloves are biennials, meaning they last two years.

Alcea starts its blooming as a tight trumpet but widens its flower mouth as the flowers mature. *Alcea* adds height to a hot sun garden so works well at the back of the border or along a wall or fence. Most Hollyhocks are biennials meaning they seed in fall, germinate the next spring and will not bloom until the following year. The fig leaf *Alceas* are the only true perennial in the hollyhock family and return year after year.

Aquilegia or Columbine has long sippy-cup spurs that fit a humming bird's long narrow bill. The long delicately shaped center trumpet in various colors is also convenient for these amazing birds. The rainbow spectrum of colors created by the easy reseeding of *Aquilegia* is appealing to gardeners and pollinators. Columbine is a native wildflower and grows happy in mountain conditions of dappled sunlight and high, cool elevations.

Campsis, or trumpeter vine is a custom-shaped meal ticket for hummingbirds. Trumpeter vine's bright-scarlet to orange flowers attract masses of these delightful birds season after season. Trumpeter vine is fast growing and vigorous, sometimes becoming invasive. The flower colors of orange, scarlet, yellow, salmon, and red are attractive additions to the late-summer fence line or trellis. Trumpeter vine as it matures will fill a fence or screen for privacy.

First they are planted, taking a full season to grow. It won't be until the next summer when they'll bloom. The foxglove flowers set seed and drop their seeds for self-sowing. Last the parent plant dies and the entire process starts over. In other words, foxglove only survives for two years unless they are like the perennial foxglove, 'Ambigua.'

Daylilies are a favorite of gardeners because they grow everywhere without a care in the world. Their zone-three hardiness and long-lived easy-care genetics add to the popularity of this amazing perennial.

There are many other lovely trumpet-shaped flowering perennials like the early budded blooms of *clematis*, blue *gentiana*, and orange creeping hummingbird trumpet or *Zauschneria*. Planting trumpet-shaped blooms in a garden especially if they bloom in hot colors will insure that hummingbirds will visit your garden but this flower shape is also attractive to all pollinators, especially the night pollinators.

Digitalis grandflora, or foxglove, 'Ambigua,' considered only one of a few real perennials in this family of plants, is "foxy." Notice the darker, tiny markings inside the delicate trumpet-shaped flowers. They must be footprints, a clue that fairies have been hiding inside.

Tiny trumpet flowers line the slender wiry stems of *Heuchera* or coral bells. *Heuchera* is a garden workhorse that blooms for six weeks or longer if the finished stems are removed. This North American native is popular for its variety of evergreen, ruffled leaves that have been bred in every shade from lime to chocolate. Clump forming coral bells bloom in June and July looking especially nice lining a partial shade porch or walkway.

NIGHT-BLOOMING TRUMPET-SHAPED FLOWERS

We often find ourselves thinking that flower's colors and fragrance are there just to please gardeners. The truth is that the shape and color of a flower's blooms only function is reproduction! Different pollinators are attracted to different things and flowers have adapted very clever ways to attract pollinators and trumpet-shaped flowers are one of them. For example, the night moths only pollinate at night, so a group of trumpet-shaped flowers bloom at night just to attract these moths.

Angel trumpet is an annual in western gardens and its self-seeding behavior ensures its return yearly. The seedlings grow vigorously into adult plants in a single season.

Gardeners are now challenged with a new decision making chore when they plan their gardens for flowers are more than a pretty face. Thought concerning not only the sun orientation, soil and climate and shape of the flowers is required but also they need to think of both daytime and nighttime pollinators for without these important insects there would be no flowers.

Penstemon is famous as a Northern Hemisphere wildflower and a hummingbird attraction. The trumpet-shaped tubular blooms of coral, pink, red, white, and purple shades fill tall spikes with masses of showy flowers in mid-summer. *Penstemon* grows best in western mountain gardens in full sun and thrives in a water-wise gardening.

Datura often called Angel Trumpet is a night blooming, very fragrant flower that opens wide at night to attract pollinators. Angel Trumpet's so pure and pristine appearance not only attracts night moths but melts any gardener's heart at its beauty. However not all is pure with *Datura*. The seeds and flowers are poisonous and is called Jimsom weed by ranchers for it is dangerous to cattle.

The blooms of *hosta* are often surprising for gardeners plant *hosta* as a shade-loving foliage plant, but in late summer, these amazing perennials produce a crop of white or pale-lavender trumpet-shaped flowers. The intoxicating fragrance not only attracts night pollinators but daylight workers too.

Oenothera, or evening primrose, has pale translucent trumpet-shaped flowers that open wider as the night darkens and close before noon the next day. *Oenothera's* fleshy deep roots give drought tolerance, so it thrives in well-drained western gardens. Evening primrose are delightfully fragrant, easy to grow and bloom from mid-summer through fall if their very interesting, pepper plant shaped seed pods are kept picked. All night pollinators including bats flock to *Oenothera's* delightful fragrance.

Yucca, or Adam's needle, is occasionally called soapweed for this prairie-native plant was used by Native Americans as soap. Yucca is dependable as an attractive focal point due to its fine sword-like evergreen foliage, but when it blooms, it is spectacular with its elegant, creamy, widened trumpets marching in mass up the stems. Because yucca blooms both daytime and at night it attracts every pollinator, bees, that sleep when its dark, wasps, flies and butterflies but at night when Yucca's fragrance becomes heavier the night pollinators flock around this unique perennial.

Lysimachia punctata
(li-si- MAK-ee-a)
YELLOW LOOSESTRIFE

SHAPE	Tall stems massed with blossoms
HEIGHT	Three-foot-tall center stalks with shorter side stalks
WIDTH	Forms clumps or colonies
BLOOM TIME	Summer to late summer
COLORS	Single, yellow five-petal cups tinged with scarlet inside the center
SITE	Thrives in rich moist soils
LIGHT	Partial sun or partial shade
HARDINESS	Zone four
COMMENTS	Mistaken reputation as an invasive perennial

Yellow loosestrife is a tall, handsome perennial that dependably colors the garden in brilliant yellow-primrose-colored flowers spikes in July and August.

Creeping jenny, 'Aurea,' is growing here with drought-tolerant Irises in the background; *hosta*, a shade-loving perennial and very young starts of *filipendula*, a partial-shade plant. Drought, shade and partial shade, shows how versatile the low growing *lysimachias* or loosestrifes are for they grow in most any situation. Loosestrife, 'Aurea's' bright lime-green foliage lights up a partial or shade garden but may, as with many hybrids, revert back to the original green colors of the species, *nummularia* or the green creeping Jenny.

'Aurea' with its pale lime, almost luminescent foliage adds bright light to wherever it is planted.

Creeping Jenny roots efficiently on top of the soil anywhere the leaf nodes touch the ground. These can be used as new plants. Sever the newly rooted Jenny and plant the new starts right in the ground. The success rate will be about 75 percent. We are so vigorous in moist fertile soils that we will choke out other not as hardy groundcovers, making us a perfect weed barrier.

ARDENERS OFTEN SHY away from perennials that are gossiped about as being invasive and I suppose this is why I'm not as popular as some perennials. The truth is, I'm not invasive and I want to clear up that myth right now. I do grow from a creeping root called a rhizome that creates underground mats that can be difficult to remove but in the dry Rocky Mountain environment and lean soils, I do not spread. I sort of produce seeds but I'm not a self-sowing perennial and my seeds are so rare they are hard to find in the market place so seeding isn't a problem and definitely not a way I could spread. Regular division when I outgrow my garden spot will keep me exactly where the gardener wants me. The low growing ground cover *lysimachia* or creeping jenny is the only loosestrife spreader in our family.

LOW-GROWING *LYSIMACHIAS*, CREEPING JENNY

Our *lysimachia* groundcovers are often called moneyworts because our rounded leaves resemble a coin laced on a cord, but we are usually called creeping Jenny. Our bright-yellow cup-shaped flowers appear in early summer and continue blooming sporadically into fall. We even tolerate some foot traffic. We are a very useful groundcover when planted as edgings or shrubbery undergrowth. Our foliage forms a leafy mat not over three inches in height and spreads easily. We give a terrific look to planters filled with *hosta* for we cascade gracefully over the edge and surrounded the *hosta* with our bright foliage. A brilliant new hybrid, called 'Aurea,' has spectacular gold foliage that glows as it spills over the front of a flowerbed or container. 'Aurea' is for gardeners who want more contrast in foliage colors as an under-planting for shrubs. Take a look at both of us in the pictures below to see the differences in our foliage.

The Jennies are not as vigorous in the lean dry soils of western gardens and is less aggressive in partial shade or shade gardens but because it can spread rapidly these are the best places to grow Jenny. Its hardy dependability has made it a favorite in the west. Creeping Jenny's spreading can also be slowed by cement edging, metal barriers, or rock and cement walls, or by being grown in containers or planters.

The elegant spilling of creeping Jenny over the edges of this cement wall is lovely. No other plant, perennial or annual could make the classic designer statement the creeping Jenny has made. Topping this is that jenny is long-lived, disease and pest resistant, semi-evergreen and will always look this delightful.

Our history is interesting and there are several stories of how my names came about. I was named after King Lysimachus of Macedonia who discovered and used my medicinal abilities to help his people. I became famous for stanching bleeding. They would bind me around a wound and I would quickly stop the bleeding and just as quickly perform a cure. My entire plant is an edible herb and can be harvested in early July and dried. I taste medicinal and can be used to stanch bleeding and as a gargle for bleeding gums in the mouth.

My common name of loosestrife was earned because of my special abilities to dissolve stress or "lose strife" in animals. I would be placed under the animal's yokes and my smell would protect them from gnats and flies, helping them to quiet down. I would also be burned in houses for my astringent smoke would drive away the pests and it was said that even snakes would disappear when the burning fumes came near them.

As a member of the *Primulaceae* family that also prefers rich, moist, wet soils and shady gardens, our growing preferences and traits are similar. Primrose is also used for edible and medicinal purposes. Primrose flowers in spring, on a low compact-clump of medium-green fuzzy leaves that will be covered with bright-eyed blooms. With the proper conditions of soil, sun, and nutrition, primrose will add beauty to a partial-shade or shade garden for many years. The annual varieties of primrose have a wide color range but do not survive western winters. Their popularity is due more to a gardener not being able to resist any plant in bloom, after a long winter, rather than hoping it is a perennial. Most perennial varieties are zoned as a high zone five and are not dependable in Rocky Mountain gardens with the exception of the old-fashioned cowslip primrose that lives a long, carefree life.

Our first start of cowslip primrose was gifted to my husband and me from his mom in the 1950s. Our property had originally been a cherry tree orchard, so we had lots of nice shady spots to plant our primrose. As years passed, our entire back fence line was edged with divisions from the parent plant. The compact, attractive primrose was simple to dig and divide. When it bloomed in springtime, the yard looked breathtaking; however, the beautiful plant would collapse in the heat of summer so we planted annuals over it. By fall when the annuals were done, the cowslips had regrouped and were once again edging the garden with their compact foliage that stayed nice throughout the winter. Without fail, our primrose would bloom every spring to again bring joy to the garden. Question: Why are cowslips not available in the green industries now? I have purchased every primrose available from auricular, a supposed zone two, and *denticula* or drumstick mix, zone four, but none have returned dependably after winter. I need the old-fashioned cowslip primroses that are dependable!

LYSIMANCHIA OR YELLOW LOOSESTRIFE

Like other primrose family members, I will flourish permanently as long as my needs for moisture and soil are met. My flowers are small, only about three-quarters of an inch in diameter with five pointed petals that form a bright cup. These glowing cups are attached firmly by a band at my stem and march proudly upward, making a stunning mass of pure-yellow spikes in a garden. My side stems branch out

Loosestrife's abundant and showy blooms are excellent as cut flowers. Cut the blooms in early morning after the dew has dried and dunk them in lukewarm water immediately. Trim all the leaves off for they will last nicely as long as their foliage is not sitting in water.

and they are also covered with brilliant blossoms so I put on a great summer show. My floral whorls have tagged me with another popular name so I'm often called circle flower.

My foliage is also lovely, forming long, oblong, lance-shaped, pointed leaves. My leaf edges are smooth and the underside's soft hairs seem to accent the veins on my leaf surface.

Companion plants are those that like the same site I do like the delightfully pleated foliage of *Alchemilla*, or lady's mantle. *Brunnera* grows at just the right height to add their spring time delightful blue colors in front of my foliage. The blues of Jacob's ladder also gives a nice contrast. Short *campanula* 'clips' and *heuchera* or coral bells are comfortable neighbors to soften the area in front of my tall foliage. Another good thing about me is that my foliage stays as a solid mass of

'Firecracker' with its bronze leaves and yellow loosestrife with green foliage make an excellent pair. 'Firecracker' is often called *purpurea* because of its dramatic foliage colors. The bronze leaves vary in coloring, some more green and others more bronze, making it even more attractive.

Okay, Let me make this perfectly clear! Now after finding out that I never waiver in heat, cold or rain and always put on a great show along with the fact that I rarely set seed and don't need dividing very often it's obvious that I'm not an out of control perennial. I also grow slower in western gardens and partial shade, so do you really think I'm an invasive perennial? Of course not!

green throughout the season. Deadheading spent flowers to freshen my foliage is a gardener's choice.

My cousin, *lysimachia ciliate* 'Firecracker,' with its chocolate-colored foliage looks good next to me. We are both lysimachias but are not exactly alike. 'Firecracker's' foliage is looser and the tips of its smaller stems will be covered with dime-sized yellow flowers in summer. 'Firecracker's' foliage doesn't hold tall like mine and will need to be cut back after flowering. Because it's a hybrid, it is not considered rampant.

Propagation of yellow loosestrife is due about every six years. This proves I'm not invasive for that length of time is longer than recommended for division of most other perennials. Dig my entire clump in early spring as soon as my shoots break dormancy. Spring is the best time to divide any perennial growing in the high elevation western gardens for fall divisions cannot be trusted time ways for a new perennial to get established and/or strong enough to survive a western winter. Lift my clump and squirt off the dirt so the roots and stems are visible, making it easier to figure out

where to divide. Either tease our roots apart or use a knife or pruner to cut us into sections. Every division needs several stems and an ample supply of roots. Plant these new divisions immediately just like any other bare-root perennial. Ground layering is another successful method to propagate us. Pull my tall stem to the ground and make a shallow cut at a leaf node. Bury the leaf node cut in the soil and pin it with a peg. Roots will form from the node. A hormone rooting power can be used to help out the process. Doing this in the fall will insure new starts all rooted and ready for spring planting!

163

SECLUSION AND PRIVACY

THE QUESTION HOMEOWNERS want answered is how can I gain seclusion and privacy on my own property? How can homeowners foster a sense of privacy and give themselves a retreat from the outside world?

For a very private retreat, use a section of your yard and cordon it off with an arch. By simply placing this arch as a doorway, back yard privacy has been achieved.

For privacy from outsiders the answer may need to simply build a barrier like a fence or wall and gate it. This is a direct, functional and logical solution.

WHY THE FENCE?

The fence or wall must have a purpose. Will it be a physical barrier from traffic and noise or create a privacy boundary? Perhaps the fence is needed to separate areas of a yard like a designated play area for children or to confine pets. Once the purpose is understood, materials for fencing can be chosen: wrought iron, chain link, wood posts, panels or even the popular vinyl fencing can be used as long as the product suits your purpose. Walls are usually masonry so the difference between the two is based on construction.

CHOOSING MATERIALS

Once the purpose of your fence is decided, the materials can be chosen. Remember to stay true to the architectural design of the home but still meet community building restrictions. Many HOA or Home Owner Associations allow certain heights in front yards and taller, usually up to six-feet-tall fences in the back. They can be real fussy about building materials and even the color of the fence. Try to circumvent any problems with neighbors.

A strong privacy fence built from masonry plus the extra height of vinyl fencing placed on top of the wall filters the traffic noises and headlights of a busy highway.

The homeowner's property was wide open to viewers, making them feel they lived in a fishbowl. The family chose to build a privacy wall out of cinderblock faced with rock. The wall also was a water conservation trick for water runs down any slope but adding the wall leveled both the upper lawn and lower lawns and the wall prevents erosion.

This log or pole fence is called a Wyoming fence in cattle country and looks right at home in the Rocky Mountains. The gate is constructed with massive logs that were probably cut by the rancher. The purpose is to keep cattle in and the fencing materials do this as well as suiting the surrounding environment.

An ornate wrought-iron fence that surrounds a Victorian style home was added to enhance the aesthetic feel of the space and to give the homeowner a place to plant flowers on both sides of the fence. Wrought iron is nearly indestructible so is easy to keep looking good and gets more beautiful as it ages.

In opposition to the simple construction of the Wyoming fence is a contemporary style of fence done in wrought iron. The fence has a simple but elegant look that suits the house. The purpose is more for design than privacy.

Believe it or not, there is a chain link fence camouflaged beneath the weighty growth of trumpter vine. Chain link is a very affordable product and looks very classy as a deer fence when set inside a wood frame.

The strong, vertical lines of a board fence line will look hard and imposing without a flower border in front of it. The versatility of wood in all of its different forms; split rails, grape stakes, poles or bamboo, to name only a few, can create louvers, slats, lattice or whatever the needs or imagination of the homeowner desires. Horizontal board fences are excellent accents to newer contemporary styled homes.

There is no doubt that this eclectic copper-colored whimsical sunflower fence line and gate will always be remembered proving a homeowner can pretty much do what they want for a fence.

BUILDING A BOARD FENCE

Wooden fences are typically the popular choice of Homeowner. They usually have three separate sections; four-by-four posts, two-by-four rails and the covering or siding. Siding can be wood, metal, fiberglass panels, or act as a background for artistic endeavors or flowerbeds. Step the fence height sections if the property is not level.

1. Lay out the fence: mark, usually the length of the rails, where the posts will go with stakes.
2. Run a tight string between the stakes to mark post positions and check for plum.
3. Dig the holes a foot deeper than the posts will set and a foot-and-a-half wider. The depth will save the posts from frost heave and the width will give room for the stabilizing of cement.
4. Add six-inches of gravel to help with drainage.
5. Center the post in the hole and surround it with cement. Add an extra three inches above ground for a slope so water will drain. Bagged ready mix is easy to use but water will be needed so follow the directions. Tamp to remove air pockets.
6. Check the post for level and wait for the cement to harden for about twenty-five- minutes then align the posts and brace them with stakes while the concrete cures.

7. Cut the posts to height after they are set.

8. Add rails, using a square to make sure each rail is perpendicular to the posts. Toenail the rail or use brackets to hold them solid.

9. Stretch a level line from post to post to mark the bottom edge of the siding and secure the boards with screws longer than the board's thickness. Check alignment as you proceed.

10. Finish off the bottom with a kick board.

11. Decorative caps add a finishing touch to the top of posts.

Your fence will do a lot more than give seclusion. They will filter sun; keep out strong winds and mute street noise. They can act as partitions to divide the yard into areas for parking, relaxing, recreation or storage, and don't forget gardening.

A masonry wall with a gate flanked with pillars and lightening assures this person's seclusion and privacy but also makes an impressive entrance!

Polemonium
(po-le-MOH-nee-um)
JACOB'S LADDER

SHAPE	Clump with straight spikes holding loose clusters
HEIGHT	Some varieties reach eighteen inches, others twelve
WIDTH	Stays slim, basal reaches fifteen inches
BLOOM TIME	Late spring to early summer
COLORS	Shades of blues, sometimes white
SITE	Moist and cool, well-drained neutral or mildly alkaline
LIGHT	Partial shade or heavy shade
HARDINESS	Zone two
COMMENTS	Famous for its unique fern-like foliage

Polemonium, better known as Jacob's ladder, is admired for its delicate sky-blue flowers on dense ferny foliage.

Jacob's ladder foliage really appears as an old-fashioned single rung ladder. The exquisite fern-like foliage grows from basal swirling rosettes that arch gracefully as they mature. The silver-foliaged *pulmonaria*, 'Diana Clare' in the background is also a fine foliage perennial for the partial or shade garden and makes an excellent companion to Jacob's ladder.

Polemonium's blue, one-inch, cup-shaped flowers are special in every garden, but when the white antlers change to orange to attract pollinators, it's an "art trip."

The word :alternate" describes the arrangement of leaves on both sides of the common axis. The phrase "odd-pinnate" means there is an odd leaf, or only one, on the terminal end and pinnate tells us the leaflets resemble a feather.

"GREETINGS," I SAYETH. I've been honored by being named after the Biblical Jacob, whose vision of a ladder reaching into heaven is a well-known story. The vision promised Jacob that his descendants shall be like the dust of the earth and shall spread to cover the Earth. When it pertains to me, this prophecy appears to have come to pass. My origins have moved from Western Europe, east through the Himalayas and into Alaska. From Alaska, I moved down through California and east to the Rocky Mountains. I'm called a native in the midwest and almost considered invasive in the eastern United States for I practically fill every flower bed. The historical value of my name should be powerful enough motivation for every gardener to make the prophecy come to pass by growing Jacob's ladder in their gardens.

My name also came about because of my evenly spaced ladder-like foliage and just may be the most interesting part of me. My foliage gives me a double season of interest in gardens for I flower in early summer and after my spent flowers are snipped my distinctive foliage thickens and takes on the appearance of an attractive fern.

It may be of interest that with my easy growing abilities I struggle in some western gardens unless the conditions of my natural environment are replicated. As a wildflower growing in the coolness of high mountain canyons I flourish for I'm right at home in a cool growing area. The solution to my short life could be that many gardens located in the Rocky Mountains are sitting inside a desert region and I have no drought-tolerant tendencies. High and dry summertime heat can cause me to languish. The ups and downs in mountain elevations could be the answer for temperatures in the mountains vary considerably. I do not tolerate direct sun so partial shade or heavy shade is my prime growing spot so if I'm planted there I usually thrive. If I still struggle, analyzing my other growing needs may give some answers.

Adequate, consistent moisture is necessary for me to thrive, but my taproot requires well-drained soil, so areas with heavy clay that doesn't drain could drown me out. When planting Jacob's ladder in clay soil, add gravel and amendments to the planting hole for standing water will result in root rot. I grow well in neutral pH soil which is the average level for most western gardens but often their water has a higher pH so I'm given an alkaline supplement each time I'm watered and this could explain why I'm an "iffy" perennial in the west. Microclimates of sun, soil and water are in every garden so if I'm not preforming these may be the reasons. Many gardeners keep replanting me because they think I'm so beautiful. Growing conditions are full of contradictions, so it would be worth it to plant me in your garden, give me plenty of water, and see what happens.

Butterflies are attracted to my stamens for pollination. My seeds that fall into the garden will choose to germinate or not for we have a mind of our own. Winter's vernalization encourages germination but we will wait until springtime to sprout. Dig any seedlings in spring and replant them to the garden. Remember, seedlings are always hardier than the parent plant but rarely look exactly like that parent. This self-seeding is uncommon but enough will start to assure I'll always be in your garden so it's easy to replace a *polemonium* that was short lived.

My established clumps should be divided every four-to-five years. Dig a ten-inch deep trough around me and lift my root ball with the shovel. Gently tease to separate my root mass or split me with a knife. Plant me back in the ground immediately for my roots will not tolerate getting dried out. Soggy winter soils can also cause me grief so add gravel to the planting hole for drainage and organic mulch for fertilizer. I do not require a fertilizer program and the mulch is all I'll need to keep my roots cool, moist, and healthy. Spread compost around me in winter to protect me from the Rocky Mountain's erratic spring weather.

If I get cut or bruised and my fragrance is released, cats will flock to me almost as if they think I'm catnip. Place citrus rinds under my clump to keep the felines away. Cats like me but deer stay away. I have no pest or disease problems. My tall stems also make excellent cut flowers for a vase.

To keep my handsome foliage tidied and looking its best cut my awkward looking flowerless stems back to the basal foliage as soon as I finish blooming. A few can be left for seeding. My alternate, odd-pinnate, bright-green leaves will continue to grow. "Alternate, odd-pinnate" is botanic flower leaf language that is used to describe my ladder-like foliage.

FOLIAGE CONTEST

I'm not the only perennial to have foliage as their main attraction. If a contest were offered asking gardeners to name their favorite foliage plants for partial sun or shade I'm sure that Hosta would be number one. Galium or sweet woodruff would be high on the list as the most delicate looking. Lady's mantle, without a doubt, would be the plant with the most fascinating leaves because of their beautiful pleating that holds water drops. Heuchera would be the most colorful with bergenia and helleborus sharing the award for being the perfect evergreens. Here are six of these wonderful shade perennials with outstanding foliage:

Hosta is undeniably the number-one foliage perennial for shady gardens and always adds a classy statement to whatever garden it graces. With such handsome foliage, hosta deserves first place.

Heuchera are often thought of as colorful foliage plants but the tiny trumpets are so lovely that it just might also win the most beautiful flower for shade gardens.

Galium forms a spreading groundcover of small, waxy, whorled, green leaves. Clusters of delicate, sweet-smelling white flowers bloom in spring.

Alchemilla or lady's mantle with its gray-green pleated leaves is spectacular especially after a rain storm when the pleated petals hold water drops like diamonds.

Two evergreen perennials, *Bergenia* and *Helleborus* have foliage so beautiful that a gardener would almost be tempted to give them the number-one spot in place of *hosta*.

Companion plants are the perennials who like cool moist gardens in partial sun of shade and all of these contest winners will make good companions. Truth be known I grow well with every perennial in chapter two and three that is how comfortable I am to be around.

Polemonium planted with white *Corydalis* in a very comfortable shady garden.

Polemonium caeruleum is the original Jacob's ladder and is still the most popular variety. The adjective marker *caeruleum* after my Latin name means "sky blue," which is my usual color, but white 'Alba' Jacob's ladder are also available. 'Alba' occasionally shows up from seeds that have germinated. The blue or white colors are attractive in any garden be it cottage, formal or contemporary. I seem to fit nicely wherever I'm planted. My symmetrical foliage is so interesting that I knew hybridizers wouldn't leave it alone so now there are new varieties being cultivated and they look amazing. New variegated Jacob's ladder foliages are really eye catching. Check labels carefully when purchasing these cultivars for hardiness. Here are a few samples to whet your appetite:

Polemonium caeruleum 'Brise d'Anjou' is a new hybrid that has long handsome yellow-edged variegated leaves. The leaves are so striking a gardener often has to touch them to see if they are real. The yellow edged leaves look especially nice with the medium blue flowers on Brise. Other variegated foliage *polemoniums* are 'Heavenly Habit' and the *reptens* variety called 'Stairway to Heaven.' 'Stairway' blooms blue, is shorter and spreads as a ground cover. *Reptens* are very hardy and will even grow in the deep shade of a walnut tree.

The incredible foliage of 'Stairway to Heaven' is heavenly.

It's been great getting acquainted and these growing tips will guarantee that I will "spread as the sand" fulfilling the ancient prophecy and beautifying the west while I'm at it.

A PLACE OF MY OWN

HOME! A PLACE OF MY OWN! What is it about a home and yard that makes it yours? Is it just a place to hang your hat or is it the one place where your deepest needs are met? Living in the Rockies, residents find their outdoor lifestyles have a way of connecting to the heights and lows of the mountain elevations and temperatures where they reside. Outdoor areas seem to be where personal needs differ with the exception of everyone wanting the seclusion or privacy as seen in the last side sketch. But there are other innate needs tied to the earth that may be every bit as important as privacy and again the garden is where they can be satisfied.

The power of a seed and earth can be shared no matter how small the student. The pleased feeling when the seed has become an edible, organically grown commodity is a self-sustaining lifetime skill for these children will never be afraid of going hungry.

OUTDOOR NEED #1: EDIBLE GARDENS

Gardeners are passionate about growing their own food! Growing edible gardens in the Rocky Mountains presents overwhelming challenges with short cool summers and frost often occurring every month of the year. Mountain homeowners, as they always do, have discovered creative methods that circumvent the temperatures. A Utah homeowner with a small shaded back yard "needed" to grow tomatoes for Utah tomatoes grown in alkaline soils and water are unsurpassable in flavor. Tomatoes require heat for as long as they are growing, so this is how this gardener makes sure his vegetables are the best.

The hottest spot in the garden just happens to be along the south foundation of the home so grow boxes for growing tomatoes, cucumbers, and peppers were built. Notice the dripper system and bug distracting marigolds in the corners. Needless to say he always wins the award for the earliest tomatoes in the neighborhood.

Where seasons are short choose cool weather, quickly maturing edibles like radishes, leaf lettuce, onions and peas. In Idaho where they are famous for growing potatoes, underground potato pits dot the landscapes. Potatoes are frost sensitive so must be stored where they won't get damaged and these root cellars storage units are excellent for storing potatoes as well as other crops. The underground pits keep items naturally cool, in the dark and the humidity remains relatively high so vegetables stay fresh. Root edibles like carrots, squash, parsnips, turnips or cauliflower will stay as fresh as the day they were harvested as long as they were rescued before the frost hit. Many potato pits have turf roofs planted with self-sustaining perennials like *sedums* and *Sempervivums* that provide extra insulation for the roof.

For mountain dwellers, the supermarket is often not around the corner so saving their vegetables in a naturally cool, 32 to 40 degree F. root cellar gives them a year-round supermarket just outside their door. Without some type of ventilation with pipes, fans or ducting the vegetables may spoil. My husband installed small surplus computer fans in ours for they are long-lasting and cheap to run.

Wyoming gardeners know that trying to grow tomatoes without a long season of high heat is never really successful for tomatoes stay small and the skins will be tough as leather. Cucumbers and peppers also require summer sun and heat. Many gardeners will compensate by using a section of their yards for a low structure called a cold frame that can be quickly covered if frost is forecast. Cold frames are designed in several ways. Some have hoops that cover a row crop. Others are lowered into the ground while others are made of solar plastic that can be closed in cold and opened during sunshine.

OUTDOOR NEED #2: STORAGE

Too much "stuff"! I hear this all the time. I hardly have space for my flower garden with all the "stuff" that needs a place to call home. Organization takes a great deal of time in the beginning but once it's done it saves homeowners more time than they thought possible. So just bite the bullet and browse these ideas to see if any of these organization tools would work for your "stuff."

Outside garage walls are prime spots for storing all kinds of items but to look good and stay useable "stuff" needs to be off the ground. Lean-to sheds can be built against the garage wall for cabinets to store bicycles, garbage cans or firewood.

Garage storage units multitask to meet a homeowner's needs. There are overhead storage units and giant hooks that attach to the ceiling and will pull down for easy retrieval of big items like camping gear, bicycles or Christmas decorations. Lockers can be installed side by side for tons of

The cold frame is made of a solar plastic covering a wooden frame. The enclosed frame keeps the growing area warmer and frost cloth adds an additional ten-degree heat factor. The frost cloth can be tucked around the plants at a moment's notice of freeze warnings. Compost clippings like fall leaves gathered and chopped with the lawn mower along with manure and soil are mixed in the cold frame. The decomposition of the mixture produces heat to also booster the length of the growing season and ensures great soil for planting a great crop.

This ingenious cold frame cover for when temperatures really drop is made from recycled storm doors. After the metal excesses on the doors were removed, a plastic solar covering was placed on the door frame with lath metal screws. The solar plastic really heats up the interior of the cold frame when they are placed on the frames. The door frame coverings are so lightweight that they are easy to slip into a top grove while the bottom of the door is held in place with bungee cords. Veggies will eventually freeze but will have had plenty of time to mature so they are A # 1, prime plants. Not all growers have these needs but cold climate gardeners have found ways that "needs" are easily met to successfully grow vegetables.

Three of these sturdy attractive circles hung on an outside garage wall would make a very artistic statement. One homeowner claims that when his wooden circles are full of firewood he is ready to face whatever winter dishes out.

storage area both inside and out. Secure the base of lockers against rodents thinking they just got a great house is an important issue.

OUTDOOR NEED #3: SAFE PLACE FOR KIDS TO PLAY

Children bring so much joy to lives that parents want to return that joy by creating a safe place for them to play. In

A tire swing is more of a challenge than regular swings for it circles, twists and turns. What makes it even better it will hold more than one child. Friend's interaction curbs screen attraction.

urban or suburban residences there is room for swing-sets or sandboxes that kids enjoy. Board fences can be utilized as chalk boards, climbing walls or to hold storage baskets installed on them for holding kid's trucks, sand buckets and balls. Playtime is probably the biggest health benefit we can give our children. Here are a couple of ideas:

Kids love to climb, and the straining of the reach builds strength and burns tons of calories. Active outdoor yard-toys provide many health benefits for kids who are becoming more sedentary with too much sitting static technology time.

Experiencing both weightlessness and gravitational pull is healthy for both kids and parents. The rebounding exercise reduces body fat, increases muscle agility and balance while gently detoxifying the jumper. Besides it's a lot of fun.

Rural areas typically have more space for kid's activities. Kids have horses to ride, cows to herd, chickens to feed and eggs to gather. One enterprising rural parent created a dirt track with hills, jumps and curves to keep his kids entertained at home, away from the tube and happy.

Sport activities may be high on the "need" list of parents as well as kids. Volleyball, croquet, bocce to name a few favorites can be planned for and so can a trampoline.

Looks like a competition! They know how much fun they are having, but the kids are really strengthening their legs, arms and shoulder muscles when they turn, lift and operate the bikes. Balance develops plus the ride increases their heart rate. Dirt bikes are more than exciting!

Home isn't home without a pet to greet you with an excited, loving welcome. A place for pets with a fenced backyard is typical for everyone loves their pets especially the kids. Kennels or dog runs are needs that take planning. The summer heat and winter cold in the west are important pet issues.

OUTDOOR NEED #4: A PLACE FOR THE FAMILY PET

Perennial vines allowed to climb over this dog kennel provide much needed shade in summer's heat. *Clematis*, *Lonicera* or honeysuckle, *campsis* or trumpeter vine, *Polygonum* or silver lace vine and *parthenocissus* or Virginia creeper, will furnish shade and block doggy smells. Any of these perennial vines will beautify a kennel or dog run.

Home isn't home without a pet to greet you with an excited, loving welcome. A place for pets with a fenced backyard is typical for everyone loves their pets especially the kids. Kennels or dog runs are needs that take planning. The summer heat and winter cold in the west are important pet issues.

OUTDOOR NEED #5: THE "NEED" FOR HOBBIES

Of all the outdoor hobbies, gardening is ranked number one in most areas of the country but if you live in the Rocky Mountains hunting and fishing probably exceeds gardening. Hunters are so avid they often grow their own game.

This Western hunter grows his own birds then releases them to the wild when they reach a stage of maturity so he always has a good supply for hunting. He grows quail one year, then pheasants another but this year he raised guinea hens and he swears he will never make this mistake again. "Oh, they are not all bad for they eat ticks and snakes plus they squawk and screech when a something comes into the yard," he explained. "But they are the dumbest birds alive, even more stupid than turkeys. They travel in flocks and were released months ago but they still come home to roost. I doubt they will ever leave home!"

PARTIAL-SUN AND PARTIAL-SHADE PERENNIALS SUMMARY

A partial-shade or partial-sun garden is a comfortable home in the west for more perennials than any other garden area. In the higher elevations, the sun is harsher and hotter but the summers are shorter and cooler, so the spectrum of perennials to plant in these areas crosses into the boundaries of full-sun perennials and into the shade perennial category.

THE LINE BETWEEN full-sun, partial-sun and partial-shade perennials wobbles all over the garden. The high elevations of mountain gardens can deplete the energy of drought or full-sun perennials because in the higher elevations the sun is hotter. It seems most perennials actually grow and bloom better with a little afternoon shade. On the other spectrum are the shade perennials. Many gardens vary their sun and shade daylight hours as the seasons of the sun shift. For these reasons many full-sun perennials are a part of this list and so are the shade perennials. I've found in western gardens that partial shade/partial sun is the favorite spot for most perennials so the list is long, but that's a good thing. Perennials that are not included in the list are probably acidic soil lovers or are zoned out of our regions. I've grown all of these between my Utah and Idaho gardens, but it is still a good policy to check labels and other gardens in your community.

SPRING-TO-SUMMER-BLOOMING PERENNIALS

SHORT TO MEDIUM HEIGHT

Alchemilla or lady's mantle

Ajuga or bugleweed

Anemone or snowdrops

Arabis or rockcress

Armeria or thrift

Aubrieta or purple rockcress

Aurinia or basket-of-gold

Avens or geum

Bellis or English daisy

Bergenia or heartleaf

Brunnera or Siberian bugloss

Convallaria or lily-of-the-valley

Corydalis lutea

Doronicum or leopard's bane

Euphorbia or spurge

Galium or sweet woodruff

Geranium or cranesbill

Hedera or ivy

Helleborus

Heuchera or coral bells

Heucherella

Hyacinths

Iberis or candytuft

Iris, dwarf crested

Lamiastrum or Herman's pride

Lamium

Linum or flax

Myosotis or forget-me-not

Narcissus or daffodil

Phlox, creeping

Primula or primrose

Pulmonaria or lungwort

Ranunculus or creeping buttercups

Saponaria or soapwort

Scilla siberica or snowdrops
Tiarella or foam flower
Tulipa or tulip
Veronica reptens
Vinca or periwinkle
Viola or violet

MEDIUM–TALL

Allium or ornamental onion
Aquilegia or columbine
Centaurea or mountain bluet
Dicentra or bleeding heart
Dictamnus or gas plant
Hesperis or dame's rocket
Iris or flag
Papaver or poppy
Polemonium or Jacobs ladder
Tanacetum or painted daisies
Thalictrum or meadow rue
Thermopsis or false lupine
Trollius or globe flower

SUMMER-TO-FALL-BLOOMING PERENNIALS

SHORT–MEDIUM

Artemisia or wormwood
Aruncus, dwarf, or goatsbeard
Callirhoe or winecups
Campanula clips or bellflower
Cerastium or snow-in-summer
Coreopsis or tickseed
Delphinium, short, or 'Summer Blues' and 'Summer Nights'
Dianthus
Filipendula or meadowsweet
Gaillardia or blanket flower
Gaura or apple blossom grass
Gentiana or gentian

Geraniums or crane's bill
Goniolimon or statice
Gypsophila repens
Helianthemum or sun rose
Hosta
Liriope or lilyturf
Lychnis haageana and *viscaria*
Lysimachia or moneywort
Oenothera or evening primrose
Potentilla or cinquefoil
Salvia or sage
Scabiosa or pincushion flower
Sedum, low varieties, or stonecrop
Sempervivum or hens-and-chicks
Silene or catchfly
Stachys or lambs ear
Veronica, short, or speedwell

MEDIUM–TALL

Achillea or yarrow
Aconitum or wolfsbane
Anthemis or golden marguerite
Aruncus or goatsbeard
Asclepias or butterfly flower
Aster
Campanula persicifolia
Centranthus or red Valerian
Chelone or turtlehead
Chrysanthemum or dendranthema
Coreopsis or tickseed
Delphinium
Digitalis or foxglove
Echinacea or coneflower
Echinops or globe thistle
Filipendula or queen of the meadow
Genista or broom
Gypsophila or tall baby's breath
Helenium or Helen's flower

Heliopsis or sunflower
Hemerocallis or daylily
Hibiscus or rose mallow
Iris Sibirica or Siberian flag
Kniphofia or red hot poker
Leucanthemum or shasta daisy
Ligularia or leopard plant
Lilium
Lupinus or lupine
Lychnis or campion
Malva or mallow
Monarda or bee balm
Nepeta or catmint
Paeonia or peony
Penstemon or beardtongue
Perovskia or Russian sage
Phlox paniculata
Physostegia or obedience plant
Potentilla or cinquefoil
Rudbeckia 'Goldstrume'
Salvia or sage
Sedum, tall varieties, or stonecrop
Solidago or goldenrod
Tradescantia or spiderwort
Trollius or globeflower
Veronica, tall, or speedwell
Yucca or Adam's needle

With so many perennials to choose from, there is no limit to options, so embrace a variety. With so many choices it's easy to plant perennials for contrast in colors, shapes, sizes, and season of bloom. Thumb through this book for more details and growing requirements of any perennial that looks interesting, and if possible have a copy of *Powerful Perennials* for information on cold climate, drought tolerant, wildlife resistant and which soils the perennials prefer.

*Resolve to unplug
and disconnect,
Find a sweet shady
spot to reconnect.*

SHADE PERENNIALS

GARDENERS MAKE ME laugh! Those just starting to landscape a new yard are so infatuated with the unique textures and foliage colors of shade perennials like Hosta that they moan because they only have full sun in their garden. The coin flips when years later after their trees and gardens have matured and become engulfed in shade, then they moan about not having enough sun to plant the hundreds and hundreds of colorful sun perennials. The solution to this dilemma is to probably design your garden for sun and shade situations. The main purpose of planting trees is for shade and to furnish the structure of bones and height to the garden. Planting trees is an economical way of adding value to a home but trees are available in different sizes and shapes and a forty-foot tall and wide shade tree may not add value to the garden.

Shade gardens offer many advantages like a place of quiet peace where a gardener can regroup. Gardening in shade is easier and not as time consuming because the plants grow at a slower growth rate. Perennials not only develop slower but are more permanent and live longer in shade. Plants require less maintenance like deadheading for there is less blooming, less watering because evaporation is reduced, less fertilizer because they grow more slowly and less weeding because most weeds are sun plants.

Ferns, *Hosta*, and *Trollius* add serenity to this low-care shade garden. Shade plant's foliage and textures stay fresher and more vibrant in the quiet low light of shade. All three plants bring a different texture to keep the shade garden interesting.

Here are a few pointers for making the most of a shady garden.

1. Light colored flowers and foliage show up better in a shade garden.

2. Variegated, silver or the bronze foliage like that of the *ligularia* shown above brings all season color to a shade garden.

3. Spot bright colored containers like a huge, brilliant cobalt blue pot filled with chartreuse *hosta* in the garden to add a full season of color.

4. Shade plants planted in groups of three or more plants will look more dramatic. Many shade perennials have small leaves giving a dainty look like that of lady's mantle but grouped will give a stronger garden impact.

5. Spring-blooming bulbs add a carefree season of color and by the time the trees leaf out the bulbs have gone dormant.

6. Combine different heights of plants for most shade perennials have a smaller stature. *Thalictrum, aruncus,* and *dicentra* are great choices and there are more to meet in chapter three, shade blooming perennials.

Shade gardens grow depending on what level of shade a garden has. Light shade as written on a plant label means that the area is shaded for two to four hours a day during the hottest hours between 10:00 a.m. and 6:00 p.m.

Filtered shade on the label means the perennial will grow well under trees. Sunlight penetrates and shines through the trees leaves depending on how dense the tree canopy is. The lower level of evening and morning sunshine usually shines beneath the branches and limbing-up or removing the lower branches will allow more light to filter in.

Full shade, usually symbolized on a label by a darkened sun sign, are spaces that are shaded all day. A dense tall thick planting of trees creates full shade gardens as well as an overhang or several tall buildings. Usually there is an element of reflected light through the trees or off the building but all living plants need some sun so hardscaping is optional at the base of these types of buildings.

Dense shade is the more difficult problem for gardens. These are the darkest areas with all day shade without reflected light. Dense shade is typical under low growing trees like a pine tree which also gobbles up any water and nutrients leaving the plant nothing in return. A tree sends out masses of roots that will also overtake and fill the top layers of soil. Root competition consumes the soil leaving nothing for other plants to grow in and is usually a bigger problem than shade. A choice of a deep rooted tree like an Oak will send less top layers of roots while a shallow rooted tree such as a willow will provide more root competition.

Shade gardens plants are full of foliage, colors, and textures. The above picture shows the bold bronze-red foliage of *Ligularia*, 'Britt Marie Crawford,' a fine shade perennial that breaks the rules, for shade plants rarely bloom in gold colors.

Anemone pulsatilla, 'Rubra'
(uh-Nem-oh-nee)
SNOWDROP ANEMONE

Pulsatilla sylvestris
(pull-su-TILL-uh)
PASQUE FLOWER

W E FEEL CERTAIN you're wondering why there are two of us introducing ourselves. There are several reasons but mainly anemone and pulsatilla at one time were considered the same perennial. That's understood for we are a lot alike, both in size and early spring bloom time. *Pulsatilla* is famous for blooming at Easter time and was given the common name of "pasque" flower for pasque means Passover in the Christian religion. I'm affectionately called snowdrop or windflower for the Greek meaning of the word "anemos" means "daughter of the wind" and I'm at my best when a breeze causes me to nod softly. We both form fluffy seed heads or fruit after blooming that are attractive for drying or cut flowers.

The attractive silky tufts of *pulsatilla* are often accused of being aggressive when seeding but this darling has never naturalized or reseeded in my northern gardens. The attractive seed heads are like another round of flowering for they look quite dramatic in the garden or the vase.

Our foliage is deeply divided but pasque flowers have finer, ferny-like foliage that stays attractive and continues growing until frost. My foliage stays small and tidy as long as I'm planted in a shade garden. In sunlight we both glisten for we are covered with fine silky hairs. Most of my hairs are on the underside of my leaves while pulsatilla is covered with a soft velvety down.

Anemone forms cottony puff ball, seed heads that reseed in many places but hasn't naturalize in my Utah and Idaho gardens. The cottony material traps the seeds in their fabric but can be easily removed along with the seed.

Anemone sylvestris's clump of palmate-lobed or hand-shaped leaves forms a tight bun after blooming but the foliage stays nice all season and often sends up another satiny flower or two throughout summer and again in fall.

Anemone Pulsatilla

SHAPE	Small clump with wiry stems holding cup-shaped flowers
HEIGHT	One foot
WIDTH	Eight-inches
BLOOM TIME	April and May
COLORS	Creamy white blooms with yellow centers
SITE	Average, well-drained, tolerates both alkaline and clay soils
LIGHT	Partial and full shade
HARDINESS	Zone 3 or down to -40degrees F
COMMENTS	Snowdrops blooms are like lights turned on in a shady garden

Pulsatilla sylvestris

SHAPE	Small clump of cup-shaped flowers
HEIGHT	Ten-inches
WIDTH	Eight-inches
BLOOM TIME	Early spring, Easter time, April
COLORS	Wine red or violet
SITE	Average, alkaline clay, well-drained soil in cool climates
LIGHT	Full sun
HARDINESS	Zones 4
COMMENTS	A very showy perennial in bloom

The bright-green fine ferny foliage of *pulsatilla* differs from *anemone* in that it keeps expanding in the sunshine of a cool weather garden like those in high mountain valleys.

The main reason we are so much alike is that we are close sisters in the Ranunculus or buttercup family. Our family has many well-known members like *delphiniums, thalictrums, trollius,* and *aconitums* and most have retained their early ancestral characteristics. Our flowers are bisexual meaning we have both male and female reproduction structures so we are called "perfect" plants for we can fertilize ourselves. Buttercups are considered "simple" flowers with four to six petals and a "simple" pistil at the center of the flower. Our golden stamens and anthers are spirally inserted and beautifully detailed. Only twenty three species out of thousands of Ranunculus are native to North America and *pulsatilla* is a famous native.

Pulsatilla vulgaris was thriving in the tundra areas of North Dakota when the first settlers arrived and are so loved they have been affectionately honored as the state flower. The plants bloom early and hunker-down on short stubby stems for protection against the cold. Fine hair on both the petals and flowers gives another layer of protection from the cold for anything that grows in North Dakota will grow anywhere. They send up a solitary bell from a basal whorl of only a couple of leaves at the start of their season.

Most Buttercup or Ranunculus family members contain compounds that are toxic to humans and animals giving us wildlife resistant qualities. We contain acrid oils so handling plants may cause a skin irritation or allergic reaction. This may be our simple way to protect ourselves for the future for we look delicious but if tasted we have a bitter almost biting taste that is hopefully, quickly spit out. There are companies who offer dried *anemone* and *pulsatilla* that are best used as a poultice similar to old fashioned mustard plasters. The part of the plant that grows above ground is dried and made into a paste then wrapped between thick cloths and placed on either male or female reproductive systems to heal and eliminate pain. It's said I will also help curb restlessness in children.

The simple buttercup shape of *anemone's* five or six-petaled blooms on twelve-inch stems are native to Central and Western European mountains. *Anemone's* glistening delicate flower's charm is like that of turning on a light switch in a shady garden spot.

Propagation of *anemone* and *pulsatilla* is best done by spring division for allowing the seeds to naturalize in western gardens is "iffy." Some seeds may germinate but divisions of the rhizome root ball are a better method in the Rocky Mountains. Dig our roots in spring for fall dividing does not give us enough time to get our root system fully developed before the onset of winter. Plant us at our previous height about a foot apart. Never plant us in lines but in a swath, triangle or half circle.

Now this is where we start differing for I grow in shade and *pulsatilla* grows in sun. Plant my starts as under-plantings beneath trees, shrubs or perennials for too much sun will retard our growth and cause us to go into summer dormancy. We grow best in loose soil but our underground stolons will sucker easier giving us a tendency to spread. Planted in clay we stay put but we grow better in loose loam like the forests where we originated. It will take a year for me to bloom. When I'm at half-height I start to bloom with my buds emerging on bent stems. The buds dangle down like the spring bulbs, *Galanthus*, called snowdrops so this is why I'm also called snowdrops. As my flowers start to open my stems magically straighten so the flowers can soak up the sunshine of spring. I'll continue

blooming for about a month until my flowers reach the stem tips at maturity.

So now you know we are very much alike in size and bloom time but our foliage is different and *pulsatilla* grows well in full sun but I need the shady part of the garden. We are natives from different continents so it is surprising we were once thought to be the same plant. However we are both excellent rock garden plants and could be called alpines for our hardiness and long lived abilities. Neither of us grows well from harvested seeds but I'm easy to divide while *pulsatilla* is safer when purchased in nursery pots. Our velvety texture

As *anemones* start to bloom they form buds when the stems are at half-mast. These downward facing buds resemble the spring bulbs called snowdrops so the name was attached to the *anemone*.

Pulsatilla planted in the gritty soil of a rock garden grows a fine alpine perennial. It will grow in any soil from chalk to loam and is not fussy about the pH of the soil.

Two weeks later the buds have opened and the stems are starting to stand straight and holding the blooms that have opened wide to the sun, another example of the wonders of nature.

I also make an excellent rock garden perennial for under the shade of a tree, and I'm not fussy about soils or pH elements. Allow my plants to send out suckers so I will grow as a ground cover. A huge swatch of my brilliant white bells will really draw attention to the classiest area in a rock garden.

and small tidy size makes us excellent in containers as long as I'm placed in shade and the other in sun. Courtyards are excellent spots for both of us for we need to be grown where our beauty can be enjoyed and easily viewed. Front edgings or under plantings in country gardens look wonderful when planted with either of us especially when we are allowed to form a huge swath of spring color.

Small, compact perennials that are dependable and care free like the anemone and *pulsatilla* are not always available so they may need to be ordered a year ahead from a grower. They promise to deliver the promise of spring into a garden. Below is a view of both perennials in full bloom. Now your only job is to find sun for one and shade for the other.

These little-known perennials need to be in every garden. They are gradual spreaders and long-lived perennials that bring a whiff of spring to any garden.

A plant this lovely needs to grace every garden.

SPRING'S "FEVER-PITCH"

I N SPRING, something's in the air besides pollination and its love, for gardeners are passionately in love with their flowers. A gardener's physiological response to spring's "Fever-Pitch" is to design garden plans bulging with plants they can't live without under the guise that there will be no room left for weeds or no need for staking. My own case is probably one of the worst obsessive spring's "fever-pitch" disorders on record. I actually started Secrist Gardens as an excuse for growing enough perennials to landscape both my gardens and the entire community.

Another spring "Fever-Pitch" symptom is the gardener returning from a plant-gathering spree and realizing every single plant purchased is in bloom. It may be due to the hope and joy flowers symbolize or the extra endorphins the brain secrets with increased sunlight. In reality it's probably that spring blooming plants are just too gorgeous for any sensible gardener to go without. Along with the enticing snowdrop anemone and pulsatilla 'Rubra' acquaintance you've made in chapter four, the following is a gallery of spring blooming, western acclimatized perennials that every garden deserves.

GALLERY OF EARLY SPRING BLOOMING PERENNIALS

It's very noticeable that many of the spring-blooming bulbs and perennials are plants that perform better in shady gardens. The logical reason for this is they bloom before trees and shrubs leaf so they are the benefactors of

Heartleaf *Bergenia* keeps its huge bronzed leaves throughout winter no matter how deep the snow. With springs first warm days, *bergenia* will start to form tight buds, gradually opening similar to how a gardener's heart starts to open as bergenia appears through the snow.

Daffodils are the hardiest and longest living of any bulbs in western gardens, for they are deer and disease resistant and thrive while dormant in our hot dry summers. Daffodils will naturalize year after year, only needing division when they cease blooming.

Helleborus, or lenten rose, often makes its entrance through the snow. The flowers are interesting, exquisitely colored bells that droop downward and will hold their blooms until summer temperatures start. *Helleborus's* handsome evergreen foliage looks fine all seasons.

Creeping *phlox* blooms in a dense carpet mass of pastel-colored flowers. The secret to growing attractive creeping *phlox* year after year is no trimming until after they bloom. Then cut the spent stems, leaving only a nice tuft of the moss like foliage. The perennial will grow throughout the summer and winter and again bloom in early spring.

Doronicum, or leopard's bane, is a surprise when it blooms because it is the first daisy-shaped flower of the year. *Doronicum's* bright look lifts the mood of any viewer. It grows about fifteen inches tall and wide with dark-green holly-like foliage that is every bit as delightful as the flowers.

Pulmonaria, or lungwort, is a pleasing addition to the early shade garden but is also pleasing in the summer and fall gardens. Its delightful silver or silver-dotted foliage is every bit as attractive as its ethereal flowers. The unique flowers start out as pinky coral buds and open into delicate shades of violets and blue.

For height in a shady spring garden, plant *Dicentra*, or bleeding hearts. The amorphous hearts of *dicentra* seems to coincide with the increased heart rate of gardeners when they gaze at this spectacular partial-shade garden perennial.

Heucherella with its high-wattage foliage brings evergreen energy to the early spring garden. This fine new hybrid blooms for over a month with fuzzy bottlebrush pink and white blooms. Their eight-inch blooms resemble excited exclamation marks shouting "Welcome Spring!"

Spring-blooming primroses are famous for leading a couple down the primrose path of courtship. Primroses are long lived and hardy as long as they are the true perennial primrose or cowslip. The pictured primrose above is called drumstick primrose and is a zone four.

Papaver, or poppies, with their enormous, dazzling scarlet, red, salmon, or orange petals surrounding black-eyed centers energizes any garden with their huge colorful blooms. Poppies go dormant after blooming and will need to be cut to the ground.

The snowflake shapes and amethyst centers on this fifteen-inch, early blooming hybrid *centaurea* will excite any senses still mired in winter woes. Cutting amethyst back by late May will ensure another round of blooms in late summer.

Which is sweeter: the columbine nectar-rich spurs or the child sampling the flavor? Columbine are versatile and grow as wildflowers in the mountains but are just as happy in a cultivated partial-shade garden. The early daisy flowers of golden *doronicum* are in the background.

The very unique and perfect proportions of the exquisite columbine with its long spurs of nectar gave it the name of *aquilegia*, coming from the Latin word for eagle.

Hesperis, or sweet rocket, is a fine spring-blooming perennial to add height to the back of a partial-shade border or flower bed. *Hesperis* will naturalize quickly, so it needs to have its seeds removed as soon as it finishes blooming.

Every garden needs a celebrity plant like *edelweiss* with its amazing survival skills. Edelweiss grows well in the Rocky Mountains and blooms with beautiful delicate white flowers in spring.

spring's full sunshine. This could also help explain how critical Spring Fever can be, for humans instinctively react to seasonal changes just as some animals hibernate in winter. Check to see if you are a victim of spring's "Fever-Pitch" by answering the following question: Have you ever bought five of the same perennial because they bloom in five different colors? Right! Well I have, now I'm questioning my motives for writing this gardening book. Is it perhaps just another symptom of the physiological response to spring's "Fever-Pitch"? Remember, gardening is the way to scratch the itch of spring's "Fever-Pitch."

Bergenia cordifolia,
Bergenia crassifolia
(ber-JEN-ee-ah)
HEARTLEAF

SHAPE	Low, thick clump of glossy leaves with pink flower clusters in spring
HEIGHT	Twelve-inches
WIDTH	Fifteen-inches
BLOOM TIME	Early spring in April
COLORS	Shades of rosy pink
SITE	Average soil, tolerant of a wide range of soils
LIGHT	Partial shade but shade tolerant
HARDINESS	Zone 3
COMMENTS	A good slug free substitute for *Hosta*

Bergenia is an outstanding, tough, classy looking perennial ground cover. *Bergenia* is famous for its large, glossy, heart-shaped leaves that change to purple during winter.

Heartleaf *Bergenia* is a long-lived, clump forming, partial or shade perennial that will perform with perfection under a porch or portico.

As the snow melts, a gardener watches in awe as the beautiful foliaged *bergenia* unfolds from its evergreen, leathery rosette and pushes up its gorgeous blooms. The glossy leathery leaves of bergenia hold their perfection and are in high demand with florists for flower arrangements.

The heart-shaped leaves of *bergenia* are remarkable for surviving intact from a winter of deep snow or even no snow. They turn a rich bronze at the first frosts of fall. Usually, they will have a few tattered leaves after winter, but once they are snipped and trimmed, they will look excellent again.

GREETINGS, I'M CALLED *Bergenia* and was named after a famous German doctor and botanist, Karl August von Bergen. My native country is Russia, so I'm sometimes called a Serbian pig squeak. This is because if my leaves are rubbed between the thumb and forefinger they give out a good squeak. Heartleaf is my popular common name and the leaves in the picture below explain this name for they are all indented at the stem and rounded like a heart.

My foliage is my best trait. It flaunts bronze-reddish color as fall temperatures start to drop. The cooler temperatures bring out the best of me, for I refuse to bloom in a hot climate. *Hosta* and I grow the same size of clump and are famous for our bold leaves. We both like partial to shady gardens, and we both grow laterally with new growth in all directions. Our main differences are that I'm an evergreen perennial and *hosta* goes underground or is deciduous in winter time. I just hunker down and enjoy the cold. This means my elegant leathery foliage stays around all winter—and all year, for that matter—and gives flowerbeds that often sought for but rarely found touch of class. Also, if a gardener has a slug and snail problem that keeps their hosta looking ratty, then I'm a good solution for I'm not bothered by these slimy creations. Slugs do not ruin my foliage, so I'm a more dependable plant in many ways than the very popular *hosta*.

Pictured in late fall, after a long hot summer, the *hosta*, shown at the top of the picture has been fried and the *bergenia* is still lovely with the exception of a few notched leaves.

I'm incredibly hardy and not bothered by hardly any pests or disease. The one exception is the black vine weevil which may chew notches along the edges of my elegant leaves. My leaves are typically slightly serrated so you may have to look close to see the characteristic notches left by this night foraging insect. The weevil is non-flying and does not destroy *bergenia*, but it does damage the foliage. Two organic treatments for black vine weevil are diatomaceous powder, which is made of fossilized aquatic organisms that damages the outer layer of the insect's tummies as they crawl toward their dinner, or a more effective product called beneficial nematodes, which uses nature's own method of killing off garden pests. These nematodes are effective against soil-inhabiting insects like weevils, grubs, cut-worms, iris borer, maggots, and Japanese beetles.

Beneficial nematodes are naturally occurring and only attack soil-dwelling insects. Nematodes are safe for humans, animals, plants, and worms. It is an organic, biologic pest control so safe that it's free of EPA restrictions. The beneficial nematodes are sprayed on damp soil and immediately go to work seeking out pests. They enter the insect or its larva and start to feed. A nematode bacteria releases and spreads inside the insect, creating a host for the nematodes to feed on that kills the insect in a few days. The high nitrogen content of fertilizers and pesticides are averse to nematodes.

I'm proud to be a member of the *Saxifragaceae*, family of perennials. There are only three of us who are garden favorites; *bergenia*, *heuchera*, and *tiarella*. We all thrive in the cooler Northern Hemisphere and the scientific meaning of our name is "of the rocks," so we are highly adapted to living in the Rocky Mountain states. The flowers of the *saxifragaceae* family are usually small flower clusters held on a stem above the rosette or basal plant. We are considered hermaphroditic perennials for we contain both male and female parts. We usually have twice as many stamens as petals and our fruit or seeds form inside a capsule. None of us naturalizes in western gardens and our tendency is to stay put, gradually expanding over time and staying somewhat evergreen.

Authors note: The first time I saw *bergenia* was fall semester, under a portico on the humanities building at a local university. The new recently planted *bergenia*, and there must have been several thousand clumps, was so consistent and healthy that I found myself wondering what it could be. The outstanding foliage was a shiny green and seemed to have wrapped itself in its beautiful, rounded thick foliage. I watched the *bergenia* throughout the school year and marveled at it when day after day of the January and February below-zero temperatures never caused it to stutter. As the weather broke in late March, it seemed to unfold slightly and opened its leathery leaves for a red-stemmed cluster of pink and rose blooms to lift up from the middle of a center rosette. The plant was enchanting. I watched and finally found this glorious plant at a nursery, took it home to plant and still find it enchanting. That is exactly what the perennial *bergenia* is and every garden that grows *bergenia* becomes enchanted!

Adding microscopic nematodes to the area around *bergenia* will eliminate the notched edges on the plant's beautiful heart-shaped foliage. Only spray nemotoides in the early mornings or late, late afternoons, for they prefer cool temperatures.

SAXIFRAGA FAMILY FAVORITES

Saxifragas grows in the same locations as *bergenia*, *heuchera*, or *tiarella*: partial shade or full shade. These small, spring blooming perennials all have clusters of flowers on stems topped with exquisite flowers. The new spring foliage is edible.

I'm noted for my low-maintenance and long life. I grow slow and my zone-two hardiness protects me in extreme temperatures. About my only requirement is to have any winter damaged tattered leaves removed in early spring. I spread by rhizomes that will grow together so I make an excellent ground cover. Propagation by spring division is the most successful method. When I get overcrowded with too many crowns, dig my entire clump and pull it apart. Trim off the foliage and replant. I grow well in normal, sandy or clay soils with a ph of neutral, alkaline and even acidic. Never divide me and trim my foliage in fall for this foliage is what gets me through the winter months.

My seed can be germinated, but this means my spent flowers would have to be left on the plant as they dry and start looking unsightly. If you are determined to try to seed me, collect the seed capsule that forms in my flower centers. Some may have lots of seeds and others may have only one. Place the seeds in a container and place in the freezer for two weeks. Move the seeds from the freezer for another two week period then sprinkle my seeds onto a germination tray filled with potting soil. I may germinate in a couple of months or it may take six -months. It will take several years until the plants are ready for the garden. If this is just too much of a process, I understand. This is the reason why divisions are so much easier and successful.

With time, my rhizomes can become thickly overcrowded and blooming will slow. Now It's time to divide me. As soon as the weather cooperates, gently pull the flower stalks out of

As *bergenia* matures, it appears more like a groundcover and is great for a shady spot in the rock garden.

the damp ground with a piece of the root or rhizome attached. Plant me directly into the garden and I promise you a good percentage of success. This easy propagation method keeps the perennials from getting root bound and the mother plant will seldom need division.

As *bergenia's* flowers fade, a seed capsule will start to form in the middle of a bloom. Wait until the capsule is completely dry before removing the seedpod, then start the cold vernalization. Wait two weeks after removing the seeds from the freezer to seed them on a peat filled nursery tray.

I'm a favorite of bees, birds, and butterflies seeking out an early feeding. I'm noted for being deer resistant; however, in higher elevations deer will eat any evergreen perennial. The removal of my greenery by browsing deer in fall will probably result in my demise, for without my foliage food, I will not get through winter. A covering of shade cloth placed over me in October will prevent me from getting chunked by deer.

Shade cloth is a green, knitted or woven fabric that allows water but does not rot, mildew, or become brittle. Cover my foliage loosely and use the U-shaped landscape pins to hold the cloth to the ground. Most deer leave gardens in populated communities to move into higher country for the summer.

Mongolian and Siberian teas are made from *bergenia* leaves and have a gentle pleasant taste similar to black teas. Collect any tattered leaves from my foliage as soon as the snow melts. Wash, chop, and allow the leaves to dry. Seep or infuse these leaves like regular tea but increase the amount of leaves to enrich the taste and color in your cup of tea.

Each *bergenia* rosette will furnish a new division or start as long as it is attached to a root or rhizome and planted quickly. Do not allow the roots to dry out.

Being planted along a north facing front porch is a gift from *bergenia* to gardeners who want their front yards to look sharp all year. My short, compact size will never spill over to crowd out the sidewalk. My foliage will give a perfect, all year, look to a front yard. Once I'm established the gardener's work is pretty much over for I'm more maintenance free than most other perennials. My huge rounded heart-shaped leaves are a wonderful companion to shade-loving annuals or my dense foliage will cover up taller perennials knobby knees. Of all the available perennials, I promise I'm the perfect plant for the front of a home.

Use only the tattered *bergenia* leaves to make tea for they have begun fermentation. When cutting back these evergreen perennials, take care. Reach to the basal stems to cut out old growth. It won't take long for the fresh new foliage to fill in.

Brunnera macrophylla
(BRUN-er-uh)
SIBERIAN BUGLOSS

SHAPE	Mounding clump with clouds of lacy flowers that morphs into a sturdy clump of huge heart-shaped leaves by fall
HEIGHT	One foot
WIDTH	One and a half feet
BLOOM TIME	Early spring
COLORS	Tiny sky-blue flowers
SITE	Not fussy about soils
LIGHT	Full shade or partial shade
HARDINESS	Zone 3 to 8
COMMENTS	Consistent moisture is the key for success with this plant

Stage one of *brunnera's* shapeshifting begins with a rhizome root that is usually harvested and planted in the fall, but in high mountain gardens, spring is a better time to divide *brunnera*.

Stage two of *brunnera* starts as the very first rays of early spring sunshine touch the ground notifying *brunnera* that it's time to wake up. The leaves are a little tattered and soiled but the big mystery at this point is to visualize what several weeks of metamorphic change will bring to *brunnera*.

WOW! *Brunnera's* stage three arrives with the early days of spring. This fascinating perennial turns gardens into a glamorous haze of sky blue as *brunnera* turns on it divine powers and sprinkles its lovely forget-me-not flowers above, around, and through the garden. Everything about *brunnera's* spring show is light, airy, and lacy.

By late summer's stage four, *brunnera* is no longer light and lacy but has shape shifted into a squat bristly basal heart-leafed plant that stays attractive until frost when it will again go underground and start the metamorphosis process all over again. The common name of bugloss is Greek and means "ox tongue," referring to the appearance of *brunnera* in its late season shape shift.

IN EARLY SPRING, my delicate, slender stems lift airy clouds of diminutive flowers up into the sky and dance above and around the other perennials. My stems of lacy blue flowers with yellow centers resemble my relative, the appealing, ever-favorite forget-me-nots. These form a hazy, energy-filled blue mist that floats above the other spring perennials.

By late summer, my shapeshifting has turned me into a basal clump of heart-shaped five-inch-long bristly leaves, which still look attractive but are a complete opposite of my dancing spring blooms. I look nice until frost when I'll go completely dormant and shapeshift again to an underground rhizome and spend the winter resting, getting ready for my next spring entrance.

Shade perennials are some of the strongest survivors on earth. We grow slowly, so it takes longer for us to mature. We also live longer and need less care, so if a carefree garden is on your agenda, a shade garden is the answer. These traits are an apt description of me for I grow slow, live longer and never require division to stay healthy. I'm one of many shade perennials that can be planted and left alone. I'll gradually reach full size and will stay about the same size from then on. It takes longer for shade plants to grow, and we compensate by living longer. So I'm slow growing, carefree, and long lived, and that's three pretty important character traits.

Brunnera is deer resistant in both my Idaho and Utah gardens. The fine hair-like down that covers the perennial is probably why the deer do not browse it. This perennial is adaptable to growing conditions and soils, as long as it gets enough water, and even thrives beneath a pine tree in my Idaho garden.

Another important trait I have is that I'm never browsed by deer. Many of my companion shade plants are deer resistant also. It's as if nature knows that growing in shade gardens takes so much more energy than growing in sunny sites so we are given extra compensatory strengths. Here is a list of a few shade and partial-shade perennials that have protection from wildlife and are not browsed in western gardens. Some shade perennials like *digitalis*, or foxglove, are protected from deer because they are poison. Others such as *dictamnus*, or gas plant, with its citrusy smell drive deer away for they dislike smelly perennials. Native perennials like Jacob's ladder or coral bells have developed their own unique protection. For example, coral bells has an alum taste that puckers the mouth, so deer must find it distasteful. Perennials with soft, felt-like or hairy foliage like us, the *brunneras*, are also not appealing. Hybrid perennials are more prone to getting browsed than specie plants.

EXAMPLES OF DEER-RESISTANT SHADE PERENNIALS LIKE *BRUNNERA*

- *Aconitum*, or monkshood, blooms in late summer.

Brunnera is covered with fine hairs giving it a texture that deer won't eat. The following list contains other perennials that deer shy away from.

- *Alchemilla*, or lady's mantle, blooms in mid-spring.
- *Anemone sylvestris*, or snowdrop anemone, blooms in spring.
- *Aquilegia*, or columbine, blooms in late spring.
- *Aruncus*, or goatsbeard, blooms in mid-summer.
- *Bergenia cordifolia*, or heartleaf, blooms early spring.
- *Dicentra spectablis*, or bleeding hearts, blooms in late spring.
- *Dictamnus*, or gas plant, blooms early summer.
- *Doronicum*, or leopard's bane, blooms early spring.
- *Digitalis purpurea*, or foxglove, blooms early summer.
- *Eupatorium*, or chocolate eupatorium, blooms in fall.
- *Euphorbia polychrome*, or cushion spurge, blooms late spring.
- *Matteuccia*, or ostrich fern, does not flower, but its fronds stay green.

Authors note: Shapeshifting or metamorphosis is often the speculation of fiction but the plant world does it all the time, and no perennial does it as well as *brunnera*.

- *Helleborus*, or lenten rose, hybrid orientals, bloom as the snow melts.

- *Heuchera*, or coral bells, natives like 'Ruby Bells' and 'Firefly' bloom late spring.

- *X Heucherella*, or foamy bells, blooms spring to summer.

- *Iris*, crested, and spuria are native iris and bloom in late spring.

- *Lamiastrum galeobdolon*, or 'Hermans Pride,' blooms spring to summer.

- *Lysimachia nummularia*, or creeping Jenny, blooms most of the time.

- *Myosotis alpestris*, or forget-me-nots, blooms mid-spring.

- *Penstemon digitalis*, 'Husker's Red,' blooms summer.

- *Physostegia virginiana*, or obedient plant, blooms late summer

- *Primula vulgaris*, or old-fashioned cowslips, bloom in early spring.

- *Polemonium*, or Jacob's ladder, blooms in early summer.

- *Pulmonaria*, or lungwort, blooms spring.

- *Silene dioica*, 'Clifford Moor,' blooms summer to fall.

SHADE PERENNIALS THAT HAVE NEVER BEEN BROWSED IN MY GARDEN

There are many new cultivars of brunnera, but the common all-green leafed species is hardier in high mountain gardens and none of my family are happy without a cold winter. The variegated forms of brunnera are breathtaking, expensive and touchier to grow. Honored by Colorado State University in 2015 as a "Too Good to Wait Performer," 'Alexander's Great' is a larger sized, variegated brunnera. 'Alexander's Great' with its heart-shaped silver-dusted leaves with green veins and edges is a dramatic accent to any shade garden. Its hardiness through hybridizing is no longer a zone three but a zone four.

Aquilegia or columbine is a native wildflower perennial, so deer never bother it.

Dicentra spectablis is a poisonous native perennial, so deer leave it alone.

Euphorbia polychrome, or cushion spurge, has poisonous sap, so deer are savvy enough not to sample this perennial.

Helleborus, or lenten rose, is poisonous and is also called stinking *helleborus*. The poison and smell are why deer have enough sense to stay clear of it.

Another award-winning brunnera is the very famous 'Jack Frost.' Its gorgeous translucent overlay on its green leaves appears to have been dusted with silver. It is so eye-catching that it won the Perennial Plant of the Year award in 2012 and the Royal Horticultural Society's Award of Garden merit. Other new brunnera cultivars include 'King's Ransom' with blue undertones in its foliage and more sun tolerance. 'Sea

Native iris, spuria, and crested or dwarf iris have their natural immunization against invading deer. Other hybrid irises are not so lucky.

Penstemon, 'Huskers Red,' is a hybrid mix of a native *penstemon* perennial mixed with the poison of digitalis, so the two parents team up to chase deer away.

The soft, felt-like foliage of *primula*, or primrose, does not taste good to marauding deer. After all, one of their favorite meals is rose bushes.

Pulmonaria with its felt-like foliage is not appealing to wildlife. The silver *pulmonaria*, 'Diana Clare,' is deer resistant due to its toxic tendencies.

Heart' is like 'Jack Frost' on steroids with tougher foliage that isn't bothered by the intense summer heat in the mountains. The newer brunnera cultivars are zone four.

Spring division is the most successful method of propagation for brunnera in Rocky Mountain gardens. My seeds may self-sow but never stay true to the parent plant, so it's advantageous to remove my spent blooms. Wait for brunnera to stop blooming, about ten weeks, before dividing. Using a digging fork that is less damaging to the roots, remove the entire clump and gently pull my rhizomes apart into pieces. Replant me into a well amended soil in a shady area and water well. Consistent moisture is necessary for my health and good looks, for without it, my leaf edges will turn brown, I'll look burned, and I may need to be cut back to the ground. Mulch is always the answer to conserving moisture. Place a good three-inch layer of mulch over my roots to conserve moisture and keep me cool. With the mulch, I'll have no need for fertilizer. Next spring, I'll fill a larger section of your garden with all my new starts and my shapeshifting abilities.

Brunnera, 'Jack Frost,' with its outstanding silver-frosted foliage is a winner in shade gardens in the Rocky Mountains. I have it planted with the plain green *brunnera* and the combination is eye-catching especially in shade. Both plants form nice mounding clumps of excellent foliage, but 'Jack Frost' is not as long-lived as the common brunnera and starts to dwindle after a couple of years.

Brunnera thrives in moist shade, so pair it with other moisture-loving companion perennials like those shown in the above picture: *hosta*, *tiarella*, and *lamium*.

Hellebore or *Helleborus*
(he-LE-bo-rus)
LENTEN ROSE

SHAPE	Compact clump with cup-shaped flowers
HEIGHT	About fifteen inches
WIDTH	About a twelve to fifteen inch spread
BLOOM TIME	Very early, late winter to early spring
COLORS	Shades of maroon, wine, rose, white, pink, pale yellow, and lime
SITE	Neutral to alkaline, well-drained soil
LIGHT	Under trees in a shaded area
HARDINESS	Zone 4
COMMENTS	*Helleborus* is frost resistant

Helleborus is an unusual and elegant perennial in both foliage and flower. Plant *helleborus* in a north-facing flower bed, by a porch, or along a sidewalk. They enjoy the alkaline lime from the cement in these areas.

The exquisite, waxy, beauty of lime-colored *Helleborus niger* with its zone-four and possibly a zone-three hardiness with snowcover thrives in the temperate, cool regions of the Rocky Mountains. With the cooler mountain temperatures, *niger* is never bothered by a frost/freeze cycle but just keeps blooming. The flowers persist or dry after blooming but still look like flowers.

Helleborus resembles a rose but does not smell like a rose, and a few varieties are often called "Stinking *Helleborus*." How can something so lovely can have such negative traits?

Look carefully around the base and to the left of the beautiful nodding *Helleborus* and you will see germinated seedlings. Leave these starts alone until they form a double leaf on the end of their stem. Dig with a trowel and transplant the seedlings into the garden or pot up for neighboring gardeners. Be ready for a surprise, for *helleborus* crossbreds easily and may bloom in a rare color or type. Many of new colors and petal patterns are the results of self-seeding.

OLD MAN WINTER has no power over me. My year-round attractive foliage persists through the deepest snow, and then in early spring I bloom with the tulips and daffodils. In fact, for me to be my most attractive requires the freezing, frosty periods of winter.

I hope you will like my history. I'm a native of the mountainous, rocky regions of Greece and Southern Europe, so I'm right at home in the limestone rocky regions of the North American mountains. In most gardens around the world, I flower around the period of Lent, the forty days of moderation before Easter, so another name for me is Lenten Rose because my flowers resemble roses. My entrance welcomes spring, so I often poke my flowers up through a snowdrift. This is how another common name, Christmas rose, was pinned on me. In the warmer gardens of North America, I often bloom at Christmastime, and some gardeners will grow me as a house plant to help celebrate that holiday.

Helleborus's exquisite flowers and outstanding foliage won the family of *Helleborus orientalis* the coveted Perennial Plant of the Year Award in 2005. Orientals are noted as having zone-five hardiness or minus eighteen degrees F, so they perform best in areas of the west with milder winter temperatures.

My flowers resemble old-fashioned wild roses, but I have no genetic relationship to roses for I'm a member of the *Ranunculaceae* or buttercup family. We also differ from roses in that roses are edible, but most of the *Ranunculacean* families are known to be toxic to humans, animals, and slugs.

Our poison made us famous as the first chemical or biological warfare agent used to win a war. In 600 BC, the Athenians were fighting with the city of Kirrha over the sacred land of Delphi and put *helleborus* in their drinking water. The Kirrhas became so ill and weak that the Athenians were able to easily regain the Corinthian Gulf. Our alkaloids and glycosides not only won a war but are also a deterrent to pests and wildlife like deer and rabbits. Other well-known *Ranunculaceae* family members famous for poisonous qualities are *Delphiniums* and *Aconitums*. My Greek name is of "Hellenic" origins, but the meaning of *Helleborus* also warns about my toxic qualities for the root word "elle" means "to injure" and bora means "food."

My designer-beauty flowers have five petal-like sepals surrounding an intricate center ring. The petals do not drop after blooming, as most petals do, but stay on the plant. This flower staying power is called "persisting" and means my flowers dry on their stems and still remain attractive. With only a glancing look, I appear to still have flowers into the summer season. This petal persistence protects my seed pods and contributes to a huge amount of seed development and dropping. These seeds are the best way to propagate me. My deep roots resent dividing and these divisions will not bloom any sooner than my seedlings. *Helleborus* seeds are a fine bonus for any gardener and they will settle happily beneath a pine tree or nestle into other perennials or at the base of the mother plant. My seeds require a sixty-day moist chilling to germinate and Mother Nature and our cold western winters do this best. In a couple of years, my seedlings will have sent down roots and will show up everywhere even inside many of the other perennials. Some of these starts will turn out lovely with rare or spotted colors, but many may look like mud and are easily weeded out. Transplant your favorites these into your yard while still young for the best success. You will be glad for I'm an expensive perennial when offered in box stores.

A gardener may be really surprised when finding an array of *helleborus* in new colors and patterns when their cross-pollinated seedlings start to bloom. Many of the new *helleborus* colors and patterns are the results of hybridization by botanists.

Hybrid breeding has even introduced double-petaled flowers in myriad colors. Wedding Party Series are an example of hybridizing and are known by names like the white 'Maid of Honor,' the pink 'Blushing Bridesmaid,' and the shaded-pink, 'Flower Girl.' More varieties of hybrids are being developed as we speak, so there is no end to the varieties of *helleborus* that will soon be on the market.

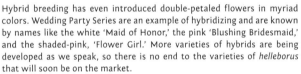

Different varieties of Hellebore plants offer a range of flower colors from white to black. Below are a few of the colors.

Spring purchasing of potted *helleborus* for intermountain gardens is difficult for we bloom so early and the ground is usually still frozen. Also we may have been forced on greenhouse shelves for a quick sale and are offered to customers at our prime, in full bloom. We can't be planted in frozen ground for we've been grown in a greenhouse, and even if we are frost tolerant, the shock would kill us. We still need to be held outside but protected until the ground has thawed and warmed up. Purchasing from a grower who winters their perennials in a cold frame without heat is a smarter place to purchase *helleborus*.

Once I'm planted and growing, I'm totally carefree. My excellent flowers and foliage will add to the lush look of a shady garden spot. I never need trimming or deadheading, just a little cleanup as the snow melts. Never remove my foliage in fall, for I'm evergreen and this is when I start to set buds.

The cold issues facing our hardiness are because we are totally evergreen. We stay looking flawless during the cold of winter. Wind is our worst enemy so if there is snow cover our low growing large pointed leaves are protected from wind damage and with the melting of the snow we will still look pristine. Preparation of the planting spot for me is a must for like clematis I'm pricey and often hard to get started. Amendments of compost or old manure will help create my favorite woodland preference. Hopefully I'll be left in the new spot for a long, long time. I'm not a heavy feeder and rarely require fertilizer. Too much fertilizer will result in an excess of foliage and fewer flowers. Planted in rich composted soil in western gardens is all I require to live a long life of happiness.

SUPERB FOLIAGE OF HELLEBORUS

Evergreen plants bring an architectural quality to a shady garden. In western gardens, many of us bloom in early spring as soon as the frozen ground thaws. We are resistant to the western problems of deer, voles, and rabbits, so we will not be devoured by the hungry wildlife before we get to bloom even when late winter is a prime hunger time for animals. Our pleasure is to provide our exquisite blooms when flowers are a scarcity. We are easy-care perennials, for once established we are drought tolerant, but we are at our best with regular moisture. The only fertilizer needed is a light application of granular, well-balanced fertilizer in spring. The only trimming required is careful removal of tattered or disfigured foliage in early spring before my new growth occurs. Caution when trimming: only remove the damaged foliage so as not to take flower buds with it. We are long-lived perennials, and our good looks will not decline with age but only become more beautiful with maturity.

The evergreen foliage of *helleborus* could easily be its best trait for it stays perfect all year. Planting me along north-facing foundation plantings of evergreens will not only improve the appearance of the evergreens but I'll be easily viewed as the snow melts. My waxy foliage with its shinning leaves are so carefree and perfect throughout the year that I'm a custom plant for a front yard. I also add to alpine or rock gardens dappled with sunlight. Container pots planted with my bold-shaped smooth texture will look attractive year around.

The classic good looks of *Helleborus's* impeccable serrated-edged foliage make it a top contender for container planting. Do not remove or trim *Helleborus* foliage in fall because this is when the perennial starts to form buds. Leaving the foliage will help the flower pot remain attractive during the winter but keep the pot moist and away from damaging winds.

FROST-FREE PERENNIALS

SPRING IN THE western Rocky Mountains has nothing to do with a calendar but is dictated by the elevation and the weather. Mountain heights and very low spots are generally colder than valleys so spring comes later to these areas. South facing foothills, nears lakes or pavements have a warmer microclimate. Just when gardeners and plants are suckered by warmer weather Jack Frost pays a late season visit and wreaks havoc on tender new perennial growth. Plants are at their most venerable period as they break spring dormancy. An early unseasonably warm period that initiates perennials to wake up early, followed by more freezing temperatures is the culprit. Spring freezing temperatures usually result in temporary leaf damage. Most perennials will outgrow the curled, white, bleached leaf tips but if they don't the damaged portions should be pruned off. This isn't lethal to the plant but it is lethal to the upcoming season's flowers for the flower buds were probably what were just pruned from the frost damaged plant. Frost injures plants by causing ice crystals to form in the plant cells thus disrupting any movement of liquids. Here are a few suggestions for mountain gardening in springtime.

1. SELECT PERENNIALS IN THE HARDY ALPINE, DROUGHT TOLERANT, AND EVERGREEN PERENNIAL FAMILIES.

FROST-TOLERANT PERENNIALS PROFILE

Frost Tolerant Perennials usually fall into the tough Alpine groundcovers, drought tolerant or evergreen categories or sometimes a combination of two or three of these. Helleborus is an excellent example of a perennial that fits into two categories; it grows low to the ground like an Alpine groundcover, and its foliage stays evergreen through winter. Many frost tolerant perennials like Iberis or candytuft has waxy leaves that hold moisture-like anti-freeze inside their leaves. Here are several other perennials that are completely free of damage caused by late spring freeze/thaw conditions

Armeria's stiff leafless stalks stay evergreen over winter and if they should get nipped with a late freeze leave their flattened clump alone and when the weather warms they will stand up again and the delightful flowers will not be far behind.

Ajuga is an outstanding evergreen groundcover for shade and admired for its distinctive variegated foliage and toughness. Not much bothers *Ajuga* so it can be depended on to come through a late season freeze without any damage.

Alpines like *Aubrieta* with its thick ground hugging carpet are so adapted to mountain up and down elevations and temperatures that they are rarely bothered by anything. Spring bulbs are noted for their weatherproofing or perhaps they have a canny instinct about when to push up through the ground but both will not be bothered by Jack Frost.

Bergenia thumbs its nose at old man winter and its beautiful heart-shaped foliage that has already survived winter is undamaged. Evergreen perennials like *Bergenia* never worry about a little frost.

Brunnera is indifferent to a sudden frost and simply bids its time until the sun comes out. Then they lift up their lovely, for-me-not like blue with yellow-centered flowers to greet the warm days of spring.

Doronicum is the first daisy flower of the season and its soft leathery foliage must protect the flowers buds for *doronicum* never seems to lose its buds in a freak freeze.

Festuca is a handsome selection of blue-foliaged short grasses. *Festuca* stays evergreen during winter and a spring freeze is kid's-stuff to this hardy perennial. Blue *festuca* grows in several varieties and sizes.

Dianthus's foliage stays evergreen and is very drought tolerant perennial so its foliage is never damaged by winter snow or frost. *Dianthus* is protected because their bloom time is June. Ironically this *dianthus* is called 'Frosty Fire'.

Potentilla with its native hardiness, never-misses-a-beat when a sudden late spring frost visits. *Potentilla* is very popular in even the most northern areas of Rocky Mountain gardens because of its hardiness and long bloom time.

Pulsatilla starts blooming during Lent, the forty days of moderation, before Easter. The plant is small and very close to the ground in early spring so perhaps this is why a frost doesn't damage its buds. It's not until after it blooms that the foliage really start to grow.

Yucca is not only drought tolerant, but always stays evergreen. The knife-like waxy foliage of yucca's has its own antifreeze right between the front and back of its leaves so just waits for the cold to pass.

2. DEFENSIVE MEASURES TO AVOID FROST DAMAGE

- A layer of compost or mulch over the perennials not only slows down the breaking of dormancy time by keeping the ground around the perennials froze so they won't break dormancy if a "sucker hole" of sunshine visits but holds in moisture around the plant.

- Cover plants with frost cloth, sheets or blankets when frost warnings occur. Remove the covers when the sun comes out. Make sure the covering is not touching the plants. Plastic is not an adequate cover. We use U-shaped

Sepervivium or Hens and Chicks are hardy, drought tolerant and evergreen. They never falter at the weather unless the ground is too wet. Then they made rot in a freeze situation. Each of these chicks will grow into a nice hen once they are away from their Mother.

Thyme's foliage stays attractive all four seasons. This tough perennial is a drought tolerant Alpine, and an evergreen perennial. The excellent foliage is fragrant and turns red in winter, never ever does thyme acknowledge a spring freeze.

Our first cold frame was made of windows our neighbors removed for new replacements and then kindly donated them to us. This cold frame is totally portable taking maybe twenty-minutes to put up and another twenty-minutes to take down when the weather settles. We use this cold frame for our potted cannas and dahlias so we can get a head start on growing them. Supply a heat source by installing an electric light bulb or even Christmas decoration lights that can be turned on at night if the weather takes a turn for the worse. The simple structure usually needs a window or two opened when the sun comes out.

frost cloth pins to hold the covers in place. Frost cloths are re-useable frost after frost.

- Build a cold frame.

3. DON'T GET OVER ANXIOUS

Box stores are famous for their early tempting displays of flowers in full bloom. Remember: if a perennial is in full bloom, out of season, it has been greenhouse grown and has probably enjoyed a diet of daily fertilizer. These perennials have no defense against a frost or hard freeze and if planted too early may not survive. Plants actually become established faster if a gardener waits until the weather makes it fun to be outside digging in the dirt.

4. KNOW AND UNDERSTAND THE ENVIRONMENT WHERE YOU RESIDE

A USDA hardiness zone map that divides the United States into wide strips of large geographic heat areas is a basic starting spot for finding perennials that will grow in your garden. For simplicity sake I have not included heat numbers for in the Rocky Mountains these are not important for we never reach the eight and nine heat zones of the Deep South. Nor have I included the confusing Sunset Magazine numbers for simplicity is always best. The USDA maps are color-coded and numbered with zone-one being the coldest spots in Alaska and on up to zone-nine being the warmest. Our Rocky Mountain gardens have a range of zones based on elevation. We vary between a zone-three in the higher mountains to a zone-four in the valleys and a zone-five on the foothills and in cities with lots of concrete paving. Typical spring safe to plant frost dates are Mother's Day in a zone-five and in zone-four wait 10 or so days. Zone-three gardens are usually safe to plant the first week in June.

Create a comfort zone that suits the needs of your perennials and they will reward you with years and years of beauty. Year after year, I've tried and lost the beautiful zone-four, *buddleja* or butterfly bush. They are a shrub like perennial that leafs out with the first warm days of spring and invariably will get froze as the weather changes. This freeze kills my butterfly bushes so I've choose to not include *buddleja* in this book. Microclimates occur in every garden, for example the gorgeous, zone-five, Hibiscus that gives shrub like size and red colors to fall gardens is a can't live without perennial, so I choose to plant this valuable zone-five, perennial along my south foundation. This is a warm microclimate where my *Hibiscus* does beautifully. Zone temperature on maps are not signed in cement so asking questions of neighbor, gardeners, attending classes or of course using this book as the hands on reference book it is.

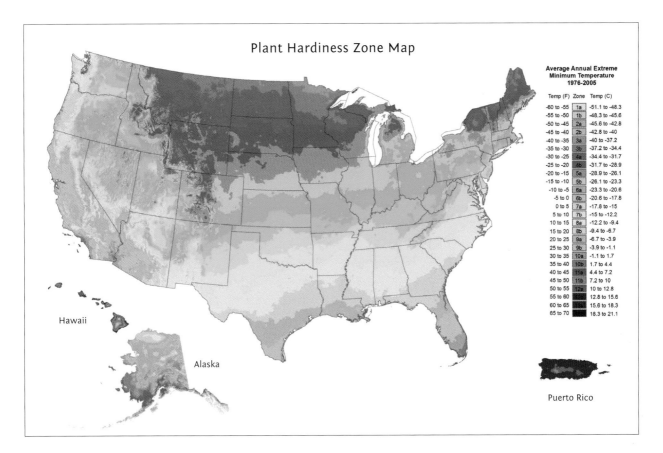

Matteuccia struthiopteris
(ma-TOO-chee-uh)
OSTRICH FERN

SHAPE	Vase-shaped bright-green foliage and no flowers
HEIGHT	Two to three feet in North American mountain gardens
WIDTH	Lateral stolons spread gradually forming colonies
BLOOM TIME	The lacy foliage lasts from spring to fall
COLORS	Fresh green with new fronds in lighter colors
SITE	Ferns originated in damp acidic soils but will perform in amended moist alkaline soils
LIGHT	Shade, even deep shade but will do fine with some morning sun
HARDINESS	Zone 2
COMMENTS	Ferns thrive in cool summer climates like that of mountain gardens

Ferns are the oldest surviving perennial on the planet, and their feathery fronds still create an unequalled lush beauty in a shady garden.

The fern fiddleheads appear in early spring. They are harvested before they completely unfurl, boiled and served as a delicacy. They are so popular in Vermont that they are the state vegetable.

The heavy elegant leaves of *hosta* are a perfect pairing with the light as feather's arching foliage of ferns. Both perennials are not famous for their flowers. Most shade perennials are modest producers of flowers due to the low light but a gardener soon learns to appreciate how attractive a fern's foliage really is and won't care about not having flowers.

Trollius jumps up through this dreamy shady garden to bring flowers to the non-blooming ferns. In the background are dried blossoms of *thalictrum* that have completed their spring show. *Thalictrum's* dried blooms persist on their stems to add another flower element to the ferns.

A SHADE GARDEN WITHOUT ferns isn't an appropriate shade garden at all. I've decorated shade gardens way back with the dinosaurs, and you might notice I'm always part of the scenery in a natural history museum in the dinosaur's section. The prehistoric creatures probably dined on my tasty fiddleheads for I'm nontoxic and very edible. I'm still a popular delicacy, but now days I'm cooked.

I was discovered growing in North America so I'm considered a native perennial. I am deer resistant and immune to most pests and diseases. All of this is important but my main attraction is my majestic beauty. Gardeners sigh with happiness when my graceful vase-shaped ostrich feathers emerge at my narrow base and unfurl into a shuttlecock shape of verdant lushness. I struggle somewhat in high mountain gardens because of the minerals from the rocks which created alkaline soils, but I still grow. I never really reach my upper heights in these gardens, rarely exceeding thirty inches. I'm also slower at getting established, so plant me in amended soil and be patient, for I'll take a little longer, but once my roots settle in, I'll fill the area with breathtaking ferns. Consistent moisture is another key to keeping me vigorous. With plenty of water and well-drained soil, within a few years, I'll start sending out offsets and will eventually colonize a huge fern-filled section. I promise, it will be the most spectacular spot in your garden. Once established in amended soils, I'll never need fertilizer, just a top dressing of compost now and then to hold in moisture. If I get dried out in summer, I have a tendency to go dormant and my beautiful ostrich feathers will collapse and die back. No worries, I'll return next spring looking even better for the long rest. In many Rocky Mountain gardens with their cooler temperatures, I do not go into dormancy until fall.

My feather-like fronds add a delicate contrast to coarser-textured shade foliage plants like hosta, ligularia, and

The contrast of the fancy colored leaves of *heuchera* or coral bells with the colored centers of tiarella and ferns is a dramatic look for any garden. Fill a garden area with ferns and *tiarella* then edge the planting with evergreen coral bells for a long season of outstanding foliage color. Who said that huge gaudy flowers are important?

Filipendula, or meadowsweet, is a tall vigorous late-summer-blooming perennial that contrasts well with the delicate lace of matteuccia. If the ferns are allowed to dry out in the heat of late summer, they may go dormant, so the *filipendula* will camouflage the fern's spent foliage.

brunnera, but in truth, I'm a great garden companion to any and all shade plants because of the light texture of my foliage.

COMPANION PLANTS FOR FERNS

Adding perennials in the same vicinity of ferns give the ferns the flowers they lack. Ferns are excellent perennials to mix with spring bulbs. The bulbs bloom early. The ferns break dormancy late so between the two perennials a garden area will always look excellent.

Many fine shade groundcover perennials like the *lamium* shown at the bottom of the picture look excellent when planted at the feet of the *matteuccia* fern. Sweet woodruff with its fragrant white blooms and circular foliage and lily-of-the-valley will also form carpets for the ferns to work their way up and through. The combinations are very satisfying.

Tiarella with its outstanding all-season, compact foliage is very appealing when fronting ferns. Shade perennials are lovely, low-care plants, and the best part of a shade garden is that it never looks weedy, overgrown, or out of control.

Don't delay, the sooner the new spring starts are dug and moved the better they will perform in the garden. Starts taken from yours or a neighbor's yard for replanting will be superior plants to any potted purchases of ferns.

DIVIDING FERNS

Once we're established, a gardener's work is done for we take complete care of ourselves. Few weeds will germinate under the shade of a fern colony and we even become more drought tolerant with maturity. There is no wildlife or diseases that give us grief so we are totally self-sustaining. A gardener often would like to spread my beauty around to other areas of the garden so here are a few suggestions for multiplying ferns. Ferns can self-sow from the single-celled spores located on the backs of my fronds. The fronds of a fern serve both photosynthetic and reproduction functions and the spores are the result. Germinating spores is a thankless job best left to Mother Nature and takes years so division is the best way to multiply us. We go completely dormant in fall so are hard to find the next spring. Wait until our fronds start to poke their fiddleheads through the ground, usually in late April or early May, and then quickly dig, divide, and replant. If I'm up and starting to open my fronds and they are touched or

To divide ferns in fall, wait until the feathers start to dry and droop in late August. A big shovel will be needed so the huge root ball, crown and all, can be lifted. Make sure the crown is full and sturdy, for without a solid crown, the ferns will not be strong enough to winter and start out spring as a full-grown perennial. A rule of thumb with ferns is the bigger the start the better.

Have nursery pots ready when dividing ferns. As soon as the root ball is lifted, stick the ferns into the pots as they are dug so they won't dry out. Two-gallon pots will be needed for some of the roots. Place the root ball into the pot and then adjust the plant and add top soil. Water well and keep ferns damp all winter. Potted ferns survive winter nicely in a cold frame. By spring, a full grown, gorgeous fern will be ready to grace your flowerbed.

The underground rhizome roots of ferns will send out runners over summer, like that shown above. This runner will send up new fern fronds in the garden the next spring. If these runners are cut by accident before they break dormancy, that fern may be a goner. In the fall, mark carefully where ferns are growing so they will not mistakenly get dug up during the spring cleaning. Many spring "Fever-Pitch" gardeners will plant a new perennial in any blank spot in the garden and may inadvertently dig up or damage ferns, and that would be a crying shame. It's really best to plant me in a shady corner area that you do not want to bother with and want to look great then leave me alone. The longer I'm left on my own to colonize, the thicker and more beautiful I become. Not many perennials are as independent as I am, but I'm more beautiful when left to do my own thing.

This is how thick and glorious ferns look when they are left alone. After all, they have been on this earth for millions of years and never needed the interference of a gardener in all that time.

damaged while being transplanted, they may just die back, so do divisions as soon as my crown can be found and is still small. If this window of opportunity passes, then dividing will have to wait until fall.

There are other family members of ferns that are very beautiful and popular. The *Athyrium* (ath-EE-ree-um), or lady fern, is smaller but has a tough constitution. Lady ferns

Athyrium, 'Pictum,' is one of many in this family of ferns. 'Pictum' is a small mound only twelve inches in height and fifteen inches around. Its silvery foliage won it the Perennial Plant of the Year Award for 2004. Display 'Pictum' where its exceptional foliage can be appreciated as along the front edge of a shady garden. Athyrium does not compete well with tree roots and needs to be kept wet.

are graceful and, like the *matteuccia*, colonize easily but are zone four, so they grow better in the valleys of mountain gardens. *Athyrium* is more receptive to mutation than I am, so has parented many different varieties of ferns. Lady ferns are found everywhere across the United States for they grow well in clay soils and even in the Deep South.

ATHYRIUM OR LADY FERNS

Ferns grow so thick that they are good back up players for a front row of annuals in a shade garden. Annuals like impatiens and begonias add the color a gardener so dearly loves and will look doubly luscious for the delightful ferns will fill the background behind them.

Wax wing *begonias* are a trouble-free annual that is self-cleaning and deer resistant so works well when planted as a colorful edging in front of a fern garden. Wax wings or 'Dragon Wings' bloom in a soft coral pink or scarlet red. They also have burgundy or bright-green foliage. *Impatiens* bloom their heads off in shade and will provide ribbons of pink, coral, red, salmon, or fuchsia to brighten a shade garden.

Hosta
(HOS-tuh)

SHAPE	Clump-forming perennial famous for its foliage more than its flowers
HEIGHT	Tall average thirty inches; medium average twenty-four inches; short average twelve inches
WIDTH	Approximately equal to their height
BLOOM TIME	Late summer
COLORS	Blue, gold, and patterned leaves are showy
SITE	Average soil, but will grow in alkaline clay
LIGHT	Shade plant, tolerates deep shade
HARDINESS	Zone 3, very hardy
COMMENTS	Like potato chips, one *hosta* is never enough! *Hosta* infatuation is a malady shared by all gardeners.

The consistent, all-season elegance of a clump of *hosta*, 'Francee,' planted along a path or pond brings a classy design element to any shady garden spot. 'Francee,' the Cadillac of *hosta* with its dark green leaves and crisp white edges, brings elegance to any shade garden.

Blue Angel has WOW POWER because of its thirty-inch-tall and twice-as-wide size that acts as a centerpiece specimen in any garden. The heavy, silvery blue-green leaves are very substantial, and if your garden is plagued by slugs and snails, plant this type of *hosta* for it is pest resistant. Choosing from the ever-growing selection of heavy, corrugated, blue-leafed *hosta* that slugs and snails ignore eliminates the heavy maintenance of hand picking snails at night.

Hosta, 'Halcyon,' is the smaller of the blue-foliaged *hosta*, reaching only about twelve inches in height and two feet in width. 'Halcyon' is one of the best and most popular of the blue cultivars for it fits in a small space or container and is a slow grower. The perfect heart-shaped leaves with distinct ribs are more blue-green than many of the other blues. 'Halcyon's' soft lavender flowers raise above the foliage clump to about two feet. 'Halcyon' won the coveted American Hosta Society Distinguished Merit Hosta award in 1987.

Hosta 'Fortunei Aureomarginata' has the colorful golden yellow margins of many of the *fortunei* "sports." The golden margin resembles an aura thus its name. Many *fortunei hosta* have white margins and are called *Albomarginata* for *albo* means "white" in Latin. Often, the stripes are centered in the middle of the leaf, and these *hosta* are called *Mediovariegata*. Most *fortunei hosta* break dormancy earlier in springtime and mature faster than the slower-growing blue-leafed *hosta*.

HOSTA IS MY PASSION! My first introduction to *hosta* was well before it gained its popularity in local gardens. A well-to-do neighbor took pity on a very young new homeowner who had no a clue about gardening, and she gave me my very first hosta start. She called it a plantain lily, named for the rounded shape of its leaves. The plant's huge lime colored foliage stood out with a light-like radiance that easily gave it status as the most gorgeous perennial in the garden.

Early each spring, when only the "eyes" or growing tips of the *hosta* had broken through the soil, I carefully dug around the *hosta* plants and pulled root sections away from the mother plant. Dividing *hosta* before its sumptuous leaves emerge guarantees the foliage will not be damaged. Divisions never missed a heartbeat, always regrouping into a magnificent clump after several years. Soon I had an elegant half circle of *hosta* surrounding each fruit tree that dotted the back yard. They looked spectacular and this success bred a passion for gardening that has never faltered over years and years of gardening and I owe it all to one start of Plantain lily.

Hosta's history is short compared with many perennials for it wasn't until the mid-nineteenth century that it started to infiltrate European and American gardens. My scientific name is *Hosta plantaginea*, and all *hosta* are clumped as plantain lilies. Our genetic roots are from the Asian countries of Japan, China, and Korea. In 1812, we as a group were named in honor of a highly esteemed botanist and physician Nicholas Thomas Host. Philipp Franz von Siebold a famous German physician and scientist also brought many specimens of hosta that are the large bluish-colored *hostas*. The elegant *hosta sieboldiana*, are named for him. A Scottish botanist

Robert Fortune introduced many new varieties of colored leaf and striped *hosta* from Japan so the *hosta* fortunei are his namesake.

Today's *hosta*, *sieboldiana*, with its blue glaucous foliage and broad ribbed elegant leaves are not the original Asian species but are hybrid relatives that contain genes of the early species. The many variegated, slick-leaved types of *hosta* still carry genetics from the original *hosta fortunei*. *Hosta*, like so many of our perennials, still carries the original species genes but has been bred to enhance size, leaf coloring, and vigor, making it one of the most popular and stunning perennials in the garden.

Hosta, 'Patriot,' with the dark-green leaves of its parent, 'Francee' *fortunei*, and wider cream margins that turn white as summer progresses, won the *Hosta* of the Year Award in 1997. 'Patriot' does not have blue tinted foliage but the substance of its foliage gives it slug resistance. The popularity of 'Patriot' started a full family of patriotic named *Hosta* such as 'American Hero,' 'Liberty,' 'Loyalist,' 'Minuteman,' 'Old Glory,' 'Pure of Heart,' 'Revolution,' and 'Victory.'

If my garden was limited to only one type of *hosta*, it would be *Hosta sieboldiana* 'Elegans.' This stable perennial has served for multitudes of blue-foliaged "sports" (off-spring) for all of these types of *hosta* have *sieboldiana* in their make up. This classic award winning, mid-size *hosta* forms an upright, sturdy clump of large corrugated, puckered, heart-shaped leaves that give it slug resistance. *Sieboldiana* is one of only a few blue-leafed hosta whose flowers are fragrant and as with most *hosta*, their lovely flowers open toward evening and last only one day.

The creamy-white center stripe on *hosta*, 'Night before Christmas,' gives this mid-size perennial presence in the garden. The white stripe draws the eye furnishing a showy, ornamental excellence in shady gardens. The dark, olive-green foliage is deciduous like all *hosta* and evaporates at the first fall frost. *Hosta* never needs deadheading or other maintenance but stays in neat, lush clumps, never straying out of bounds.

Saying a gardener has a favorite *hosta* is like saying you have a favorite grandchild, but *Hosta*, 'Francis Williams,' sits at the top of my chart for it always breaks dormancy early and survives winter stronger and more beautiful every year no matter how rough the weather was. The spring coloring of 'Francis' is turquoise and gold, but the colors change as the season progresses as pictured above. The heavy corded, waxy-coated leaves of the *siebolds* are evident, but 'Francis Williams' has the eye-catching coloring of the *fortunie hosta*, so it's obvious that genes from both plants were used. The wild geranium, 'Johnson's Blue,' with its contrasting lacy foliage is an excellent companion plant.

The reproductive organs of the *hosta* are referred to as a perfect plant for they contain both male and female organs. The long protruding, sticky, female pistil will need fertilizing from the fluffy pollen on the male stamens. The pods will close protectively and develop *hosta* seed in about six weeks.

Hosta is expensive and so desirable that many gardeners want to propagate *hosta* without dividing their mother plants for hosta rarely needs division. Hybridizing *hosta* seed should be left to botanists for the pollen from the selected male parent must be placed on the selected female parent without contamination. But gardeners always like a challenge so here are some steps to hybridizing *hosta*. The procedure is easier to do early morning before the bees wake up and get to the flowers first. First open the flower to expose the long female protruding pistil reproduction organ. The male parent anthers will show fluffy pollen that is to be placed on the flared sticky end of the female pistil. Using a small paintbrush, repeat the process of dusting the pistil with the pollen. A light covering of material like netting will now help keep the bees from cross contaminating the hybridizing. Wait for six to eight weeks for my seed pod to open. *Hosta* seeds are small dark one-winged specks that can be harvested and planted in peat-filled pots. These are called pod babies and are slow to produce. My seedlings are usually 99 percent all green and rarely resemble the parent. If the parent has *H. sieboldiana* in its background, some blue seedlings may show up and gold *hosta* may produce all three colors, but it is rare that variegated *hosta* produce variegated offspring for the initial variegation was caused by a genetic mutation.

The popularity of *hosta* due to their good looks and ease of care have increased the demand in gardens. Sprouting the pod babies takes three or more years for a seed-germinated *hosta* to reach a workable size. Divisions are the primary method of propagation, but the results are a clone of the mother plant. Tissue culture has now made it possible for *hosta* to be in every landscape. The tissue, florets, flower scapes, or shoot tips are used for cultures but don't always come true. Tissue culture also has helped eliminate the *Hosta* virus X which hit in the early 2000s. Virus X is spread by any means that moves plant sap from infected plants to healthy plants. Commercial field-grown plants were the worst offenders. Contaminated hands or tools, mechanical weeding in host production fields or even power washing before shipment spread the disease. The symptoms of virus X is a bleeding of color, mosaic ring spots, twisted leaves, or no leaves, and then death. Virus X is more prevalent on gold varieties or on variegated foliage.

Golden *hosta* like the gigantic slug-resistant much awarded 'Sum and Substance' are more susceptible to *Hosta* virus X disease than other colors. *Hosta* with symptoms of the virus need to be destroyed, roots and all. Never place infected *hosta* in the compost—remove them from the property. Fortunately, virus X has become more rare due to the tedious works of tissue culture hybridizing and fewer field-grown bare-root plants.

Hostas are relatively pest free, but the main problem is that slugs and snails love them. Those in the cooler regions of high elevation gardens are blessed because these voracious feeders prefer the warmer areas of the west. Slug- and snail-resistant *hostas* are the heavily corded leafed varieties both blue, gold, and variegated. With so many varieties of mollusk-resistant *hosta* available why would a gardener plant a *hosta* that will be snail bait?

Pictured is an overnight snail banquet on a once-beautiful *hosta*. Check the internet for hundreds of slug-removal methods. Be prepared to laugh, but methods like mulching *hosta* plants with pine tree needles and eggs shells under the assumption that soft-bellied snails will not cross the sharp lines do work. But here is a warning if using egg shells in alkaline soil gardens: egg shells in mineral-rich soil will all but sterilize the soil. Personally, I find picking the slimy creatures at early dawn or dusk most effective. Always place the picked up snails or slugs in a zip-lock type of plastic bag for they will still breed when thrown onto the road or placed in a garbage can. In other words, the bottom line for controlling these obnoxious creatures is to plant snail- or slug-resistant varieties of *hosta* to begin with!

Accenting hosta with well-chosen companion plants ensures they get the attention a nonstop, perfect perennial deserves. *Hosta* are late-breaking perennials, a perfect reason to surround *hosta* with the early spring bulbs like tulips, *daffodils, hyacinths,* or the smaller species bulbs like crocus and snowdrops. The bulbs will bloom in the early sunshine of spring and then go dormant. The *hosta* breaks dormancy mid or late May and gracefully covers the spring bulbs' remains.

Accent the variegated varieties with the color of the flower blooming next to them. Avoid too many variegated *hosta* sprinkled around, for it will appear spotty, but planting them in drifts will draw the eye along the border. *Trollius,* 'Golden Queen,' accents this perennial well when planted as a background, especially when planted with *hosta* with gold in their leaves.

Hosta with its consistently excellent foliage is a perfect plant for pots and containers. The zone-three hardiness of *hosta* also is receptive to being wintered in a pot or container.

This striking combination of *hosta* and *trollius,* 'Golden Queen,' both shade-loving perennials, gives a sumptuous, lush look to this garden. Of course, the maidenhair ferns that grow well in the same environments add another excellent companionship dimension. Ferns and *hostas* are like salt and pepper, always belonging together.

A new *hosta,* 'Praying Hands,' presents a fresh new look to a pot or container. The best part of using hardy plants like *hosta* in pots is that they will usually make it through a winter as long as they do not dry out or get too wet.

GO BOLD

Going bold means simplifying the garden's look by making beds big enough to plant more of the same plant. Perennials look classy in large groupings rather than planted individually. Pick a core of six to eight plants and stick to it as in the above photo; 'Karl Foerster' fountain grass and huge clumps of bold foliaged *hostas* are the basics of this flowerbed. Shown below are a few more of the best bold perennials for thriving in our environment in shade gardens.

BOLD DESIGN NUMBER ONE: CONTRASTING

FOLIAGE COLOR

Going bold is a design that never looks chaotic or busy. It usually stays away from perennials with fine, lacy foliage. One of bold's first techniques is to use perennials with bolder foliage. It may be a unique color with big leaves, big flowers, or just big! An example is *ligularia* with its rich purple leaves that is so outstanding in shade gardens it is often mistakenly assumed will not survive our mountain climate but is one of the best bold shade plants available.

Ligularia

Hosta and fern are classical shade perennials, but if you want to add more excitement to your garden, then add in a big plant with a bronzed foliage contrast, and *ligularia* does both of these. *Ligularia*, or leopard's bane, grows from three to four feet tall and about as wide. I usually plant three of these beauties together to get the biggest impact. In late summer, they brighten the garden with their single, daisy-shaped flower that stands out like a spotlight against the dark foliage.

The seed-propagated *ligularia*, 'Midnight Lady,' with its huge five-inch dark-purple toothed-edge foliage and robust orange-yellow flowers are hardier than other types of *ligularia*. It winters well in high valley mountain gardens for it has zone-three toughness. Look at the contrast between the bright-lime hosta and the burgundy *ligularia*. It's hard not to fall in love with *ligularia*.

EXOTIC TROPICAL FOLIAGE

The tropical foliage of canna lilies is an outstanding look when wanting to add a bold flair to a garden for their size and leaves are massive. Cannas' majestic leaves can be green, striped, or bronzed with rich dark colors. Cannas can be planted in a clump or solo in container pots. In the cold climates, cannas require harvesting so they won't freeze and rot. But harvesting these beauties is a good thing for they multiply like rabbits, so dig them about a week after the first freeze and store them in a non-freezing but cool area.

'Chocolate *Eupatorium*'

A splash of dark-burgundy shrub-shaped foliage in a moist shady garden is eye-catching. Look no further than 'Chocolate Eupatorium' *rugosum*. Its dark coloring with delicious dark bronze leaves sprouting from purple stems is handsome. As summer cools into fall, there's a creamy icing of white lacy flowers that forms on the stems of 'Chocolate.' The pollinators flock to the nectar-rich blooms, adding another delightful garden dimension.

The bold tropical foliage of canna lilies is untouchable for majestic beauty. Cannas are easy to grow. Plant them in the ground after the last frost or start them early in nursery pots and place them in a warm area to get a head start before planting them in the garden.

Eupatoriums are rugged, pest-free choice selections. *Rugosum* or 'Chocolate *Eupatorium*' is a zone-four perennial that performs better in a warmer microclimate or lower foothills. Its saving grace is that it breaks dormancy late, into May, so rarely suffers from freezing frostbite.

BOLD DESIGN NUMBER TWO: CONTRASTING SHAPES OF FOLIAGE

ADDING HEIGHT

Mix shade plants artistically, placing the taller perennials like *filipendula* and *thalictrum* in the back. Don't leave out the colored foliage on trees and shrubs to provide the contrasting background colors. Shade shrubs like *Daphine*, 'Carol Mackey,' with their tight variegated greenery with creamy edges look lovely under a red-foliaged maple tree and thrive in mountain conditions. Any contrast between foliage adds drama or boldness.

These shade-appropriate trees, red leaf maple and shrub *Daphine*, 'Carol Mackey,' are planted at the back of the flower bed to add height and structure and provide a background for shorter plants to play off.

Clematis

Perennial *clematis* adds boldness to a boring area with their magnificent six-inch flowers. The 'Jackmanii' group of *clematis* with their huge long-flowering brilliant colors bloom during peak summer periods and are the hardiest of the big flowering *clematis*. With their zone-three minus 40-degree F hardiness, they grow vigorously in my Idaho garden. The high arch for 'Jackmanii' to climb on also adds bold structure to a shade garden. *Clematis* likes their feet in the moist conditions of a shady area and their heads in the sun. Once *clematis* gets established, it is relatively easy to grow. The main task to keeping clematis looking good is cutting the entire vine to the ground, no higher than twelve inches, in early spring. Do the trimming before the stems start to bud, usually March, or as soon as possible. This pruning is crucial, for without it, the vine will get too heavy to climb properly and will fold down over itself. Winding their leaf petioles on the arch is a regular, enjoyable, flower-fussing activity. The *clematis teuiflora*, or

'Sweet Autumn' *clematis*, is also hardy in mountain gardens. The vigorous vine blooms with delightfully small creamy lacy fragrant flowers.

To achieve a bold look like this, install arches for height and cover them with *clematis*.

Tall and skinny mixed with short and round foliage gives a dynamic contrast to often boring shade gardens. Repeat and space this planting in clumps of five or six plants along the shady fence for a showpiece design.

CONTRAST FOLIAGE SHAPES AND SIZES

Use perennial shapes as well as foliage color to draw the eye into the shade garden. Below is the tall, skinny, elegant, and rare white *spuria* iris backing a rounded clump of round-foliaged burgundy *ligularia*.

BOLD DESIGN NUMBER THREE: CONTAINER PLANTING

To add a splash of boldness into a shade garden use container pots of bright colored shade annuals placed to highlight or hide an otherwise unnoticed area. The best shade

The colorful leaves of the annual *coleus* tucked into a bright bowl can be placed anywhere in a shade garden for a bold accent. This pot was placed right against the base of a shade pine tree where not much else grew and looked spectacular all summer.

Placing colorful containers of burgundy foliage similar to this 'Dracaena Spike' and 'Dragon Wing' or baby wing *begonias* adds an eye-catching boldness to this shady spot filled with *hosta*, ferns, and columbine.

A north-facing front porch needed both the height of the 'Dracaena Spike' surrounded with the tough, self-cleaning 'Dragon Wing' red *begonias* to lift it out of the ordinary. Both plants are drought tolerant and require less watering in a shade spot.

annuals for mountain gardens are 'Dragon Wing' *begonias*, which are self-cleaning; 'Draceana Spikes,' which are easy to save; and the coleus shown below.

Annuals add constant color to a shade garden, but they require watering and a regime of once-a-month fertilization. Deer love to browse annuals but seem to stay clear of container pots. Choose bright colors like reds for planters. The red spectrum of colors is the rarest, especially for perennials so adding these to shade gardens is definitely a bolder look in a garden.

BOLD DESIGN NUMBER FOUR: UTILIZE GROUNDCOVERS

This lovely shade garden has done all the right things to give it an appealing classic but bold look. The homeowners removed grass that was struggling for more light. They added a raised flowerbed so the soil could be amended and furnish better drainage. A flagstone path was added not only leading to the raised berm but across it for easier traffic flow and upkeep. Container flower pots give added interest and the edges are taken care of with low-care, carpeting groundcovers that crowd out weeds and give a much-needed finished look to the garden.

Shade groundcovers provide attractive edges of colorful foliage and flowers. One of the most attractive in both flowers and edging is the unbeatable clump-growing 'Herman's Pride' Lamiastrum. 'Herman's Pride' establishes easily but is not invasive. The only problem with 'Herman's Pride' is that it is a dry shade perennial and it looks more attractive when grown in a dry situation.

Lamiastrum

'Herman's Pride' grows in a neat compact habit with a slow rate of spread and is never invasive. Its height is around eight inches but spreads to fifteen inches wide or so. 'Herman's Pride's' superb foliage is silver streaked and holds nicely without flopping the entire summer. In late spring, the perennial covers itself with luscious pale-yellow pearl-like blooms. Hardiness is zone four and it's deer resistant. *Lamiastrum*, 'Herman's Pride,' should not be confused with *Lamium* or deadnetttle or the spreading variety of *lamiastrum*, so watch the label at purchasing time for they are very similar in appearance and they are both shade plants. 'Herman's Pride' is very drought tolerant and grows best in a dry shade situation.

By late fall, 'Herman's Pride' has stopped its long two-month blooming streak and settles down to wait for frost, for it is totally deciduous but its compact clump is still very attractive. The outstanding perennial never needs to be deadheaded or trimmed and always looks excellent. Part of the reason is that it is not a seed-grown perennial but a hybrid that is propagated by cuttings or divisions—in other words, it is a clone. This fine perennial wears a variety of skill hats that few perennials can achieve: it can be planted under a deck or sunless eaves and will still look fresh and vibrant all summer.

A few other shade groundcovers that do a great edge carpet are the following:

Galium or sweet woodruff

Lysimachia nummularia or creeping Jenny

Pulmonaria, 'Diana Clare'

Convallaria or lily-of-valley

BOLD DESIGN NUMBER FIVE: ADD IN SOMETHING THAT MAKES YOU SMILE

A copper couple playing hide-and-seek will surely make everyone smile!

Pulmonaria, 'Diana Clare'
(pul-mon-AIR-ee-a)
LUNGWORT

SHAPE	Low clump with tiny spring-blooming bells
HEIGHT	About ten inches tall
WIDTH	About fifteen inches around
BLOOM TIME	Early, with daffodils
COLORS	Interesting buds change color as they open
SITE	Moist, damp area
LIGHT	Shade, under dappled trees
HARDINESS	Zone 3
COMMENTS	Silvery spotted foliage

The silver-sheened long-pointed leaves of *pulmonaria*, 'Diana Clare,' shine at the bottom of the picture, planted on the left is *lamium* for spring bloom, wild geranium 'Johnson's Blue' is summer flowering, and aconitum adds color and height to the fall garden. At the right bottom of the picture, notice the drying daffodil stems from early spring. One small spot in this shade garden furnishes elegant foliage and flowers for a full season of colorful perennial beauty.

Pulmonaria 'Diana Claire' forms drooping clusters of half-inch flowers in early spring before the perennial's foliage starts to grow. Flower production on all *pulmonarias* is typically low, but 'Diana Clare' is more generous with her ethereal colored blooms and flowers that last for over a month.

Leaves grow long and large by the end of the season, developing an excellent consistent circular mound of ground cover in shady areas. Many varieties have silver-dotted or blotched edges along their leaves while others are almost all silver.

'Diana Clare' is far easier and more vigorous to grow than other *pulmonarias*. The twelve-by-eighteen-inch clumps form dense multicrowned plants, custom grown to light up the darkness of a shady garden.

I'M A LONG-LIVED, slow-growing perennial that makes a beautiful statement in a shade garden. There are wars, death, and taxes, and there are gardens. Gardens or their plants last longer and *pulmonaria* with its patient resourcefulness is one of the best plants to prove this, for I actually was discovered as a seedling in a garden!

I appeared by luck, found by nurseryman Bob Brown in 1995. He was so delighted with this new vigorous *pulmonaria* that he named it 'Diana Clare' after his wife and offered it to gardeners everywhere. When Mother Nature decides to show puny botanists how *pulmonaria* really should grow, she cross breeds and comes up with perhaps the best perennial available, especially for shade gardens. So allow me to tell you about how remarkable I really am.

I'm a hybridized seedling of a *longfloria pulmonaria* and an old-fashioned specie cowslip lungwort, which gives me my long, pointed silver leaves and hardiness. When I emerge in early spring, I'm breathtakingly beautiful for I'm covered with exquisite bells of such a soft almost ethereal presence they almost look unreal. My flowers are small rosettes of notched funnel-shaped blooms that start out about an inch tall, but over the next couple of weeks I'll reach my full height of about eight inches. My delightful buds usually start out pink tinged, but I open to new shades, usually reddish violet, and then mature to azure and royal blues.

Like all *pulmonarias*, my delicate two-toned blooms change colors from bud to bloom and present a mystery of how such an exquisite flower could be out-shined by its foliage, but in the case of 'Diana Clare' it's true for I'm the best pulmonaria of all. My silvery leaves brighten shade gardens with such ease that my foliage takes first place, and like *hosta*, I'm valued more for my foliage than my flowers. I'm the only *pulmonaria* that does not require cutting back after I finish blooming. By summer, I will have formed basal clumps about ten inches tall and fifteen inches around. My long narrow leaves are broader than other *longifloras* and grow in an interesting silver rosette that adds elegance to the edgings of a shady garden or underplanted beneath perennials or shrubs. My silvery foliage adds a new color and texture to a shade garden and can be used as an accent between other shade perennials like dark-foliaged coral bells, *hosta*, or ferns.

I grow from thick white-colored fibrous roots that were used in early days to treat bronchial and pulmonary diseases, thus my Latin name *pulmo* meaning "lung." My common name, lungwort, derived from the lung shape of my leaves and it was thought the leaf spots resembled a diseased lung.

My leaves are fuzzed with fine silky hairs, a trait of drought-tolerant perennials, but this is not true in my case. I do not really thrive under a hot dry summer sun, but I tolerate more heat than other members of the *pulmonaria* family and require minimum leaf cutting because of deteriorating foliage. I also do not perform in southern climates but prefer the cooler northern, zone-three mountain climates of the Northern Hemisphere. Unlike other *pulmonarias*, I'm not at all fussy about soils and grow equally well in clay, chalk, or loam types of soils. Acidic, alkaline, or neutral soils' pH factors are also fine with me. Compost, manure, or peat moss amendments will help with feedings and moisture retention and so will a consistent watering system. Fertilizing me in early spring and fall at the same time lawns are fed will satisfy those needs. It's so rewarding to add my attractive foliage and luscious flowers to the garden for I have absolutely no negative characteristics. I'm even deer and rabbit resistant with slugs not readily attracted but taking only an occasional nibble. So plant me in a shady area under deciduous trees (for I'm actually a woodland

Pulmonaria, 'Bertram Anderson,' is an older cultivar that has proven its worth. Its larger size and long, pointed, spotted leaves gives this fine perennial focal point presence in a shady garden.

plant) where I'll get spring sunshine and morning light, and I'll return yearly, slowly and surely becoming more beautiful as the years pass.

Many other fine varieties of *pulmonaria* are top-rated shade plants and have been around for many years. Most of these have the traditional spotted lung foliage and all of these must be cut back after blooming to encourage foliage production. They all require shade, amended soils, and consistent water.

Pulmonaria, 'Bertram Anderson'

'Bertram Anderson' is a *longifolia pulmonaria*, meaning it has extra-long, lance-shaped leaves that are pointed on the ends. Its distinctive dark-green leaves spotted with silvery mottling are superb, staying vigorous and consistently robust throughout the growing season. 'Anderson' is not adversely affected by low winter temperatures and survives minus 40 degree winters. 'Bertram Anderson,' sometimes called 'E.B. Anderson,' blooms later and opens to bright-blue flowers from early May through mid-June. Like all *pulmonarias*, 'Anderson' never spreads or is invasive but stay nicely put right where planted. 'Bertram's' foliage forms a larger mound of almost two feet. 'Bertram's' flower stalks with their moderate bloom will need to be cut back to a few inches from the ground before fresh mounds of foliage will emerge.

Pulmonaria, 'Roy Davidson'

'Roy Davidson' is another excellent *pulmonaria* for high valley gardens and has the distinct long, pointed foliage of longifolia mixed with the hardy European species or original wild pulmonaria parentage. 'Roy Davidson' sets buds of pale pink that almost look white, and its flowers are a soft pale periwinkle blue. 'Roy' is a smaller perennial and stays in a tighter clump and grows to only ten inches. The foliage of 'Davidson' is heavily spotted with almost-white dots. It adds a bright cheerful specimen planting to a zone-three garden with

Pulmonaria, 'Roy Davidson,' with its smaller size of only eight to ten inches in height, is a great container perennial. Plant this splendid shade perennial along with a red-foliaged *dracaena* and red or pink wax wing *begonias* in a colorful container for a shade garden focal point.

its compact loveliness. As soon as the flowers are removed, the unique foliage of *pulmonaria* starts to develop. Removing the flowers also removes the seeds which develop one seed per flower but take an eternity to germinate. Seedlings can be germinated, but will be different from the parent plant.

Pulmonaria, 'Mrs. Moon'

Pulmonaria, 'Mrs. Moon,' often called Bethlehem sage, has handsome medium-green foliage dotted with pale-green spots. The buds are violet and open to pink. 'Mrs. Moon' is an early bloomer and colors in early April to late May. Its height never reaches over twelve inches, but with maturity, its spread can reach forty inches, so it will eventually fill a good-sized space along a shady border. 'Mrs. Moon's' main difference is the rounded oval-shape of its leaves. Should browning foliage occur, simply cut them to the basal rosette for this is often typical of 'Mrs. Moon.'

Don't be deceived by the mound of small-leafed foliage in the above pictures for they are portraying bloomtime when the leaves are still small. The real appeal of pulmonaria is after the flowers are removed and the foliage starts to do its huge resplendent leaf show. *Pulmonaria's* foliage is every bit as showy as *hosta*, and it is not slug bait.

New *pulmonaria* are being introduced all the time. Several offer cultivars that bloom in reddish shades. 'Red Start' sets red buds that open to pink blooms. 'Red Start' has dull-green leaves and spreads so it works well as a ground cover. It is the earliest to bud but is not as hardy in western gardens. 'Raspberry Splash' is a raspberry pink with more upright foliage with long narrow sharply pointed and distinctly spotted leaves. It is a hardy zone three and is gorgeous. All of these are choice perennials with traditional spotted green foliage, but none have the health and vitality I do.

PLANTING AND PROPAGATING PULMONARIA

Plant and propagate *pulmonaria* using standard planting procedures. Purchasing bare root plants from reputable nurseries may be the best source for a specific variety. Order

The distinctive, trademark foliage of lungwort are always eye-catching in a shade area; their light colored dots grab and reflect light due to the silky hairs that cover the fine perennial.

bare roots early and plant them as soon as they arrive because most nurseries ship their plants at the correct time for planting. Remove plants from shipping containers immediately on arrival. Clean off any broken or damaged roots and soak the plants overnight in temperate water. Dig a deeper hole and add a phosphate fertilizer to the bottom then place soil over the fertilizer. Plant the roots, leaving the plant crown about an inch from the surface. Fill with soil and tamp down the soil, water immediately.

When planting potted plants, wait until danger of frost has passed for *pulmonaria* is frost sensitive. Plant potted perennials at the same level as they are in the pot. Follow the above same steps for planting bare roots.

The best method for propagating *pulmonaria* is to wait until after they have bloomed. Dig the entire clump and divide the rhizomes into sections containing ample roots. Plant the same as bare roots and water consistently. Plant starter can be added to the final watering to give the plants a jump start.

Seeding is possible but takes tedious time with harvesting, chilling and heating. 'Diana Clare' sets seeds occasionally without intervention in the garden, and the plants seem even more vigorous than the parent plant. No matter what the situation, you will find that I'm a dependable and an award-winning *pulmonaria*.

These 'Diana Clare' seedlings showed up in my shade garden among hosta and lamium. Their dark royal-blue blooms and silver foliage will stand out like a beacon in next year's shade garden. The gifts and rewards plants bestow on gardeners bring an over-the-top happiness when we discover them.

Trollius chinensis, 'Golden Queen'

(TRO-lee-us)
BUTTERCUP OR GLOBEFLOWER

SHAPE	Clump-forming with double buttercups of globular flowers
HEIGHT	Twenty to twenty-five inches
WIDTH	Stems above the foliage stand straight above the twelve-inch clump
BLOOM TIME	Early summer
COLORS	Golden-orange or yellow
SITE	Moist even wet clay and alkaline soils
LIGHT	Partial shade or shade
HARDINESS	Zone 3
COMMENTS	An undemanding member of the buttercup family

Trollius chinensis adds an explosion of color to the shady garden with its translucent bright-orange or golden cup-shaped flowers and prominent stamens.

Trollius, 'Lemon Queen,' with its double flowers and nice compact habit is often called buttercup. Even the glossy-green five-fingered foliage could be mistaken for buttercups.

The strong stems that never droop along with the attractive finely divided foliage give *trollius* top status in damp, high mountain gardens of the west.

Trollius is such a cheerful accent, adding flowers to the stability of this clump of *hosta*, 'Francis Williams,' that a gardener will wonder why they took so long to add *trollius* to the garden.

I'M *TROLLIUS* OR better known as queen of the buttercups! Buttercups are favorites for our cheerful sunny blooms dazzle a shady area in a garden. The meaning of my name *Trollius* or Buttercups is lightness and joy. Often we are rubbed beneath the chin of a child to see if they like butter and one of our symbols is that of playful childishness. As a member of the *Ranunculaceae* family, we are happy growing in the Northern United States but are wildflower natives of Siberia.

There are delightful legends pertaining to my golden blooms that go way back in history. A Libyan youth named *Ranuculus* became so entranced with his beautiful singing voice, he kept singing until he collapsed and died. The god, Orpheus transformed him into a tiny buttercup and named it Ranunculus in honor of the poor boy.

Another legend says the fairies are responsible for buttercups. A group of fairies saw an old miser struggling with a heavy pack of gold. They stopped him to ask for alms. The old miser refused so the naughty fairies cut a hole in his heavy sack. As he made his way his golden coins dropped, scattering on the ground from the bag. *Trollius* or buttercups sprang from each coin.

A western story tells of coyote fashioning new eyes from a dainty buttercup after his were stolen by an eagle. Today in many areas, buttercups are referred to as coyote eyes.

The magic of stories share my message of joy and cheerfulness and I'll bring that feeling to any garden.

My vibrant golden-orange colors are not easy flower colors to find in a partial shade or shade garden, but I certainly light-up any Rocky Mountain gardens. In fact everything about me from my native wildflower Siberian roots and preference for the cool regions of the northern hemisphere to my love of the West's typical heavy, wet clay soils makes me at home in the high mountain gardens of the United States. I'm a cool weather perennial with a cold hardiness of a zone three that is simply not suited to the dry hot summers and acidic soils of Southern gardens where I'll waste away.

Adding compost to clay soils will also help trap moisture and release the life giving minerals locked in clay. The minerals will deepen the color of both my flowers and my beautifully cut leaves, one of my best features. My attractive foliage grows as a fifteen-inch compact, basal clump of deeply divided, glossy-green serrated leaves. The stems rise above the clump to about twenty inches in height and need no staking. My strong stems with their smaller leaves may seem solitary but each stem launches hot-colored balls of flowers. Fortunately my strong basal leaf clump provides solid grounding.

The explosion of my rare orange and golden shades of color from mid-June into July brings a different element to the garden. I'm not a well-known, popular item at many nurseries, but if a gardener wants something impressive for a shade garden, request the grower to stock *trollius*. Planting the round buttercup flowers as a contrast behind the huge-leaved stability of plants like *hosta* looks enchanting. Mixed with ferns or other open leaved perennials, especially if they are blue, creates an eye-stopping WOW factor of color. The energy between the primary greenery color of other perennials against my orange-gold make the shade garden pop! A gardener will question why *trollius* has not always been a part of their garden and will never go without it again. They will probably wish that I was invasive but I'm not.

Slow starters are usually late bloomers, meaning I'm slow to establish, slow to germinate, and never invasive. It may take me three years to reach peak performance, but the positive aspects of taking time to establish gives me an easy-care,

Trollius seed heads, trimmed and lying on the ground in the lower left of picture have been dropped into the garden to allow Mother Nature to use her simple method of snow freezing the seed to vernalize it for germination.

well-behaved spot in the garden. I rarely need division, but my performance is intensified when I'm planted en mass, so a gardener may choose to divide me to gain more plants. Spring is the best time for division of perennials in high elevation, cold climates for it gives a full season for roots to establish.

Trollius chinenis, 'Golden Queen' and 'Morning Sun,' a compact version of 'Golden Queen,' are grown from seeds and are the easiest *trollius* perennials to locate. Both of us will reseed so let our sticky flower heads that resemble green raspberries go to seed. My seeds are slow to mature and may take two years to germinate. Seeds can be harvested but must be germinated immediately through a long and tedious heat and cold process. Allowing me to reseed naturally might give the same or better results than to try to start seeds in a potting tray. Take care when spring weeding so as not to weed out some of my new baby starts. It helps that the newly germinated seedling's foliage is an exact replica of mine. It's also comforting that when my buttercup flowers bloom I'll look just like my parent.

Looking at a close-up of the intricate details of a bloom of *armeria* makes a person wonder how such miracles occur without divine intervention!

'Golden Queen' seedlings have established themselves among ferns and cover spent daffodil foliage along with staying true to their parentage. *Trollius* plants prefer the same moist shady area of the garden as do ferns and hosta so they make excellent companions.

Bellis opens dazzling rounded heads of red, rose, pink and white in early spring. *Bellis* reseeds nicely which is a good thing for it is a short-lived perennial or biennial.

Hybridized *Trollius cultorum,* known by names like 'Alabaster' or 'Cheddar,' will not reseed, as it is with most hybrids. Their blooms may have variations of colors and heights, but the straight seed-grown *Trollius chinenis* are much hardier and perfect and need no hybrid improvements so should be a western gardener's first choice.

My name *trollius* means "globe" in German so a noticeable part of my charm is my striking unique globe-shaped flowers. The hybridized *Trollius cultorum* petals curve over and are more globe-shaped than *Trollius chinensis* with its more open flowers. Round-shaped perennial blooms are not really common so act as a counter point to the daisy-shapes and

Allium blooms in a sunny late spring garden. Their flowers bloom in a variety of round globe-shaped flowers in various heights and shades of purple.

The rounded ball-shaped globes of garden *phlox* are fragrant late-season-blooming perennials.

and tall sizes have a ferny foliage that performs well in moist, alkaline gardens and compliments *trollius* in every way. I think the most outstanding perennial companion for me is the dark-chocolate foliage of *Eupatorium rugosum* 'Chocolate.' The dark foliage of 'Chocolate' is a striking accent backing the brilliant orange of *Trollius*, 'Golden Queen.'

'Golden Queen' is both deer and rabbit resistant, and I have my very own pollinator called the small globe-flower fly. My chiffon-like flowers in brilliant and rare orange-gold add a new flower form to brighten difficult shade gardens. My rate of growth is slow, so I'm never demanding or invasive. My entire plant can be mildly poisonous and cause regurgitating when eaten fresh and has almost no medicinal value when dried. I'm native to colder regions of the world and thrive in the high mountain elevations. Because I am a wildflower, plant me near a pond or stream to give me my moisture quota, but in a regular watered garden, I'll perform well with typical watering. All in all, it's plain to see that I belong in Rocky Mountain gardens.

bolder blooms in a garden. Most globe-shaped flowers have an intricate protruding center like the small *armeria*, called thrift, or *bellis*, called English daisies. The larger rounded shaped flowers such as *allium* and garden *phlox* are examples of the excitement that round flowers bring to a garden. Round has such a solid feeling of simplicity that it contradicts the reality of so many tiny florets packed so successfully around a single center.

Excellent companions for *trollius* are other moisture-loving perennials. *Primula* varieties are cold hardy, zone-three, shade-loving perennials and blooms in a mix of colors thrives in front of trollius as do the amazing foliage perennials, *heuchera*, *heucherella*, or *tiarella*. Mix *trollius* with *polemonium* or Jacob's ladder, for they both enjoy the same environment. When they bloom together, visitors stop to gawk at the delight of their blue and orange flowers hanging out together. *Thalictrum*, or meadow rue, with its columbine-like foliage and airy clusters of rose and white cotton-candy-looking flowers acts as a backup, and *trollius* dazzles when growing in front of it. *Filipendula* and *aruncus* in both small

'Golden Queen's' bright blooms gain intensity against the burgundy foliage of *eupatorium* 'Chocolate.' *Trollius* blooms early, long before the fall-blooming 'Chocolate,' so the two perennials that thrive in the same moist conditions bring two seasons of color to a garden.

SYMBOLISM OF FLOWERS

A WORLD WITHOUT FLOWERS is like a face without a smile. Flowers communicate well by exchanging information without language interaction but through symbolism. The symbolism of flowers is often romantically alluring or mysterious. Sometimes it is based on ancient legends or myths but flowers have special ways of revealing their messages. In Victorian times, flowers were used as a method of appropriate courting that would not cross the straight-laced lifestyles at that time. Flowers have an ability to relax and reset a stressed mind in under sixty seconds by their fragrance alone. This is why the essential oils from flowers have become so in demand for healing purposes. Flowers given as a gift always symbolize love or caring. The gift may be flowers for the landscaping of a family member's yard or a pot of bleeding hearts given a grieving friend. In the language of flowers, receiving a plant is always saying you are loved. Exploring the symbols of flowers shows they open our hearts to unexpressed, nonverbal feelings of love, friendship, tenderness and hope. Here are a few popular symbols and fables attached to some of our favorite perennials.

Achillea or Yarrow

Achillea, or yarrow, symbolizes the military, war, healing, and protection. *Achillea* was named for the Greek hero whose mother, holding him up by his heel, dunked him in a bath of *achillea* as protection throughout his life. The protection worked and he heroically survived battle after battle until he was mortally wounded in his heel, the same heel his mother held when she dunked him. Unfortunately the heel did not get the powerful protection of the yarrow. Now his name, *Achillea* symbolizes a weak spot in our genetic nature.

Aconitum or Monkshood

Aconitum, or monkshood, symbolizes poisonous words. The symbolism comes from the Greek legend of Theseus and Medea. Theseus was the long-lost forgotten son of King Aegeus. When he surfaced at Aegeus's throne, Medea, the king's consort, schemed to rid herself of the son by poisoning his wine with monkshood. The king suddenly recognized his son and dashed the cup from the boy's mouth. *Aconitum* was also used during wars to poison enemy water supplies and coat the points of war arrows.

Aquilegia or Columbine

Aquilegia, or columbine, symbolizes the resolve to win and proves this by its survival in our challenging environment of the Rocky Mountains. It also bestows seven gifts of the spirit: wisdom, intellect, reverence, strength, advise, knowledge, and fear of doing wrong in God's eyes, therefore it is considered a protector against evil. Survival and protection is the gift of the columbine. Other negative traits pinned to columbine are the emblem of deceived lovers, ingratitude and faithlessness.

Artemisia or silver mound and silver brocade

Artemisia's silver sages symbolize absence in a relationship. It is said these sages will ward off evil, even keeping snakes away. The silver sages have fraternal properties that say "abuse not" and protect against this type of behavior. *Artemisias* have the reputation of being a potent antidote for a malicious magic potion. Historically, *artemisia* was named for the goddess Artemis, the twin of Apollo. Artemis rules over wildernesses, wild animals, and the hunt. No wonder sages are so at home in the Rocky Mountains.

Anemone, snowdrops

Anemone's delicate beauty symbolizes the Christian Trinity and is often found in the background of religious art. The early spring-blooming snowdrop *anemone sylvestris* symbolizes hope as it pushes up through a blanket of snow in anticipation of the revival of life. The fragile-looking blooms are tougher than one would think for they symbolize health, protection, and healing.

Aster

Aster flowers symbolize love and are also considered to contain magical properties. The ancients burned *aster's* enchanted leaves to drive away evil spirits. *Aster's* love symbol is derived from ancient legends of Virgo and the goddess Astraea, whom Zeus placed in the constellation stars of Virgo. Astraea's tears and Virgo's stardust were scattered onto earth creating asters. The Latin word *aster* means "star," symbolizing the legends and the shape of bloom. *Asters* are the birthday flower for September and relate to the inner being of the receiver, saying, "I share your thoughts and feelings."

Campanula

Campanulas with their pure blue or white colors are symbols of unwavering love. The legend of bellflowers came about because the goddess Venus lost her magical mirror. A poor shepherd boy found the mirror and became very attached to it. Venus sent Cupid to retrieve the mirror, but the boy refused to give it back. Cupid shot his arrow, missing the boy's hand and smashing the mirror into a million pieces. Each tiny piece of mirror magically sprouted Bellflowers all over the world.

Centaurea

Centaurea, or Montana bluet or cornflower, was the favorite flower of the goddess Flora who ruled over all the flowers. She is portrayed on Roman coins as a crowned image, holding or scattering *centaurea* flowers. Symbolic meanings of cornflower are delicacy, refinement, and celibacy, explaining another common name for *centaurea* which is bachelor buttons.

Chrysanthemum

The symbolism of the chrysanthemum offers abundance, health, and love. A great modern-day example of the chrysanthemum's symbol of love is portrayed in the John Steinbeck's short story "The Chrysanthemums." Elisa Allen, the main character, is a lonely rancher's wife who spends her entire life polishing the house. Her one freedom is her garden where she grows lovely chrysanthemums. She is visited by a charming peddler, and Elisa grows attracted to him. She presents him with the only gift she had to give, her treasured chrysanthemums, which he threw away down the road. Chrysanthemums are the birthday flower of those born in November and a gift like Elisa's gift of these glorious perennials is saying you are loved.

Dianthus or Carnations

Dianthus, or carnations, symbolize the strongest love on earth: a mother's love. This is probably why carnations are a favorite in Mother's Day bouquets. The blooms have a long reputation of being used as a form or divination or fortune telling.

Ferns

The tightly curled ancient fronds of the fern are symbolized by their unfolding representing an awakening of our consciousness. Their mystery seeds that appear as spores on the back of the fronds were once thought to be invisible, so collecting these would bestow the gift of invisibleness on the taker and the pixies that hide under the fronds. Ferns stand for sincerity, ancient wisdom, and faith in the magic of love. As greenery it correlates to the heart chakra.

Gypsophilia or Baby Breath

Gypsophila, or baby's breath, symbolizes everlasting love recognizing that it is a naturally everlasting dried flower. The white flowers convey the pureness and innocence of love and the coming together in marriage with open honesty, making baby's breath the most popular perennial for brides' bouquets.

Helleborus

The biblical-like story of *Helleborus* or Christmas rose tells of a young shepherd boy traveling to worship the Christ Child. He wished passionately for a gift to give the child and as his tears fell flowers as beautiful as the rose sprang from the winter ground. The boy not only gifted the Christ child but gifted us with *helleborus*.

Hibiscus

Hibiscus symbolizes feminine energy with each of its five petals representing delicate beauty, unity, peace, immortality, and happiness. To receive a *hibiscus* is telling that you are beautiful. The blooms of *hibiscus* are short blooming and fleeting, so the *hibiscus* means "don't delay" and "seize the opportunity."

Lilium

The White Easter Lily has always represented the Virgin Mary and is shown being held by her in multiple religious paintings. But there is another lily symbol due to the very protruding blatant pistils of the flowers used for fertilization, so the Greeks held it as a symbol of eroticism. A famous Greek legend tells that lilies were created at the breast of the goddess Hera. Zeus was determined that his illegitimate son Hercules become a god and knew that suckling from the breast of Hera would insure this status. He used the power of the god Somnus to place Hera in a deep sleep. Hercules suckled so vigorously at her breast that the milk spilled to form the Milky Way with the overflow falling to Earth and becoming white lilies.

Paeonie or Peony

Peonies have two interesting Greek legends. The peony was named for a young student of medicine. He was so gifted that his instructor became jealous, so Zeus changed him into a peony to protect him. The other story is that the nymphs would hide their nakedness in the peony blooms and this has given the flower the symbol of bashfulness. The peony is now honored as nobility and represents good fortune. Peonies are the official emblem of China and the word translates to "most beautiful." Peonies are often referred to as a metaphor for female beauty.

Veronica

Veronica is symbolized by the plant itself. The carefree nature of *Veronica* symbolizes the sign of a no-stress situation. The steadfastness of the *Veronica* perennial represents fidelity in marriage. Even Veronica's deep-blue color demonstrates faithfulness in feelings especially in the female side of feelings.

These symbols attached to flowers are fascinating to gardeners probably because gardeners feel sure they communicate with their flowers. They certainly react when they are told they are loved because they are so beautiful. I've seen blooms stand straighter after a compliment like this so it is reasonable that over the year's conversations translate to symbols due to behaviors of flowers and the reactions gardeners have toward their flowers.

Thalictrum aquilegifolium
(tha-LIK-trum)
COLUMBINE MEADOW RUE

SHAPE	Mound-shaped blue-green foliage topped with fuzzy clusters of white and orchid clusters
HEIGHT	Thirty inches tall
WIDTH	Spreads to fifteen inches
BLOOM TIME	Late spring through mid-summer
COLORS	Shades of orchid and white
SITE	Any well-drained moist soil, alkaline, acid, or neutral
LIGHT	Cool, partial sun or shade
HARDINESS	Zone 3
COMMENTS	One of only a few perennials that adds height in a shady garden

Graceful, tall, columbine-like foliage topped by orchid or white cotton-candy-type flowers with fuzzy petals are the uniqueness of *thalictrum*. In late spring or early summer, *Thalictrum's* fluffy blooms on tall wiry stems decorate the garden with graceful, columbine-like foliage.

Columbine meadow rues are separate male and female plants. It seems strange to look at a flower without any petals and realize its blooms are prominent fluffy reproduction organs. The main point is I'm really attractive in a weird sort of way.

The budding branches of *thalictrum aquilegifolium* are fine textured and attractive. They stand above the deeply divided blue foliage and furnish a bright lacy look to a shade garden or a vase.

Thalictrum looks like long-legged little fillies in the garden. This gives the delightful perennials a see through quality that adds an open and light-hearted look to a shady spot and floral arrangements.

IT COULD BE SAID my flowers are out of the ordinary or peculiar, maybe even odd or "kooky," but I prefer to think they are surprisingly exceptional. Every garden needs a touch of the unconventional, and I like to think my flowers add off-beat freshness. The reason I'm so different is that I really don't have petals. Sepals on most flowers stay green, but mine color up and hold my reproduction organs that form my fuzzy pom-poms. Some of us are female and others are male. The male blooms are larger and more showy probably because their stamens are larger sized than the female pistils. I'm sure when admiring my fuzzy flower heads that you had no idea they are colored sex organs.

Historically, I'm a native of Europe and temperate parts of Asia. My Latin name *thalictrum* is a Greek word meaning "plant with divided leaves," but I have naturalized in the Northern Hemisphere and could have been found in your grandmother's garden. Our family roots belong to the *Ranunculaceae* or buttercup family, and out of over one hundred species of thalictrums, I'm the hardiest, a low zone three, for Rocky Mountain gardens.

Note: the *Ranunculous* family are noted for toxic qualities. Both poisonous *aconitum* and *delphiniums* are family members, so caution is advised before consuming *thalictrum*.

Botanists are trying their best to improve me through hybridization and have come up with some new *thalictrums*. 'Purpureum' is outstanding in every way for it grows taller, has a more conspicuous floral display, and blooms lavender. 'Illuminator' blooms yellow with yellow and bluish foliage. And 'Purple Mist' reaches the amazing height of six feet. Generally, all of the new hybrids receive good ratings . . . that is, if you garden in warmer zone areas of the country. I'm the only *thalictrum* that grows well in colder climates and even received the Royal Horticultural Society's Award of Garden Merit. This award requires high marks after several years of testing. The perennial also must be available, not susceptible to pests and diseases, and must perform for amateur gardens in average gardens.

Many gardeners think my foliage is my outstanding quality for it remains fresh and pleasing, spring through fall. Both my Latin name *aquilegifolium* and my common name, columbine meadow rue, are words that describe my foliage for it resembles columbine. The word *aquilegifolium* means *aquilegia* or columbine leaf, but I never suffer any of the mildew or pest problems that bother columbine's foliage.

My superb bluish-green leaves are beautifully cut giving me a graceful, well-formed look. In June, wiry stems rise above my foliage and may look delicate but are sturdy so I'm one perennial that will never need staking unless planted in deep, deep shade. This tall strong stem shape is an ideal size for cut flower arrangements, so I'm popular in the floral trade.

Seeds from *thalictrums* are generic and their flower color will be a surprise. The pendulous winged shapes of the seeds are not spread by birds and bees but by insects and the wind. The seeds can be harvested and sown directly in the garden as soon as they are mature.

Flowers are fleeting but great foliage lasts all season. It's the perfection of my foliage that gardeners come to appreciate after they have grown me for a while. To freshen me up for the rest of the year remove my spent blooms as soon as I finish flowering. The seeds are spread only by wind and insects for my silly flowers do not contain nectar-producing structures. I'm never invasive but will only reseed now and then and that is best done in home gardens by Mother Nature. My seedlings usually bloom in white but may surprise you with various colors. *Thalcitrums* are secretive and there is no positive way to tell what color a bloom will be even with packaged seed or unblooming plants purchased from a nursery.

I look better when growing in a group of columbine meadow rue, so placing fresh seeds around my feet may help germinate a group of us. Fresh seeds will be more likely to germinate but won't show up until next spring.

Spring sowing of *thalictrum* seeds in germination trays inside a heated greenhouse only requires a well-draining, seeding soil. Barely cover my seeds with peat and keep moist. Germination should occur in two to three weeks. Thin the seedlings when they have developed three proper leaves and are large enough to work with. Let me grow on, conditioning me outside until my root ball holds together then plant me in my permanent spot. I usually bloom the next year.

I'm easy to grow with minimum maintenance. I'm a long-lived perennial that rarely needs division unless a gardener chooses to move or divide me. I really prefer to be planted and left alone, but clumps can be divided in early spring. I'm slow at breaking dormancy so mark my location in the fall so you'll know where to dig. It's best to divide me carefully while I'm still dormant. Dig the entire clump and pull apart my rhizome roots being sure to have a good sized clump of roots with a strong basal center start. These can be planted out into permanent spots and will probably bloom the same year. Pot up smaller starts being sure to grow them on in a shady area.

The rewards for allowing *thalictrum* to self-sow or to propagate by division are a garden filled by a soft cloud of orchid and white puffy flowers. These delicate-looking perennials are really tough plants that come back year after year without much intervention of the gardener.

My special talents I bring to the garden are my tall height and fabulous foliage that grows nicely at the back of shady flower borders. In the wide world of shade perennials, there are only a few tall types of flowers that can be used as background plantings. *Dicentra* or bleeding hearts, *eupatorium* 'Chocolate', ostrich ferns, and *ligularia* are excellent examples of perennials that add height to the back of a shade garden border. All of these perennials grow well in cool, partial, or shade areas. They also thrive in the same deep, damp, humus-rich soils that I prefer. Pictured below are few others.

TALL SHADE PERENNIALS

Aconitum, or monkshood, reaches four feet in height and never needs staking. Its showy flowers in shades of blue, are one of the last perennials to bloom. All parts of the monkshood plant are poisonous.

Aruncus, or goatsbeard easily reaches four feet and its spectacular plumes bloom in summer. Columbine has self-seeded at the base of the *aruncus*.

Digitalis purpurea, or foxglove, will reach three feet, and its tall elegant flower spikes bloom in early summer. Allow foxglove to reseed for it is a biennial.

Iris spuria is the only iris that enjoys shade. Its elegant, sturdy spike foliage easily reaches thirty inches, blooms in early summer, and maintains its perfect spike until deep frost.

Filipendula, or queen of the meadow, stands tall at a handsome five feet. Its lacy clusters bloom in summer, lighting up a shade garden with white- or rose-colored flowers.

Lilium's elegant foliage reaches three feet or more in height, depending on the variety, and its exquisite blooms unfold in hundreds of colorful shades in mid-summer.

Tall garden *phlox* is so flexible about its site location that it blooms both in sun and partial shade but its flowers last longer in partial sunlight. *Phlox's* delightful globe-shaped blooms stand on top of strong stems that reach about thirty inches in height.

Thalictrum in all its blooming glory mixed here with some of its favorite shade garden plants. At the bottom is *alchemilla*, or lady's mantle. To the left is the dark-green, glossy foliage of *aconitum*. By mixing any of this unit's arrays of shade perennials, your gardens will become not only your favorite spot but a work of art.

All of the above tall perennials for shade like the same growing conditions as I prefer and make great companions. We thrive in dappled sunlight or partial shade. Water us regularly and thoroughly so we will bloom well and our foliage will stay fine looking. Should we wilt or start looking ragged in the heat of summer, it is better to cut us back to the ground so we can start fresh. In shade gardens, soil has a tendency to lose its vitality so always add plenty of amendments when planting. A top dressing of compost in spring helps trap in moisture eliminates weeds and is a natural fertilizer for us. This is how my companions and I will stay splendidly healthy and have long, long lives. We also are perfect companions to many of the shorter shade perennials for we contrast nicely to their bolder, heavier foliage. Allow us to be the background for many of the popular shade plants like the shorter *bergenias*, *brunneras*, *hellebores*, and *hostas* for an outstanding landscape.

Western gardeners will be happy to know I'm deer and rabbit resistant and not bothered by pests or diseases. I fill the tough-to-grow shade areas with height, color, and outstanding foliage. I compliment other shade perennials by bringing a touch of airiness to flower beds. I'm long lived, never invasive, and very low maintenance along with being a hardy zone-three perennial. What more could a gardener desire?

SHADE PERENNIAL SUMMARY

Anemone sylvestris or snowdrops is one of the early blooming perennials that welcomes spring to the garden.

SHADE PERENNIALS ARE on the short list and most of the short plants bloom early spring before trees leaf out and bring more shade to a garden. Shade perennials have a tendency to grow slower and live longer. Most shade perennials have excellent foliage that gives color and fullness to the shade garden all season and many are evergreen. Astible is a well-known shade plant but prefers acidic soils and does not grow well for me in our mineral alkaline soils so is not listed. Perennials with invasive tendencies are also not listed. If a favorite shade plant is not here I apologize for unless it has grown in my Idaho or Utah gardens I will not recommend it.

SPRING-BLOOMING PERENNIALS

SHORT

Ajuga or bugleweed
Anemone sylvestris or snowdrops
Bergenia or heartleaf
Brunnera macrophylla
Filipendula (short) or meadowsweet
Galium or sweet woodruff
Hedera or English ivy
Heucherella or foamy bells
Houttuynia or chameleon
Lamiastrum or 'Herman's Pride'
Lamium or spotted deadnettle
Liriope or lilyturf
Myosotis or forget-me-nots
Pachysandra or Japanese spurge
Pulmonaria
Vinca or periwinkle
Tiarella or foam flower

MEDIUM–TALL

Dicentra or bleeding hearts
Hesperis or dames rocket
Polemonium or Jacob's Ladder
Trollius or 'Golden Queen'

SUMMER-TO-FALL-BLOOMING PERENNIALS

SHORT

Lysimachia or creeping Jenny
Lamium or moneywort, spotted deadnettle
Potentilla neumanniana or verna

MEDIUM–TALL

Aconitum or monk's hood
Eupatorium, 'Chocolate'
Ferns
Hosta
Thalictrum

SUMMARY AND NATURE'S GARDENS "LIVE LARGE"

THE PERENNIALS HAVE spoken and told their stories. They have described how each one is unique and differs from each other in appearance and the many individual ways they grow. Some are tough alpines and others have rounded daisy petals around a center cone while many bloom in spikes, trumpets, and globes. Flower colors are the full spectrum of a rainbow. Their foliage styles vary, some being tall, medium, or short and their leaves are soft, smooth, coarse, or ferny. Some foliage is dull and others glossy or waxy and their foliage colors may be green or bluish, bronze, gray, red, purplish, silver, or yellow. About the only way they are alike is that all are considered herbaceous perennials meaning they generally die back at the end of the season and reemerge in spring.

The perennials have shown that they grow in any light conditions and the right placement of a perennial results in more colorful brilliant flowers and luxuriant foliage.

Full sun perennials like heat, meaning six hours of sunshine a day.

To achieve a full-sun cultivated garden like this takes the right choices of perennials like the *sedums*, *daylilies*, *achilleas*, and *veronicas* for they are comfortable in a full-sun garden spot in amended soils, adequate water, and heat.

Mother Nature never has a problem with finding a comfort zone for plants in her gardens. Her landscapes are the original gardens that serve as our models or basis for imitation. She has provided an inexhaustible supply of gardening ideas that we, as puny gardeners, try hard to mimic. Her authentic full-sun landscapes are part of the environment and the plants grow comfortably with what exists. They require no watering, no fertilizing or amending of soils but are long lived primordial landscapes that were growing long before human culture got involved. Perhaps as gardeners we need to pay closer attention to her aboriginal landscaping techniques.

Mother Nature's full-sun garden is very different from a cultivated garden but none the less is magnificent, remains totally self-sustaining, and belongs exactly where it is. A rock wall curved for strength helps hold erosion and drought-tolerant alpine-type plants dot the steep hill.

A favorite perennial in the western mountains is the native alpine wildflower, Indian paintbrush. It is interesting that Mother Nature is the only gardener who seems to be able to grow Indian paintbrush for when moved from its natural site to a cultivated garden, it dies. For all of our hybridizing smarts, we can't compete with Mother Nature, even on flowers.

Mother Nature is who we thank for a wide variety of native plants that when found in this country were untouched from human influence. Native perennials have a low input need for water, fertilizers, herbicides and pesticides. They are adapted to natural conditions and provide food and shelter for wildlife

Wildflowers, columbine, sweet rocket, and Queen Anne's lace grow in full sun in a mountain, snow-field garden. Cultivated varieties of these perennials are tidier and more consistent in size and flowers. They also do not look so weedy so most gardeners appreciate the hybridization of native perennial just because they look nicer and bloom longer.

Perennials that grow in partial shade enjoy light that plays over them for a half day. They prefer morning sun or a full day of dappled shade. The intensity of the sun in high valley gardens causes many full-sun perennials to grow better in partial shade.

Delphiniums have the reputation of being full-sun perennials. They grow beautifully in partial-shade gardens due to the sun's intensity and cooler temperatures of high mountain gardens. The meticulously-trimmed lawns, trimmed tree branches, and shrubs in this formal-looking garden work together for to create a spot of comfort for visitors.

Mother Nature's partial-shade gardens grow in the cooler wooded areas of mountains and require zero maintenance. Nature plants fewer species allowing them to seed into huge swaths so nothing appears random or thrown together. In fall, the leaves and foliage decompose into rotted organic debris, creating nature's own organic compost. This soil holds moisture and is firm enough to hold plants but loose enough for water to penetrate. The organic soil contains the essential nutrients to provide a home for microorganisms and a pH level so plants are able to absorb nutrients. Pictured below is a sampling of nature's partial shade gardening.

The soft curving berms of the rolling hills are home to a lovely partial-shade garden that faces north-east so never gets hot sun in its location. Notice how nature has used different heights of plants, tall at the back, medium in the middle, and short along the front. Nature must have taught us how well plants display when planted this way.

Shade gardens are often called understory gardens for they grow under trees in shade or against tall building where little sun penetrates. Shade perennials only require two to four hours of sun a day and their favorite spot is in dappled sun under a high trimmed tree canopy. Perennials in shade gardens grow slower and live longer.

Notice all of the design elements in this lovely shade garden: hardy shade perennials, a flagstone path, statues, container plants, and a bench where the garden can be enjoyed. The cement edges keep everything tidy making for easy mowing and a sharp-looking garden.

Western mountain gardens are easier going than in many places but still contain intrusions like fences, roads, paths, and parking lots. These man made design elements are important to man's lifestyles, but nature's formative landscaping like arches, rock walls, color drifts, focal points, lighting, and a place of privacy are so inspiring that we can't help trying to emulate them in our own gardens.

PROFILES OF GARDEN GEMS BY MOTHER NATURE

Below are a few more pictures of nature's landscapes that are way to fantstic for man to ignore, so we try to copy these for our own landscapes. We'll start with A for arches and trellises.

Rock walls are a signature landscaping concept for western gardens. Rocks are available and can be stacked for erosion but also to give level flat areas for planting. In the above picture, nature really demonstrates how effective rock walls are in landscaping.

Arches add much needed height to a garden and fit nicely over a path or as a break in a fenceline. Arches in our gardens are very decorative but not anything in comparison with nature's arches.

In this book, we became acquainted with a method of planting perennials in large groups, giving gardens drifts of color with only one main swatch of color per season. Here nature shows us how effective color drifts work with her fall display.

How fortunate homeowners are with an outdoor space they can call their own. How fortunate we are to live in our mountains to be able to bring nature as close as your own back yard. May this book help you create this space that will bring so much joy into your lives.

Happy Gardening!

Paths welcome visitors to the front door or give a simple way from point A to point B. Any area that is always trampled by traffic is a great spot for a path. Materials can be flagstones, cement, or even grass—or like the natural path above, dirt.

INDEX

ABOUT THE AUTHOR

NEDRA SECRIST is a retired schoolteacher who teaches gardening seminars at libraries, churches, garden clubs, and civic groups. She has been growing perennials for over fifty years. She and her husband own Secrist Gardens, a home-based perennial nursery with locations in Brigham City, Utah, and St. Charles, Idaho. She uses "green" gardening methods and hands-on training courses to help gardeners succeed.

SCAN to visit

www.powerfulperennials.com